THE
DRAW OF
THE
SEA

PRAISE FOR *THE DRAW OF THE SEA*

'A compressed rectangle of pure sea'
Adam Farrer, author of *Cold Fish Soup*

'A beautiful, wise and charming book'
Charlie Carroll, author of *The Lip*

'Menmuir's novels are full of beautiful language
and this, too, is a book that sings'
Alex Preston, *The Guardian*

'The best compliment I can pay *The Draw of the Sea*
is that the moment I finished it I signed up for
lessons with the local sailing club'
Andrew Watts, *The Spectator*

'Much more interesting than simply another
bound-beating book about Cornwall. In Wyl's adventures...
he meets conservationists, surfboard designers, modern-day
mermaids and record-breaking free divers'
Luke Thompson, *Caught by The River*

'Beautifully written and wonderfully reflective'
Miranda Krestovnikoff, diver and author

'It is impossible to read this book and not long for the sea'
Bec Evans, author of *How to Have a Happy Hustle* **and** *Written*

'If you have the slightest interest in the sea then
I can highly recommend this'
Paul Cheney, *Halfman, Halfbook*

'Drips with a gentle authenticity that makes it a joy to read'
David Harris, *Blue Book Balloon*

'Roger Deakin would have been proud to have
written it himself. Brava. It's a masterpiece'
Liz Jensen

THE
DRAW OF
THE
SEA

Wyl Menmuir

Aurum

First published in hardback in 2022 by Aurum,
an imprint of The Quarto Group
One Triptych Place, London, SE1 9SH
United Kingdom

This paperback edition published in 2023

www.Quarto.com/Aurum

A catalogue record for this book is available from the British Library.

ISBN: 978-0-7112-7397-9
E-book ISBN: 978-0-7112-7398-6
Audiobook ISBN: 978-0-7112-8090-8

1 2 3 4 5 6 7 8 9 10

Cover illustration and design by Holly Ovenden

Map by Martin Brown

Typeset in Adobe Caslon Pro by Tetragon, London
Printed and bound by CPI Group (UK) Ltd, Croydon, CRO 4YY

FSC
www.fsc.org

MIX
Paper | Supporting
responsible forestry
FSC® C171272

The travels and conversations portrayed in *The Draw of the Sea* took place over three
years between 2019 and 2021. Some events have been compressed and some names,
locations and identifying characteristics have been changed to protect the privacy of
those depicted. The author would like to express his gratitude to all the people who
have generously shared their stories with him for this book.

For Alana and Tom

Photograph by Emma Menmuir.

Isles of Scilly

White Island
St Martin's
Bread & Cheese Cove
Great Bay
Bryher
Little Bay
Daymark
Wine Cove
Tresco
Nornour

Atlantic Ocean

Samson

Hughtown
St Mary's

St Agnes
Gugh
Bishop Rock Lighthouse
Troytown
Beady Pool
Western Rocks
Wingletang Down

0 ___ 2 miles
0 ___ 2 km

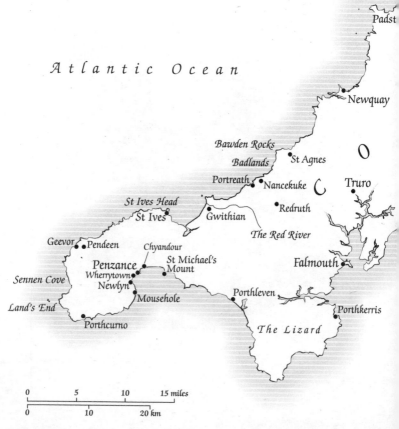

Atlantic Ocean

Padst

Newquay

Bawden Rocks
Badlands
St Agnes

Portreath
Nancekuke
Truro

St Ives Head
Redruth
St Ives
Gwithian

The Red River

Geevor
Pendeen
Chyandour
Falmouth

Penzance
St Michael's Mount
Wherrytown
Newlyn
Porthleven
Porthkerris

Sennen Cove
Mousehole

Land's End
The Lizard

Porthcurno

0 ___ 5 ___ 10 ___ 15 miles
0 ___ 10 ___ 20 km

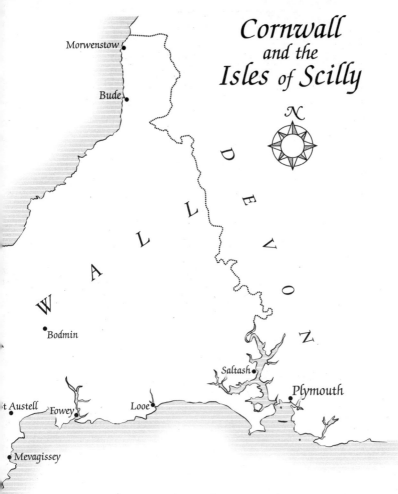

Cornwall
and the
Isles of *Scilly*

N

Morwenstow

Bude

D E V O N

W A L L

W

Bodmin

Saltash

Plymouth

t Austell   Fowey   Looe

Mevagissey

E n g l i s h   C h a n n e l

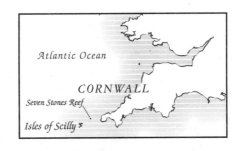

Atlantic Ocean

CORNWALL

Seven Stones Reef

Isles of Scilly

'It's the beginning of the day, you're alone, first on the beach. No footprints, there's a gale blowing, gigantic sea running, and there's wreck as far as you can see. You're alive. Your eyes are everywhere, your heart's thumping, you've got such a sense of anticipation – some people jump out of aeroplanes for that kind of thrill. I just walk onto a beach.'

NICK DARKE, *The Wrecking Season*

CONTENTS

Winter swell in Cornwall's Badlands.

Strandline Gleaner

Beachcombing & wrecking around Cornwall's coast

T HERE WAS A STORM COMING. Or, more accurately, there was another storm coming. It was the end of October and we were sitting in a lull between two areas of low pressure, a lighter patch between two bright purple bruises on the weather charts. Over the previous 48 hours, the west coasts of the UK and Ireland had been battered by the tail end of hurricane Epsilon. I'd spent the last few nights listening to the wind attempting to rip the tiles off the roof of my family home, close to Cornwall's exposed north coast, and thinking about what I might find washed up on the shore in the morning.

I had been tracking the dark blots on the weather charts for several days, watching as they raced eastward across the North Atlantic. Just a day before, the M6 buoy, 210 nautical miles off the Atlantic coast of Ireland, registered a wave 30 metres high, just shy of 100 feet, one of the tallest waves ever recorded. I'd been keeping an eye on chatter on the socials, too: the storm chasers were out in force, and big wave surfers; and though they were quieter about it, Cornwall's wreckers would be on the case too.

It was a year of broken records. There had been more storms of a strength that meant they required names than at any point

Goose barnacles on cork.

on record. We were only a few weeks into the new storm season and the storm namers had already turned to the Greek alphabet after exhausting the Roman one. The winds had been high and the seas too.

I had not been surfing (which I do badly), sailing (at which I am a little more competent), canoeing or sea swimming for weeks. Instead, I'd been haunting the coastline close to home, picking up bits and pieces I had found and bringing them back in my coat pockets. It was during these long walks and following the conversations I had with the people I met by the shore, that I began to conceive of a series of essays about the ways in which we are drawn to the sea, though really it was an idea that was returning to me.

In 2016, I published a novel, *The Many*, which was set in a small fishing village on a coast very much like you might find in Cornwall. My research involved walking around the fringe of the county, spending time in small coastal communities, listening to the stories of people who make their living from, or who find inspiration or solace, in and around the sea. Following *The Many*'s publication, wherever I went to publicize the book, at festivals and bookshops, above everything else I found that readers wanted to talk about the sea: the ways in which they responded to it, the way it held them, the ways in which they felt drawn to it. It makes sense: we're an island nation; we're shaped by the sea. It's natural, surely, that we'd want to dissect the ways in which we gravitate to the element that surrounds us, that comforts and threatens us, that gives joy and takes lives.

I live a mile from the Atlantic and there are few days when I don't go down to the sea for one reason or another. It's ritual and routine. I swim, surf, bodysurf, sail, paddle and splash. If I want to solve a thorny problem in the novel I'm writing – which is regularly – I head to the coast path and stand at the very edge of the land, looking out across the water. I cast my characters onto

Bawden Rocks, the two tiny islands just off St Agnes Head and leave them there a while to see what they are made of.

Much of life where I live revolves around the sea. On my desk I have a tide clock and a storm glass and, bookmarked on my computer, the Magic Seaweed website, which gives a surf forecast for local beaches. I could do without all of these, as there's a far more accurate way of finding out what's going on around the coast. When I collect my children from the local school, I can tell how good the surf is by the number of parents who turn up with salt-streaked hair. One of the other dads squeezes as much out of his surf as possible and sometimes turns up in the playground in his towel-coat. Like in playgrounds across the country, the parents split into their various tribes. Here, the surfing parents gravitate towards each other. They exchange notes about which break they've been surfing in between jobs, the early start they made to squeeze in a surf at the end of the day, or the dawn patrol. They talk in terms of sea state and board type, how crowded the line-up was, the beaches to which they'll be heading come the weekend.

In this surf-heavy community, life is ruled, to an extent, by the tides and the surf forecast. For many of the kids here, the first stop after the school bell rings, is not home, but the beach, the car already loaded with wetsuits and boards. On Saturdays, although there is football, cricket and rugby on offer, the surf lifesaving club heaves with the 120 or so children who pile down the beach to throw themselves into the waves each weekend, with or without boards. They can all identify a rip tide, know how to duck dive an incoming wave and, at ten, many of them already surf far better than I ever will. They, like my children, Alana and Tom, see the waves as their birthright.

I grew up in Stockport which, as the crow flies, is almost 40 miles to the nearest coastline, not far at all from the most land-locked point in England, just around the corner in Derbyshire. Stockport is a town so ill at ease with water that in the 1970s the council concreted over the River Mersey to make way for the brutalist Merseyway shopping centre. The glimpses of the river I remember, as we crossed the bridge into town to do the weekly shop, were of stacks of jettisoned shopping trolleys sticking out of the brown water, taxed and dumped bikes and a gaping maw-like hole beneath Asda where the river disappeared, a churning, frothing torrent. I remember clearly the sense of expansion I had on days out to the coast and the corresponding sense of being hemmed in when I was not by the sea. I have Stockport to thank for my own obsession, at least in part. We always want what we don't have, but it's more complex than that. When I celebrate, I turn to the sea; when I need inspiration too. And when I have needed to grieve, when my life felt upended, the sea's presence comforted me and gave me solace in ways I still find difficult to explain.

My earliest memories of the sea are of family holidays in France, of playing games in which I waded into the surf and tried to remain standing stock still as a big set came in, being delighted when I failed, being washed around in the breakers. It was after one of these long games of playing chicken with the waves on a beach in Normandy with my family at the beginning of a glori-ous summer, after being called out of the water for sandwiches, sifting through the sand, I found a brass shell casing. Later the same day, I found a stone buried in the sand which came apart in my hand to reveal a perfectly preserved fossilized limpet. I lost the shell casing almost immediately. At that age, I couldn't connect that object with the D-Day landings. I wasn't capable of seeing beyond the parasols and windbreaks to war. I'm still not capable to connecting with the fossil, with life turned to rock, with something that lived hundreds of thousands of years ago. I forgot about the bullet casing for years but kept the fossil, and for me it was the beginning of a long-held interest in the things that wash up on the shore, or which are uncovered from the sand by wind and wave.

Last year, I found another rifle shell casing, similar to the one I had found in Normandy, only this one I found 3,600 kilometres further north, on a beach in Svalbard, Norway. My hands saw it before my eyes and, as I picked it up instinctively, the memory of finding that first rifle shell came back to me with all the force that only a childhood memory can hold. Moments after, recalling the lecture I'd been given about the law that prohibits visitors to Svalbard from picking up anything manmade that might predate 1946, I returned the shell to the beach. My Arctic guide, Emil, nodded his approval, although he said the next person to find it would probably pocket it. He explained that during the Second World War, two SS officers were stationed on Svalbard, just a stone's throw from where we were and – bored, and with little but a huge store of ammunition to keep them company – they shot anything that came into view: birds, bears, seals, walruses. They set up a rudimentary and brutal polar bear trap, a rectangular box on stilts, with an opening at one end into which they placed food. The bear, on putting its head into the box, tripped a mechanism that triggered the rifle at the opposite end. The casing I had picked up was almost certainly one of theirs and was possibly from the trap, the remains of which were still standing just a few metres from us. From this one small object I tried to build out the picture of the lives of these two men there, their small hut, the isolation, boredom and the cold.

When I returned home from Svalbard, I found myself looking down at my feet more when I was on the beach, more interested than I had been in thirty years or so in the things I might find there. And the more people I met, the more diversity I saw in the reasons people are drawn to the sea, not just in the summer season but later in the year when the waves are coloured lead and seem laced with ice.

Storm-worn dragon's wing.

Ask ten different people what they see when they look at the coastline and you will get eleven different answers. Wreckers watch for the approach of storms, for weather that will wash in or wash away and uncover what may have been buried there for decades. They scan the online forums for news of container spills, hurricanes and recent finds.

Through the salt-rimmed windows of pick-ups and panel vans, surfers watch for the emergence of clean lines heading shoreward, for the tell-tale signs of the rip that will carry them out back, for an empty, peeling wave. Or they watch from low in the water, semi-submerged on their boards, the longed-for offshore breeze on their necks, and scan for lumps on the horizon, for the arrival of a promised swell. Gig rowers and sea swimmers seek out flat, sheltered waters across which to pull or swim, over which to glide or into which to immerse themselves. Sailors judge wind strength in white horses and windsocks, pick out tidal races, judge fickle breezes, gusts and lulls. Like fishermen, they overlay that which can be seen with knowledge of the shallows and the deeps, of reefs and submerged rocks, with knowledge of what lies beneath the surface, the ways in which the water moves in this particular place.

This assessment of the sea, part scientific, part mystical – the poring over of charts and apps, of long-range weather forecasts, watching the approach of weather fronts, building clouds, the sense of a stiffening of the breeze, signs that something is building – is a form of scrying. There's only so much you can tell for sure and it's always a punt. When you're out on the water, however well prepared you are, there's always an element of luck. Wreckers are no different in this respect. Many of the wreckers I've met engage in an activity I might call *flotsamancy*, a prediction of where the most interesting wreck will wash in, based on a combination of hunch, experience, tip-offs and weather tracking.

The question for me, staring at the charts, was which beach to choose. Cornwall's most celebrated wrecker of modern times, the playwright Nick Darke, described wrecking as a secretive business. The locations of beaches on which the best wreck lands are closely guarded secrets and it's a general principle that you find your own beach, make your own predictions, cast your own dice. My flotsamancy generally produces mixed results, but I chose my beach, 10 miles or so from home, and arrived just after dawn, as the tide began to fall, at a stretch of sand where, if I had timed it right, I knew I could walk for several miles along the strandline before having to turn back. From the carpark, I could see the Atlantic was unaware of the supposed lull between bouts of weather; it was still boiling white, the waves huge and messy.

There was no one else around when I arrived, though after 15 minutes or so a couple of kite surfers appeared, to take advantage of the storm winds. I found a spot out of the wind with a flask of coffee and waited for it to get a little lighter. The kite surfers looked tiny against the incoming rollers and even they were playing it safe, emerging from the water every few minutes and struggling their way back up the beach to re-enter where the water was flatter.

Later, the lifeguards arrived and set about red-flagging the beach – no swimming, no surfing – along with four men and women in their seventies or eighties who unfolded chairs and sat below the dunes and valiantly ignored the sandblasting to which they were being subjected by the relentless crosswind making a sandstorm of the dunes.

In the rapidly ebbing tide, the beach became huge and I felt the usual draw to the waves and walked right down to where they were breaking. The outgoing tide had revealed a lobster pot, which was still half-submerged in the sand and proved impossible to shift. There was still a sheen of water over the sand which, in the onshore wind, looked as though it was mounting a campaign back up the beach, serried ranks of wavelets fighting the ebb tide as the autumn sun crested the dunes behind.

Cornwall has the longest shoreline of any county in the British Isles; 326 or so miles of it. Richard Carew, in his 1603 *Survey of Cornwall*, described it as being 'so besieged . . . with the ocean that it forms a demi-island in an island'. Demi-island or not, because of the way it juts out into the Atlantic, Cornwall acts like an outstretched arm, its north coast open to the wild weather and putting it in the path of the Atlantic gyres, perfect for the gathering of flotsam and jetsam. The set of the tides and the wind, and the type and structure of beach and the seabed offshore, all contribute to determining what washes up where. Ghost nets, lobster pots, Coke bottles, buoys, fisherman's kisses and yellow fishermen's wellingtons, Nike trainers and nappies from cargo spills and wrecks, sea beans carried on currents from the United

States, Canada, the Caribbean, fragments of lives being led in other places.

In Cornwall, beachcombers are known as wreckers; in Shetland, they are scranners. There's something wonderfully disreputable about both terms and the activity itself, picking through the strandline seaweed for valueless scraps and fragments, is somewhat outré. And while the term wreckers brings to mind false lights and ships lured onto the rocks, there is little evidence for this ever having happened, though the myth lives on in family stories, in fiction and film. The first recorded beachcombers – castaways, runaways and those living on the margins in poor coastal communities – relied on selling, trading or using their finds. In Cornwall and on the Isles of Scilly, and in Shetland too, where life was hard for those living on the fringes, wrecking (or scranning) would have supplemented incomes at best, the finds making life slightly more bearable, and every scrap of wood or metal being put to use.

Most of the wreckers I met on my travels were in it for the fun rather than relying on what they found for income. The closest I've come so far to finding someone who makes their living from what washes in from the sea, aside from a few artists who use driftwood to make mirror frames they sell on Etsy, was an elderly man on a beach near Lyme Bay, who I found dismembering a driftwood tree with a small axe, which he uses to carve walking sticks to sell.

The Cornish, like the Scillonians, are inveterate wreckers. One of my favourite characters from Cornish history, the Reverend Robert Stephen Hawker – most famous, perhaps, for writing the words of Cornwall's national anthem, 'Trelawney' – was said to have smoked opium with Samuel Taylor Coleridge in the tiny hut Hawker made for himself on the cliffs at Morwenstow, in the north, from a combination of timbers of the wrecked brig

Caledonia, in 1842, and those of two ships that wrecked there over the next year. Morwenstow was, by all accounts, a poor parish and wrecking was a common way of supplementing meagre incomes. When Hawker arrived there, the residents of Morwenstow had a reputation for cruelty towards shipwrecked sailors, prioritizing salvage over life. The hut aside, evidence of a more benign sort of wrecking, Hawker became known for his efforts to ensure the crews of wrecked ships were rescued, and that those who died at sea off the coast of Morwenstow were given proper burials.

The desire to wreck still runs strong down here. Although, technically, everything that washes up on the shores of most parts of Cornwall and Scilly belongs to the Duchy, a high proportion of the homes along the stretch of coast where we live have a wreck, in some form or other, either in the house or in the garden. Part of my house, which was built just twelve years ago, is constructed with wreck timber, Nigerian iroko that fell off a ship off Penzance and which was used for some of the structural beams.

The more people I talked to locally about wrecking, the more I found it was still ingrained. The name of the house of one of our neighbours came from that of a boat on a crate they found washed up. Several years later, another neighbour found a crate from the same boat in almost exactly the same place, washed across the Atlantic to the same beach. Another yet has the ribs of an enormous drift whale lying around in his garden, which he carried off a beach and buried in a field for several months until the stench had died down, then unearthed again. The most common signs of modern wrecking are the strings of colourful buoys found on fences or on walls, as seen in gardens all along the coast.

I was almost two centuries too late to talk with Hawker and fifteen years too late to talk with playwright, fisherman and wrecker Nick Darke. Although Nick died in 2005, shortly after he and his wife, Jane, finished the documentary *The Wrecking Season*, Jane invited me to the family home to look at her collection. When I arrived, she showed me in through the porch, where various desiccated fish hung, into a lean-to on the side of the house made almost entirely of driftwood the couple collected. There she talked to me about their life together and the time they spent on the tideline.

In the study, more like a chaotic museum than a workplace, there was a lampshade made, appropriately, of a dried pufferfish and, piled on shelves, stuck to walls, filling windowsills was the evidence of the couple's obsession with wreck. Jane opened drawers filled with hockey pucks, dart-like gannet skulls, dried sea beans – the seeds of tropical plants, some of which she grows against sunny walls, each one a surprise and a thrill – and rolls of silver-grey birch bark that have floated across the Atlantic. One of the drawers contained a dish-shaped bone and it took me a moment to realize I was looking at part of a human skull they had found washed up. There were drawers full of more prosaic items, too – crisp packets dating back decades, plastic ducks, lighters, small parts of a violin, tiles from a backgammon set, lead weights, a Scooby Doo doll encrusted with barnacles, glass ampules, their medication still sloshing around inside them – Jane has no idea what is in them as they are untraceable – the product of decades of wrecking. Jane has been wrecking here for thirty years, and Nick, until weeks before he died, wrecked here since he was a boy.

'All this could so easily not have been found,' Jane told me, holding out a block of lignum vitae, the material once used to make the wheels for blocks on sailing ships. 'Somebody made that and it ended up here. It could be from the Caribbean; it could be from anywhere. These things make the whole world seem a whole lot smaller, a lot more connected.'

Nick delighted in tracking down the original owners of items he could identify, conducting transatlantic conversations with fishermen in Newfoundland whose tags had made land on the beach by the couple's house. Jane recorded their finds, creating an archive of wreckage that now spans decades, though the story started much earlier when Nick's grandfather moved to the cove from Padstow. He was a sea captain who sailed the world and had been wrecked twice himself. When he was at home, he would scan the beach for wreck and carry his finds back to the house. In a notebook Nick kept towards the end of his life, he documents a story about his father, who had been stationed on the beach as lookout for the custom's officers, as various valuable items were carried off. It was, for him, in the blood.

Later, we walked down through the garden, past a driftwood table on which sat a horde of more recent colourful plastic finds, from golf balls to the arms of Barbie dolls and pieces of pottery, past a huge red buoy and the driftwood fences Nick had built from wood that washed into the cove.

'The beach is different every time you come down,' Jane said as we made our way between the wreckage and out of the gate that led straight onto the beach. 'The stream carves different routes down to the sea, storms shape and reshape the face of the dunes, pools come and go, seaweed washes in and rots down. You never know what you're going to find either. The beach is wiped clean twice a day. That's part of the appeal: what was there yesterday is not there today.'

Picking our way through the seaweed, I could see nothing promising though. Just as we were about to give up, Jane laughed loudly, bent down and lifted a small, brightly coloured object which she held out to me. At first glance, it looked like an orange ball of fishing line, though on closer inspection I could see it was woven into a very definite pattern, like a tiny rope ladder, or a nylon corn dolly.

'I've got seven of these now,' she said. 'The last one I found was two years ago. Somebody's making them and letting them go. They're a message from the sea. On my thirtieth anniversary of getting together with Nick, a string of green buoys washed up here and I thought, this is amazing – a huge necklace for our anniversary – though it wasn't until about a month later that I realized there were thirty buoys in that string, one for each year we'd been together.'

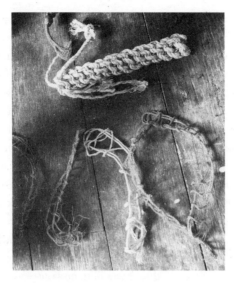

Woven dollies in Jane Darke's collection.

Wreckers, like Nick and Jane, are in conversation with the past and the present, with the vast, unseen networks that link a hockey puck from Canada to a small beach in Cornwall. And now, for Jane, it seems to me that wrecking is still part of her conversation with Nick.

'I still find Nick in out of the way places on the shore . . . that's where he is,' she told me. 'Nick was sea-made. Close to here, there was a shack his grandfather built in 1910. It was just two sheds and a 1940s stove, mildewy and damp. When Nick first took me there, it was because there was an exceptionally low tide. I remember going down some steps from the shack and I was on the sand. It was my idea of heaven.

'Nick grew up in this place, he knew the name of everything, every rock. This bit of coast was just another part of him.'

After visiting Jane, I started to make inventories of the things I found. Plastic bottles, nylon rope, cotton buds, shoes, the shells of violet sea snails which eat the by-the-wind sailors, the almost alien hydrozoa that float on the open ocean and wash up on Cornish shores in the autumn and winter, net hooks, flags, floats, lighters and plastic pipe stems (lots of these, still washing up after a container spill in the late nineties), plastic plants, golf tees, rolls of caps, combs, toothbrushes, decorating spacers, fisherman's kisses, knotted and discarded fishing net. As I did, I began to covet certain things – wrecking taps into the obsessive – and at times, I began to feel like an intertidal Womble, picking up the everyday objects that other folk had cast off.

Of all the activities you can do, by or on the sea, wrecking seems to me the most democratic. There's no industry around it, no merchandise. Unlike surfing, there's no associated fashion clothing, branded boards and wetsuits, leashes and fins, and unlike sailing costs don't spiral. There are no maintenance or mooring fees. Even sea swimming, which is undergoing a real resurgence now, has its own 'merch'. Wrecking is a decidedly anti-commercial activity. The only requirement is access to the beach, a bit of time and a little understanding of the winds and tides – a pair of wellies comes in handy, a bag perhaps for finds and one for rubbish. Really, the only real cost with wrecking is time.

However, there's a subtle hierarchy among the wreckers I met, from those who have been at it for decades to the newcomers. There are, though, a few things they all seem to agree on. First, that wrecking beaches are kept secret – few people will discuss their favourite spots. And there's a loose code. What you touch, you take home – if it is manmade that is.

As I made my way west along the beach from the lobster pot, I set about making my usual internal bargain. The deal I offer is that if I pick up enough pieces of plastic rope and bottles, the world will karmically deliver me something really interesting like a lobster tag or a sea bean. I'm aware that life doesn't work this way, but it doesn't stop me thinking it. It's gambling think-ing – if this, then that, when the system doesn't work like that. If I shake the dice so many times, they will come up sixes. And aside from the outside chance of stumbling across ambergris, the paradoxically valuable faeces of a sperm whale, sought after for its use in the perfume industry, there is little of monetary value to be found on the shoreline, which seems to have an effect on wreckers themselves.

In the wreckers I have met, I've seen none of the treasure-seeker's thrill or avarice. This is a meditative practice, in a way that fossil hunting and metal detecting just aren't. On a recent trip to Charmouth in Dorset, I watched people with picks and shovels, digging away at the cliffs in the hope of unearthing plesiosaur bones. Theirs was a kind of desperate, rough excava-tion, often taking place right next to signs warning about the erosion of the cliffs and the dangers of rock falls, pleas not to do the sea's work for it.

After half an hour, I got my eye in. Several dogfish cases, their tendrils still clinging on to wisps of seaweed. An orange lobster tag from Canada. A few rolls of birch bark, probably from the States. The child in me always desperately wants to find a message in a bottle, a note from another time and place, and every time I find a bottle with the cap still on, my heart leaps, even though I have yet to find one with a letter in it. The chances are that if I did so now, it would be part of an oceano-graphic study exploring the distribution of oceanic plastics, but I would most like to find something along the lines of the note the eighteenth-century treasure hunter Chunosuke Matsuyama wrote when he was shipwrecked on an island in the South Pacific. Matsuyama carved his note onto coconut wood before casting it off in a bottle. The story goes it washed up in his native Japan in 1935, at the village where he was born.

With many of the things I find, like Jane's mystery woven dolls, the meaning of the messages has been slightly obscured, a radio dial a few notches off from a clear signal. The sense of interconnectedness, though, is entrancing, a reminder that in times of separation, the sea connects us to one another.

Most of what I find, in terms of monetary value in any case, is worthless to anyone other than me. It's the connections that draw me to them: a mangled dragon's wing to the child who played with that dragon twenty years earlier; a roll of birch bark to a tree that fell some 4,000 miles away. Narrative drawn from rubbish. In many ways, it's like the writing process itself, a wandering, sifting, picking up and looking with new eyes approach that asks questions of the things that wash up on the mind's shore. Oh, that's interesting. I wonder if . . .

It feels strange to be excited to find shaped plastic that has been thrown up or uncovered by the waves. In his 1972 *Shell Book of Beachcombing*, Tony Soper insists that beachcombers must 'adapt to the change and learn to enjoy the plastic artefacts which decorate the tideline'. Perhaps this is an unsurprising sentiment in a book sponsored by the oil industry. This is the plastic that is breaking down into ever smaller particles in our seas, being eaten by the fish we eat, making its ways into the stomachs of birds and whales, all the way up the food chain, leaching into our bodies, our organs and which will almost certainly outlast all of us. But there is undeniably a thrill to finding something that connects us to our past, or to another part of the world.

I throw away most of what I find. The fisherman's kisses – knots cut away while fishermen mend the nets and jettisoned in their thousands – balloons, bottles and shards of unidentifiable plastic. The rest, the interesting, join my other finds in bags in the van, in bowls on the kitchen table, in smaller bowls on the French dresser.

Sorting through them later, I would see that my myopic wanderings were anything but. In the microcosm of the things we find on the shore, I experience the occasional vertiginous journey upward to bird's eye level, at which I can see the curve of the horizon in a lobster tag, the downfall of a civilization in a popped balloon, a nurdle or a Coke bottle. Or I am hurled back to a childhood – mine or someone else's – soaked in nostalgia at finding spokey dokeys, rolls of caps and limbless action figures.

Emma, my wife, asks how long the finds are going to stay on the kitchen table. Some of them are beginning to smell. I hide them in a box marked 'items with narrative potential' in a desk drawer. Emma tells me they still smell terrible; they can live outside, preferably in the bin.

Among the stones beneath a steep, eroding cliff I found the legs of an entirely bleached white plastic cowboy figure (talk about undergoing a sea change). I'm drawn to the uncanniness of sea-worn plastic soldiers with lost arms and legs, twisted and frayed, dolls' heads in which the eyes are long gone or replaced with small stones that have lodged themselves in the eye sockets. They are traces and echoes, suggestions of other lives lived. These items, washed clean by the sea, rolled around on the seabed and returned to us, slightly strange, appeal to our sense of pareidolia.

Half a wrecked cowboy.

'That's Action Man's arse.' Photographer and beachcomber Lisa Woollett handed me the bum-shaped piece of pink plastic.

'I know it's from a 1966–78 Action Man because in 1978 he became blue pants Action Man. I found that out from an Action Man expert. It's thrilling when you find out something like that. The experts call him "blue pants, tanned Action Man". Officially this is called his hip section. This is the sorts of nerdy information you pick up when you go spinning off on a little trail of research into something.'

We were standing in Lisa's office, sifting through a collection of beach finds that entirely covered her desk.

'I like finding plastic dinosaurs and small figures, things that are quite poignant. I really like plastic plants, too. In fact, I've been really disappointed when I've discovered that the thing I've picked up is a real plant rather than a plastic one, which is a bit perverse, I suppose. I'm disappointed at my own disappointment. That's when you realize your balance between being thrilled by finding something and being appalled by the state of the beach has shifted. You realize you shouldn't be so thrilled about finding a plastic Kellogg's toy that came out of a cereal box fifteen years ago.'

Lisa started beachcombing as a child on the Isle of Sheppey, off the north-east coast of Kent, and then later mudlarking on the Thames, before arriving in Cornwall, when she rediscovered the beach, as a means of escape, at first from the intensity of having children, and later when her partner became ill.

'I'd been used to being out working and suddenly I was spending what seemed like years at a time with the kids,' she explained. 'Being by the beach was totally opposite to that. That solitude was an escape. The whole thing has been an escape. It was elemental, so different to everything else that was going on in my life.

'It started when the kids went to pre-school, when you get that government two-and-a-half hours a day, so I was going to beaches I could get to in that two-and-a-half hours. There's a liberation in that. When they went to primary school, I began to go further and further away. It started out as an antidote to the kids but then when they got a bit older, they loved it too.'

As she was saying this, she lifted out of her office collection prosthetic fingertips, ceramic fingernails, the arms and legs of dolls, mangled spoons, tea pods (each used to make a single cup and then discarded), toy soldiers in varying states of decay, bone toothbrushes and combs, the plastic soy sauce fish you get from take-outs, sea combs, a type of seaweed which gathers fishing line, rope, fabric.

Lisa Woollett's collection.

As with Lisa, each trip to the sea that I take by myself is a kind of escape, the interesting items I find there evidence of those moments of freedom from all my other responsibilities.

I thought of Lisa's collections as I sifted through the flotsam, jetsam and the items that had been pulled out of the eroding sand dunes at high tide. Further down the beach, I found two dead seal pups being fought over by a crow and a seagull – it was pupping season – and further on still, a porpoise with marks of a propellor strike on its torso. I called them into the Cornwall Wildlife Trust strandings hotline, which organizes the collection and autopsy of such birds and mammals, in order to build a picture of the causes of death of coastal wildlife. At first, I wasn't sure what they were: neither had a head.

'[They] are the first things to go,' said the cheerful volunteer on the other end of the line. 'The seal's neck goes limp and, being soft, it doesn't survive the beaching.'

Looking at the seals, it was impossible not to think of other bodies washing up on other beaches. Only that morning, after I had scanned the weather forecast, I had flicked to the news pages and read an article about a family of four who drowned in rough seas trying to cross the English Channel in a small, overcrowded fishing boat. Two of Rasul Iran Nezhad and Shiva Mohammad Panahi's children were aged just a year younger than my children and I got that telescopic sense again. There but for the grace of God.

Sobering, too, was the thought that less than a mile from the beach I was walking along is a site known more for the number of suicides than anything else, the sign of which is the number of stickers for The Samaritans along the low fence by the clifftop. A beachcomber friend had told me only the week before that she has a constant low-level dread of discovering a body washed up on the beach.

What washes up on the shore has made other headlines recently, too. Eleven containers lost overboard in the Bristol Channel and their plastic-heavy contents – nappies, incontinence pads, sanitary towels – heading towards the beaches of South Gower: Rotherslade, Langland, Three Cliffs Bay.

According to campaigning charity, Surfers Against Sewage, the plastic that washes in is not the biggest problem; it's the plastic that swills around the seas that poses the greatest threat. What we see on the strandline is just a message, an indication of the estimated eight million pieces of plastic that enter the sea every day, amounting to almost 270,000 tons.

The things we find on the shore are memory. They delight and connect. They throw us into fits of nostalgia. They are horror and shame. Our detritus returns to us, bit by bit, pushed up the beach on the tide, changed by the sea. On my strandline walk, I started to think about what it would be like to carry everything we ever bought or were given around behind us, to feel the sheer weight of it, to be hampered by it. It sometimes feels as though this is what the sea is reminding us by coughing up these plastic gobbets. You're connected to this whether you like it or not, it's saying, just like we are connected to the families who drown in the sea, heading to a better life. All this stuff we thought we were ridding ourselves of, it all comes back to us.

The tide had turned by the time I was returning to the lighthouse and carpark. On the way back, I saw several walkers almost swept out in the tidal surges that come out of the blue, or rather out of the foaming white. A couple in jeans, T-shirts and trainers gave up on trying to stay dry and waded through the tidal pools, having misjudged the speed of the incoming tide. A father was ushering his two small children in wetsuits down towards the boiling pit of sea, struggling against the wind with two neon yellow bodyboards. He seemed determined they should get in the water despite the lifeguards' red flags. One of the kite surfers was losing his battle with his kite, which seemed determined to drag him out to sea. The storm was approaching.

2

Island Fisher

Eel fishing & lobster potting in
St Martin's & St Agnes

I F THE STORM did not manage to shake the walls of the granite cottage, it still shook the windows hard enough to make me think they might give under the pressure, and to hope there would still be a roof on the bed and breakfast the next day. It pressed down the chimney and pushed coal dust back into the room. Electric light seemed out of keeping with the wildness of the evening and I listened to the storm rage as I studied old maps of the island by firelight. Later, in bed, it was easy enough to imagine the same scene played out at any time in the island's history. I might have been sheltering from it under a different roof, but the storm itself would have been the same, tearing across these exposed rocks in the Atlantic and churning the sea into a fury.

By morning, though, the storm had passed over and the island was calm. What was left in its wake was a warm, almost tropical day in which all trace of the rain and winds that kept the island's boat owners awake in fear for their moorings was entirely gone. Like countless others before me, I found it difficult not to indulge in anthropomorphism. The morning seemed to be saying, 'Oh, that? Last night? I'm sorry about that. I was a

J of Hicks's dipping lugger at Periglis, St Agnes.

bit out of order, I suppose. Never mind, I'll make up for it today. We'll do something nice. You forgive me, right?'

This same sou'westerly storm had torn at the Cornish coast too, though the cottage from which I experienced it was some 28 miles further west of Land's End, on St Martin's on the Isles of Scilly. This gale had the same quality as the storms that tear up and down the valley where I live, though this one felt more elemental, less mediated by the land. Low lying and unprotected, Scilly bears the full brunt of the Atlantic storm systems.

A two-faced Celtic idol overlooks the stretch of sea between the islands of St Martin's and Nornour, on the eastern edge of the islands. A stone's throw from the former's huge white and red daymark, which sits atop the island's highest point, the granite idol is all but invisible from the sea. In comparison to it, the daymark, built in 1683, is still a child.

The Celtic menhir known as Billy Idol, Chapel Down, St Martin's.

The idol has watched over the boats that approached Scilly in storm and calm weather for somewhere between 4,000 and 5,000 years – no one really knows exactly. It has watched over arrivals and departures to the islands in heaving winter seas, over the final tacks and gibes of those who managed to navigate the passage from the mainland, the tearing ledges and the Atlantic's fury and those who faltered on the rocks. It has watched over countless shipwrecks too, including what remains one of the world's worst oil spills, that of the SS *Torrey Canyon*, which wrecked off St Martin's in 1967. It has watched over the incursion of the seas that transformed the island of Ennor into the archipelago we now call Scilly, and it continues to watch as the seas rise in the time of manmade climate change.

It is mottled with lichen, a squat, weatherworn thing. Most archaeologists agree that at less than a metre tall, the Neolithic or Bronze Age statue was part of a taller sculpture at one time, a more imposing menhir. On one side, the side that faces out to sea, the indentations on the roughly carved face indicate eyes, nose and mouth; on the opposite face, fainter markings suggest it is a kind of Janus figure, though I can see nothing of the second face, no matter how much I adopt the scientific method for seeing things more clearly by turning my head on its side and screwing up my eyes.

The idol had been lost for centuries and was rediscovered in 1948, by the Reverend H.A. Lewis, being used as one of the bricks in a field wall, after which it was identified as an important archaeological find. Shortly after its rediscovery though, in what can only be assumed was a show of extreme carelessness, it was lost again, spending the next few decades hidden in the gorse. When Keith Low uncovered it again in 1988, he gave it the nickname Billy Idol, after the punk singer, and concreted it into its current location. It is close to where it is thought to have stood originally on Chapel Down, with a clear view out to sea, presumably in part so it would not go wandering off again.

By the time I met Keith, he was in his seventies and had had one of his legs amputated. With his battered captain's hat, wooden leg and glass eye, he seemed to have perfected the look of a pirate from a Robert Louis Stevenson novel. Confined to a mobility scooter though, he could no longer make it beyond the paved paths across the low, scoured gorse on Chapel Down. He gave me directions and, on a morning that now felt more like late summer than winter, I found myself sitting with my back against the diminutive god, following its gaze across to the tiny, uninhabited island of Nornour.

I had visited Nornour a few years earlier to explore the Iron Age village that lies hidden in the grass at the point thought to be the main landing place on the now-mostly sunken island of Ennor. This time though, I was on St Martin's on commission to write a short story about the island and it seemed important to me to spend some time with its oldest resident, the one who had been given the name of a singer from the 1980s. Leaning against the god, in the sun's warmth the morning after a storm I was already beginning to believe had not happened at all, I conjured up some Billy Idol songs on my phone before remembering I was never really a fan and returned to the soundtrack of the wind on the grass and the gorse.

The diminutive two-faced god seems to me to exhibit the quality of a St Martin's islander perfectly. If you were born on the island, Keith told me later, you cultivated a particular way of looking at the world, with one eye for the land, the other for the sea.

'When I was a boy, you couldn't get away with anything, because there was always an uncle or a cousin up in the fields looking out for you,' he said. 'We always looked out for one another and we were always looked out for, but at the same time we were also looking out to sea. You'd always be on the lookout out for a boat where it shouldn't be or for the sign there might be something washed in on the shore.'

While Scillonians, like the poor coastal communities of Cornwall, traditionally supplemented their hard lives with wreck, looking at the islands now it is hard to believe that was ever the case. The same is true of the Cornish coast, where smart yachts fill spaces between the fishing boats in the harbours and the land cruisers and Teslas the driveways of chocolate box villages, during summer at least. On the Isles of Scilly tourism accounts for 85 per cent of the local economy now and almost three-quarters of islanders are employed in the tourism industry. The wrecking years are still very much in living memory though, and older islanders I spoke to bemoaned, in particular, the dawn of containerization, after which pickings became slim as less and less loose cargo fell from ships' decks.

Keith, who was born in 1946, recalled the 120-gallon cask of sherry his granddad kept in his boat shed, deck-spill from a ship that had been torpedoed in Biscay during the First World War and had shed its load of wine. With the set of the tides the casks eventually washed in on Great Bay on St Martin's. Keith's grandfather was one of the men who dragged the casks above the tideline and placed two stones on top of them – the universal sign among wreckers that an item has been claimed. He later installed one on trestles in his boat shed. The law of wreckage was an unwritten one, Keith said, though it was always honoured. Decades later, Keith came across smaller casks of brandy in the same place, slightly spoiled but, he claimed, fine to drink once it had been filtered through a pair of tights.

Everything that washes up on the shore has to be reported by law, so the men with casks sent over samples of the sherry, the claret and champagne topped up with seawater, to the Receiver of the Wreck on St Mary's. They claimed not to know what it was, nor if it was of value, but that they wouldn't mind keeping the casks for water butts, after they had dispensed with the contents, obviously.

The Receiver of the Wreck, Keith said, charged them one and sixpence for their water butts and the next Christmas several bottles of sherry, claret and champagne were left anonymously on his doorstep because, as Keith told me, tapping the side of his nose, 'he knew what was on'. The islanders were still drinking the brandy well into the 1930s.

The Receiver of the Wreck's attitude to the wine casks was indicative of a principle I came across countless times around the islands, that of turning a blind eye. Island life is governed by a whole raft of unwritten codes that allow people to rub along with one another. In a community of just a handful of people, it seems a necessity. You might always be on the lookout, though it is surely a good idea for community harmony and relations if you are able to ignore at least some of what you see and the common law, which went back further than statute or case law, stated that the sea's bounty was fair game, occasional recompense for an otherwise hard life.

Another of these codes, on St Martin's at least, surrounded the sanctity of fishing rocks. Like many families on St Martin's, Keith's had their own grounds in which they fished, through hard-earned knowledge from years of work on the waters around the island and – a closely guarded secret – from their own ledge or rock, beneath which they fished for lobster and eel. It was a way of ensuring there was enough food for each family in winter. At some point, as a child, he said, your forebears would tell you where the family rocks were, and you would learn to fish there. In Keith's case, his uncle, the man who taught him to hunt rabbits and birds, fish for wrasse from the rocks, work pots for crab, drift for pilchards, and shoot nets for mullet, taught him how to fish for eel, too.

Catching your first eel as a child was a rite of passage, Keith informed me. While lobster might have been the prize, fishing for conger eels was infinitely more fun. He recalled the day, in the late 1950s, when his uncle took Keith and a friend – a boy from Canada, the son of diplomats, who spent his summer holidays at

Keith's home – to his ledge. They were ten or eleven at the time and set out, armed with an eel crook, a long pole with a nasty looking hook at the end, for a spot just off White Island, a small hillock connected to St Martin's by a tidal causeway.

As they waded in up to their chests in the dark water, his uncle explained what would happen. He would fish around beneath the rock with the crook until he felt an eel there and then he would pull, at which point the eel would wrap itself around one of their legs or arms. Keith recalled the tension, the thrill and the terror of waiting for something to happen and then his uncle's nod that he had found something, the jerk of the eel crook and then the sensation of a large creature in the water with them. In Keith's story, the eel wrapped itself around his waist and his uncle shouted to him to hold onto the head. He recalled the strength of it and the terrifying face that came up out of the water, level with his, the rows of teeth in its strong jaws. The three of them walked out of the water with the eel still coiled around Keith, after which his uncle dispatched it with a pocketknife. There was a kind of relish to Keith's telling of this story, though I imagine that as a child I would have been traumatized by the event. He recalled they took it straight home where his mother skinned the eel and cut it into small chunks, each about the size of a Turkish delight, and fried them in a light batter. Eel, he said, is always best eaten fresh.

Early the next morning, I walked across to White Island at low tide, picking my way across the rocky bar. I tried to work out where Keith's rock was from the description he had given. Despite the fact it had not been in use for decades, I hadn't wanted to push too hard on account of it being a secret place. I hoped he had passed the knowledge of where it was to one of his children and that the secret would not die with him, regardless of whether his descendants used the fishing rock or not.

I might have walked by Keith's rock several times and wouldn't have known, though I found another rock I was looking for, one that was marked on an undated, though clearly old, map of the island I had found tucked away in a chest in the front room of the bed and breakfast. It was marked as Aunt Elsig's rock. I asked around, but no one remembered Aunt Elsig, nor why there was a rock between St Martin's and White Island named after her.

Looking back over hundreds of years of maps, it became clear that in a place this small everything has a name. The naming of the larger settlements on St Martin's is beautifully self-explanatory – Lower Town, Middle Town and Higher Town (though the use of the term Town for settlements made up of a small clutch of houses might seem a stretch) – and the larger beaches – Great Bay and Little Bay – though even on a granular level, each patch of sand, inlet and cave, each ledge and part-submerged rock, has its name. It makes sense in a place where being able to identify a particularly dangerous rock might mean the difference between returning safely from a fishing trip or drowning.

Looking at the maps, it seems the names shift with time. They are updated, adapted and renamed, or are known by entirely different names by different families. It is something the play-wright Nick Darke talks about in the documentary *The Wrecking Season*, which charted his interests as a fisherman and a wrecker; every rock and cove in the parish had a name, a fact he said showed just how heavily the coast was used. He namechecked Rubble Cove, The Turtle, The Nancy, Trescore. He worried that these names were being lost and forgotten – and with them an important history.

Standing by Aunt Elsig's rock, I wasn't sure how willing I would be, even now, to rile a large eel in the dark, kelpy waters there and nor could I imagine catching a fish large enough that it could wrap itself around my waist.

On the north of the island, I went in search of the spot where Keith's fabled casks had floated in. I found nothing so romantic washed up on the shore, though I could see from the path that part of the tideline along the beach at Great Bay was an odd shade of grey. Up close, this grey line revealed itself to be hundreds

Little Bay and Great Bay, St Martin's.

of aluminium can lids spread out along the tideline, a dull grey, metallic daisy chain the length of the beach. As I followed the daisy chain, I tried to work out how much of Keith's stories were true and how much they were embellished, but now my boat back to St Mary's was due and the questions I had would have to wait until I returned.

At the tiny airport on St Mary's, I got talking to one of the passengers with whom I would be sharing the 15-minute flight back to the mainland, a man who was visiting from Canada. He looked to be about the same age as Keith and we ended up discussing the story of the eel. He listened to the first part, then stopped me and completed it through to the cooking of the eel. He was, it turned out, the Canadian friend Keith had mentioned, though in the retelling the eel had gained another two feet in length.

When I returned to Scilly it was early July. St Martin's was on my agenda again. I had been going through the notes of my

Jof Hicks's withy pots.

conversations with Keith and trying again to pick out the facts from the stories. My first port of call, though, was St Agnes, the most eastern of the inhabited islands, where I had arranged to meet lobster fisherman Jof Hicks.

I had always assumed the owner of the concrete boat shed in Periglis Bay was a hoarder rather than someone who was doing something useful with the confusion of boat parts, bike wheels, pots, tripods, scrap metal, wood and deflated RIBs (rigid inflatable boats) in the yard. Attached to various piles of rubbish were handwritten signs that read, 'Please do not take anything – everything is here for a reason', though it was not clear at all what that reason might be.

The interior of the boat shed was much the same. Every surface was covered with a miscellany of sea-related odds and ends. There were boats hanging from the ceiling and what looked like abstract sculptures hanging from the walls. Beyond the chaos of the workshop a large set of double doors led out onto a long slipway at the top of which were several boats: a large wooden yacht covered in a tarpaulin and from within which emerged knocking sounds; kayaks; a defunct Hobie 16 catamaran with no mast or rigging; several small tenders.

On the fence, there was a handwritten sign that read, LOBSTER, LOBSTER, LOBSTER, and beneath that, 'Caught with totally, entirely, completely zero plastic fishing gear', in a somewhat incongruous echo of the GIRLS, GIRLS, GIRLS posters you might see on certain streets in LA or Amsterdam. On a hard standing, there was a contraption that looked like a cross between a dressmaker's dummy and a wicker basket, and a man in his forties was bending and weaving thin branches of willow into it.

The contraption, it turned out, was a jig for weaving the lobster pots Jof drops in the waters around the island, part of his attempt to challenge the negative impacts of the fishing industry by fishing without damaging the seas on which he relies.

If anyone is qualified to do this, it seems natural that it might be a Hicks. The Hicks family have lived and fished on St Agnes – or Agnes, as most of the islanders call it – for centuries, and the name is linked inextricably with the surrounding waters. They have been pilot boat sailors, lifeboatmen and gig rowers, as well as other things 'less regulated', as Jof described it.

In the nineteenth century, Hicks men were known, in particular, for their skill as pilots, guiding ships to safety through the maze of rocks and ledges, and rowing out to rescue those in distress on the Western Rocks, some of the most dangerous in UK waters, if the number of wrecks is anything to go by. In 1860, Sir Walter Besant wrote, seemingly hyperbolically, perhaps, that 'every rock in Scilly has a shipwreck', though the sheer number of wrecks over the centuries – somewhere in the region of 700 to 1,000 – suggest there is at least some truth to his statement.

The perilous nature of the waters around Agnes is attested to by the fact that it was the site of the first lighthouse on Scilly, built in 1680 to warn ships off from the shallow submerged skerries and ledges of the Western Rocks though, if the lighthouse on St Agnes is the clear winner in terms of age, it was eclipsed on the building of the nearby Bishop Rock, which was first lit on 1 September 1858. In 1882, the height of the tower was raised to 175 feet, yet in the stormiest conditions waves can still overtop the tower. Its two white flashes every 15 seconds can be seen for 42 miles in clear conditions. In a quirk that compounded the dangers involved in sailing these waters, the Western Rocks were inaccurately located on charts written before 1750, making them doubly difficult to avoid. This stretch of sea harbours two parallel reefs on which shipwreck sits on shipwreck, in one case literally one on top of the other, the *Plympton* and the *Hathor*, which are crisscrossed like Jenga blocks off Thicasus Ledge.

One of the last wrecks of the era of sail took place here on 14 December 1907. When the seven-masted schooner, the *Thomas W. Lawson*, was caught in a huge storm close to the Western Rocks, Jof's great-grandfather, Steven Lewis Hicks, was among the lifeboat crew that went out to the aid of the ship, which had anchored between the Bishop Rock Lighthouse and the Gunner and Nundeep rocks, hoping to ride out the gale there. The *Lawson*, the largest schooner ever built, was travelling from Philadelphia to London with 60,000 barrels of paraffin oil. She had been battered by storms for the whole journey and had already lost her lifeboats and rafts in crossing the Atlantic. Her captain, mistaking the light at Bishop Rock for a passing ship, led her too close to the rocks and decided to anchor there. The storm did not let up though and the *Lawson's* position was so perilous that lifeboats from St Mary's and Agnes were deployed, though when they arrived the captain of the *Lawson* refused help and, with conditions deteriorating, the ship eventually wrecked on Shag Rock, despite the efforts of the lifeboat crews. Following the wreck, the six-oared *Slippen*, the oldest of the pilot gig boats, built in 1830 and like the *Lawson* itself, a relic of times gone by, launched to look for survivors, though only two of the 18-strong *Lawson* crew survived, and the captain of the Agnes lifeboat, William Cook Hicks, also died in the rescue attempt.

The *Lawson* aside, the age of the motor and of the steamship had all but put paid to the Agnes lifeboat by the early 1900s. With steamships able to ignore the wind direction, the demand for pilots fell off, as did the need for gig crews and the Agnes lifeboat station closed its doors in 1920. Although the last recorded gig rescue was as late as 1955, after the turn of the twentieth century it was a rare occurrence. The building was handed over for use by the Sennen Cove fishers from the mainland, who traditionally fished from Agnes and used the island as a base, though it was later absorbed into the Hicks's farm and it is now back in use as Jof's workshop.

The family farm is still there and the Hicks family still very much in force, conducting their lives around the sea and the tides. The knocking sound I had heard from within the wooden hull turned out to be Jof's father, Johann, who was slowly renovating a 1950s Dallimore-design wooden yacht, more for the pleasure of working on the boat than any rush to get it back on the water. Later, while Jof and I were talking in the boat shed yard about fishing and making creels by hand, Jof's brother put his head round the yard in lifejacket and full waterproofs, having just stepped off his boat and shortly after that Jof's wife came down to the slipway for her daily swim. In this brief snapshot, it seemed clear that the Hicks are still very much a family of the sea.

Jof was born on Agnes, though like all islanders, he had to leave Scilly to complete his education. He trained and worked as an industrial designer. Like many of those who leave an island idyll to see the wider world, however, he was drawn back home eventually. After learning the art of creating traditional inkwell withy lobster creels from a Sennen fisherman, Jof came up with the idea of starting a commercial fishing business without the associated downsides of polluting the very seas on which the fisher relies. The bizarre sculptures hanging on the walls of the workshop, it turned out, were the product of Jof's experiments with reclaimed materials like bicycle wheel hubs to create geodesic domes made of aluminium or steel, with tamarisk to create new types of pots.

'It fascinates me,' he said as he retrieved soaked withies, inserted them into the structures, bent lashes, clamped the withies with his thumb, rotated them, twisted, tensioned, 'the idea of appropriate technologies, finding out what you can do with materials you've grown yourself or reclaimed and how that works in terms of making a living. I wanted to work out how I could take that knowledge and turn it into a business.'

The idea, which started with Jof building his own creels in an attempt to avoid having to rely on the plastic-based commercial creels that often get lost and end up being part of the problem, like so much ghost gear, extended to Jof growing his own withies with which to make the pots and then to looking at ways of dropping and pulling the pots without using fossil fuels. He was keen to stress he wasn't trying to attack the small-scale fishing industry. It's not their fault they had inherited faulty materials, he told me. Many of the local fishers consider themselves guardians of the sea.

As we talked, several people stopped by to ask about the creels, some of them visitors, others islanders who are becoming increasingly interested in the idea of seafood without climate guilt, and since starting the project he has had enquiries about it from far beyond the shores of Scilly.

'It's a sad time to find people are interested in this, as it coincides with the zeitgeist of people's general awareness of the ways in which plastic is damaging the seas,' he said in between a steady stream of people stopping to talk. 'We're more aware now of how these materials are polluting the seas, the chance of losing a pot, or of bits of plastic breaking off, which is happening continually.'

At the top of the slipway Jof asked me to take one corner of the seemingly defunct catamaran and help him to wheel it down to the shore. Up close it looked as though someone had been playing Meccano with it and it took Jof sitting in the seat to see he had retrofitted the Hobie with a sliding seat and oarlocks. It showed the same sort of ingenuity as the lobster pots – familiar technology, repurposed; scaffolding poles, chipboard and lots of string. The sliding seat catamaran, he said, was small enough to row easily and to handle in waves, and it provided a stable platform from which to haul pots. It's a constant process of design, he explained, design and redesign. He pulled on the oars and the catamaran took off, leaving me in its wake, to play catch-up in a kayak.

While Jof dropped a net to catch fish with which to bait the pots the next day, I peered over the edge of the kayak. The sea reflected a grey sky but beyond this the water was startlingly clear and I could see metres down through the thong weed and kelp to the seabed. Jof's voice brought me back to the surface. This was the part of the process he liked least, he was saying, relying on nylon nets, though he had been looking into alternatives.

When he was done, we rowed out of Periglis Cove, past the campsite at Troytown where I was staying in a borrowed tent. On the horizon the Bishop Rock light blinked at us. Beyond Troytown, we passed St Warna's Cove, behind which is an old well. In island legend, Warna, the Irish saint of wreckers, who landed there in a coracle, was traditionally invoked for the dual and conflicting purposes of both protecting lives at sea and bringing much needed wreck to the islanders. Pins would be dropped down the well along with the wish that all at sea would be safe, though there was also talk during seasons of particular hardship that some islanders would drop bent pins in with the prayer, 'to send a wreck before morning'. It is part of a long push–pull relationship with wreckage in Scilly. On one hand, the islanders, especially on Agnes, were famed for their skill as pilots, though when lighthouses were introduced to the islands, there was considerable push-back against the move. I was tempted to disregard the story of the wish for a wreck to come, though it recalled a game Keith Low had told me about in which he and his friends would throw bent brass pins filched from his mother's sewing box into the spring on Chapel Down, close to where he later set Billy Idol on the rocks.

St Agnes and the Western Rocks have always felt to me like the outsider islands of Scilly, stuck out on the edge of the edge, the most remote, the wildest part of a wild place. Rowing on a glassy sea among the archipelago of tiny islands, ledges and rocks that rear up from the seabed, the whole place took on an almost mythical feeling.

Jof slowed the catamaran and brought the two hulls over a buoy, leant forward, hooked the line and used the sliding seat to raise the pot, which was weighed down with a lump of granite. The first pot was empty and we rowed on a way to the second which was empty too. Jof seemed unfazed by the empty pots – even when the fishing was no good, it was a more enjoyable workout than the gym, he said, and far cheaper than therapy.

'It's not a cheap thing to do,' he said as we rowed between pots. 'But what we're really talking about is the price of food. Can a lobster flown in from Nova Scotia and sold for £2 be right? This is a small-scale, artisan project, but I want people to understand why they are paying £40 or £50 a kilo for lobster. I want them to say, "Yes, I'll pay that because I see that's what it should cost. I won't have it twice a week – I'll have it once a year."'

Nothing about what Jof is doing is convenient. It is time consuming and slow, fragile even. It takes time to grow the withies, time to soak them and to shape them into creels. And even then, a wooden creel may only last a season or so in the harsh waters around the Eastern Isles. It seems to point to a truth about convenience and the price of the food we eat and if nothing else, the project serves to demonstrate that we pay the price one way or the other.

How do you quantify the material, the skill and time taken to catch a lobster without ruining the sea and the seabed? How do you quantify the growing of the withies and the time and skill taken to create a creel that might last a single fishing season if the fisher is lucky? Not to mention how do you quantify the life of a creature as complex and intelligent as a lobster?

'In the past, we've paired science with economics and that has failed,' Jof called across from the catamaran. 'We've had this mystical, blind faith that somehow we'll be bailed out of this, but the last fifty or sixty years has shown us that's not going to happen. We're now entering a phase of utter frustration. So, let's pair science with art and see what happens.'

The third pot came up with a lobster under the legal size limit and after looking it over and giving it a few encouraging words he released it over the side, and it squeaked as it re-entered the water. The next two contained larger lobsters, which Jof checked to confirm they met the size requirements, turned them over in case they were carrying eggs, which would mean he would return them, then put bands round the claws and lowered them into a keep bucket.

Though the water in the bay had been almost millpond still, there was a swell as we headed further away from the shore, towards the islets off which Jof had dropped the furthest pots. The most outlying sat just off Shooting Rock, where we stopped for a while to listen to the sound of the wave as it slapped on the underside of a ledge, the noise which gives the rocks their name. A seal surfaced a few metres off and watched us listening to the boom of wave on rock. It sat there staring for a while, still and silent as the swell that passed beneath us.

'You write off the time you spend out here,' Jof said, when the seal had gone. 'You'd happily give that time instead of watching YouTube or sitting on a rowing machine in a gym.'

It was a world away from the commercial fishing fleets, a world away from the huge super trawler I had seen off the

Cornish coast earlier in the year. Jof had eight pots out, a drop in the ocean. It remains to be seen if people will continue to pay a premium price for the story of their ethically caught lobster, but against a backdrop of super trawlers decimating huge areas of sea, against mass by-catch and the industrial hoovering up of Antarctic krill, which threatens the entire ecosystem there, Jof's felt like a small, positive story.

The whole experience took me back to a conversation I had with marine conservation biologists Professor Callum Roberts and Dr Julie Hawkins, as we walked a section of the Cornish coast path, about their desire to see sustainable fisheries that do not damage the environment.

Jof Hicks pulling lobsters by catamaran.

In Callum's view, it boils down to one thing. We need to fish less, using less destructive methods, waste less, pollute less and protect more. If we were to do that, he said, the ocean would really rebound. We need to reduce the number of fish we extract and use much less destructive methods of extracting fish.

'I want to see sustainable fisheries that don't damage the environment,' he commented. 'That requires us to rethink our relationship with the sea, to stop thinking of fish as a cheap commodity that can be turned into fertilizer and turned into fishmeal or rendered down and converted into prawns. It's thinking about these commodities as incredibly important for reasons far beyond food. They are the things that keep the sea healthy – they keep life on earth ticking over. Without healthy oceans we won't have a healthy planet.'

As the American marine biologist, Sylvia Earle put it, there is no green without blue.

Both Callum and Julie's interests in the sea started thousands of miles away from the cold waters of the Fal Estuary. They met while working on coral reefs, like those off the Maldives, where the couple have completed over 2,000 dives. They describe the sensory overload of diving on healthy reefs, the sheer amount of life there and the feeling of being a visitor, privileged to go back day after day and watch the same animals go about their lives. These are habitats that are in rapid decline.

Callum outlined the problem as being one of attitudes and storytelling. Throughout history, he explained, we have had a feeling that the ocean is so big that we can put into it whatever we don't want, without comeback and take out of it whatever we want with no limit. These two beliefs have proved false, though it is hard to rethink our attitudes to the oceans as they've been built up over tens of thousands of years. It's hard-wired into us.

Throughout history, he told me, we have been doing things to fulfil our immediate needs, which has often meant eating up our local resources and then moving on. When we were bands of hunter gatherers we would move around and if local resources were depleted we would simply find some more somewhere else. We are still hard-wired to believe the world will carry on providing for us, regardless of the evidence we have to the contrary.

For Julie, some of the problem is connected with our attitudes towards the fishing industry itself. People have an incredibly romantic notion towards fishing, she said. It's a deeply engrained part of our heritage and as a result we are too tolerant of the problems associated with it. The small fishing boats bobbing on the sea, with all the memories of the seaside and childhood that brings back, act as a kind of smokescreen for the bigger problem, which is not those small fishing boats but the beamers and dredgers, the ones causing most of the destruction.

Julie's thoughts recalled another conversation I had, this one with Dr Heather Koldewey, one of the other few prominent marine scientists shouting for the ocean, as we floated on a stand-up paddleboard just off St Michael's Mount. Much of Heather's work, aside from the science itself, is about telling the sea's story better. She recalled hearing a fisheries scientist and a fisherman on an early morning call-in show on the radio at the time she was doing her PhD. The fisherman was talking about how his family had always fished and that what we need to do is fish harder. He made it a personal story, one about heritage and culture and one that lots of people could relate to. The fisheries scientist, on the other hand, was talking about what the data maybe showed. His approach, the one used by scientists across the world, was to be tentative, to stick to the data and highlight its limitations as well as its possibilities. More research is required. As a scientist, you're trained to be very boring, she said. It's always about problems and always about uncertainties, so that's what comes across to people.

There are opportunities, though, she said: 'A lot of people who are in positions of influence are also influenced by the values they grew up with. So you get people who say, "I used to go fishing with my granddad, or I used to go on holiday here." Lots of people have that experience, and you want to say to them "if you want to keep it like this, you need to protect it". We need actions not words. That's where there are opportunities for change.'

As Julie told me, before we parted ways on the coast path, 'These places will recover if we protect them. And we won't believe they are the same places once they do recover.'

That evening, from where I pitched my tent, I could see the two-masted dipping lugger that Jof had built years ago swinging on its mooring in the bay and I fell asleep to the constant shush of the waves just metres away. When I woke in the night, it was to the comforting flash of Bishop Rock – two white flashes every 15 seconds – and in the morning, I woke again to the sound of oystercatchers.

From Agnes, I headed to St Martin's. I wanted to press Keith on some of the details of his stories, to see if he could help me to separate the fact from the fiction, the yarn from events as they happened. I wanted to try again to see if I could tell where the memory ended and the storyteller began, though when I reached the house, I noticed the roses had grown across the porch of his cottage and when I pushed through the brambles, I could see the house had been cleared. In the bakery they told me that Keith had died a few months earlier. He was buried in the churchyard, near his mother's grave, the baker said, though there was no headstone to mark it yet. Instead of heading to the churchyard, though, I walked in the opposite direction to check on Billy Idol.

Sitting side by side with the small inscrutable god, it occurred to me that it was Keith who told me that the idol had two faces, that he was a Janus figure. I had come across no other mention of it in any of the accounts of the stone figure, which is docu-mented in several archaeological references to both the Isles of

Scilly and of the Celtic coast more generally. Very little is known about it at all – not its purpose, nor who carved it, nor whether it is actually in the place where it originally stood, looking out towards Nornour. In fact, most of the accounts I found seemed more interested in the fact it was found, lost and found again, perhaps as the facts around these last few years of the statue's long life were at least vaguely verifiable.

It seemed to me he made a suitable headstone for Keith, more so than one carved for the purpose perhaps. I won't get to know exactly which bits of Keith's stories were true now, any more than I can know whether Billy Idol really did watch over the comings and goings of boats five thousand years ago nor whether he had two faces or one, or what he represented to the people who carved him. There's a tradition on Scilly of, as one islander put it to me, 'trying to get as much bullshit past visitors as possible'. It's a popular game with the boatmen, she said and, when I started to listen out for it, I heard the good-natured insertion of absolute rubbish into many of the conversations I heard between boatmen and tourist. Add to that the fact that islands like St Martin's and Agnes are so thick with stories that it is difficult to pick out the strands of truth from the folklore and between the gossip, the bullshit and the tall tales it may be impossible to get to the bottom of most stories.

What most of Keith's stories speak of, though, is a deep and abiding relationship with these waters. The sea is the thread that runs through all of them and sometimes, perhaps, it takes a bit of bullshit, a bit of storytelling to get to the truth of the matter.

Scarlet and gold cup corals. Photograph by Heather Buttivant.

3

Rock Pool Pilgrim

Spring tide on the north coast

W<small>E WATCH</small> the full, pink moon rise through a stand of trees at the head of the valley. Through the branches, it looks eerily large, closer than it should be, out of proportion and alien. My daughter, Alana, asks if the moon is actually closer to the earth than usual. I toy with bluffing an answer but realize I have no idea. I tell her I don't think so, though why it should appear so huge in the sky is beyond me. She'll have to trust me on this one. Later, I do some research into it and find out that, according to NASA, no one really understands what causes the moon illusion. It is one of those things we accept happens, like the fact that Brazil nuts always end up on the top in a bowl of mixed nuts, or the fact that your bike stays upright when you are in motion, though no one really understands why these things occur. The best guess about the moon illusion is it's deeply embedded somewhere in our wiring, some throwback to an earlier moment in our evolution.

Coinciding with this most striking of moons, which comes at the end of April, is the lowest tide of spring. All around Cornwall, this super low tide will expose the remains of wrecks that are rarely seen. Huge boilers, often the last part of a ship to disintegrate, will jut out from the sand at the lowest point of tide, like crashed space capsules. At Chyandour and Wherrytown near Mount's Bay, which cradles the iconic St Michael's Mount, parts of a 6,000-year-old forest will be uncovered, the petrified remains of huge trees – ancient oak, pine, alder and hazel among which it is possible to wander. I find these lowest tides uncanny. The sunken, petrified trunks require us to look at the world anew, to imagine a time when what is now almost always covered in water, was thick forest, to imagine St Michael's Mount not as an island in a bay but a hill in the woods as it once was. The Cornish name for St Michael's Mount, Karrek Loos yn Koos, alludes to the island's terrestrial past and translates as The Grey Rock in the Woods, a memory of its former state.

I get the same feeling of the uncanny when I look over the edge of the tripper boats into the clear, shallow waters between the islands of Scilly and glimpse field boundaries among the seaweed, evidence of Ennor. These reminders of a past in which the seas were lower feed the legend of Lyonesse, the fabled land that – in some branches of the Arthurian legend – lay between Cornwall and Scilly and which, in the story of Tristan and Iseult, sank beneath the waves before Tristan could take his crown when his father died. Richard Carew in his 1602 survey claimed the bizarre catches fishermen made off Penzance, of doors and windows that came up in their nets, were proof of the lost land, though there is no real evidence to suggest that it ever existed.

The huge holes in our understanding of people's lives at a time when the sea was lower offers tempting gaps into which myths find themselves a home. I like the description that surrealist painter Ithell Colquhoun gave of Lyonesse as being lost in the depths of every mind. It does not matter that it does not exist because the idea of it, like the moon illusion, is embedded within us. On Scilly, though this low tide will not reveal Lyonesse, it will provide one of the rare opportunities to walk between Bryher and Tresco, across a temporary land bridge that opens between the islands and on which inter-island cricket matches are played.

The extreme low tides also offer a chance for rock poolers to see creatures that are normally only visible to divers. To coincide with the super low tide, I arrange to meet rock pooler and conservationist Heather Buttivant to explore the intertidal zone that is off limits for most of the year.

'All rock pools are not equal,' Heather tells me. She is crouching beside one of the topmost rock pools in a rocky inlet on the north coast, lifting stones and examining their undersides before placing them back, as gently as though she is handling ancient artefacts in a museum.

The pools at the top of the beach are exposed for longer than all the others, she says. Only a few things can survive here. The oxygen levels can shoot up and down, especially at night when the seaweeds aren't photosynthesizing and in the full glare of the sun the temperature in these pools soars to the mid-20s. As the water evaporates, the salinity rockets too and sometimes they dry out entirely, though that is not the case with this one. A freshwater stream runs through it, so the creatures here must cope with the mix of saline and fresh water too. As a result, the creatures found here, the ones we are most likely to see on a trip to the beach – beadlet anemones, barnacles and certain types of sea snails – are extremists, able to withstand the harshest of conditions. They are some of the weirdest, too.

'These little blobs of jelly don't look like they can do anything but they are incredibly well adapted,' Heather says, pointing out a gelatinous lump. 'They put their tentacles out to hunt, to trap plankton. That mouth in the middle, that's their only orifice. It's their mouth *and* their bottom, and these ones can give birth to live babies, which they spit out through there too. Everything on the shore is so weird.'

Heather has been rock pooling on this beach her whole life. Growing up in rural Cornwall, without a cinema or a shopping centre on her doorstep, she spent most of her childhood outdoors, playing with friends and exploring the beaches and pools close to home. She recalls, as a young girl, seeing hosts of goose barnacles washed up on a log, all of them opening and closing in a way she describes as 'absolutely alien', and the fascination of finding a dead whale washed up. The constantly changing environment lit her imagination and she now brings her own family here. Her partner and son, who she refers to as Rockpool Junior, are further down the beach already, armed with waterproof cameras and margarine tubs for inspecting finds.

'It's the otherness of it,' Heather says when I push her on what keeps her coming back here. 'I can get excited about things I've seen a million times. Take barnacles, for example. They're like James Bond villains, in these tiny volcano lairs. It's hard to imagine what sort of animal is in there.'

Barnacles, Heather explains, live with their heads pressed down against the rock and they build a little fortress around them with a trapdoor at the top. When the tide is out, the trapdoor remains closed, and when they are submerged, their legs emerge from the top of the tiny volcano and kick food back into their mouths.

The other thing about barnacles (a fact that seems to clash slightly with the image Heather has painted of them as classic Bond villains) is, in her words, their 'lucky dip penis', which is extraordinarily long for such a small animal, stretching up to eight times the length of their body. They reach out with it, blindly, in an attempt to mate with other barnacles. It doesn't really matter which other barnacle the penis lands on either, as barnacles are hermaphroditic.

We are crouching with our faces a couple of inches from the rock, and for a while the world shrinks to a few square inches of rock. As we sit up and readjust to the change in scale, Heather explains that, sitting on Cornwall's north coast, this particular cove is open to heavy seas and storms and the long fetch of North Atlantic waves. We are less than a mile from Jane Darke's wreck-filled, wreck-built house where flotsam and jetsam arrive with the winter storms. This beach is unusual, though, in that just a few metres offshore two small rocky islets protect the beach from the brunt of the ocean's force, creating an environment in which life can flourish. It is also protected from development, being managed, like much of the coastline around Cornwall, by the National Trust.

Heather records and reports her findings to build up a picture of the creatures that live in the intertidal zone in Cornwall. There are remarkably few records of the creatures that live on the coastline, she tells me, so it can be hard to understand how it is changing and to make a case to protect it. Although we might walk on the same beaches hundreds of times, they hold onto their mysteries and we are only just beginning to understand the range of life in the waters around our coast, the species that remain and those we are losing through over-development, pollution, warming sea waters and acidification.

Heather is one of a handful of knowledgeable amateurs who have dedicated their lives to recording life around Cornwall's rocky shores and her records have already been used in making the case for marine-protected areas around Looe, where she now lives, where she discovered four species of stalked jellyfish that had not been recorded in the area for several years. She is a strange combination of seriousness and childlike wonder. She talks rapidly, as though there is too much of interest to talk about and is entirely animated the whole time we are on the beach.

'Set me a challenge,' she says, as we move from the first rock pool. 'Is there anything you particularly want to see?'

'Anything?' I ask. 'Okay, if we could find a live cowrie, I'd be impressed.'

Challenge accepted, we move down towards the sea, which is still retreating. I've been collecting cowrie shells with my wife, Emma, since we first met; she searched for them for years before that. Neither of us has seen a live one though and it seems unlikely to me that a cowrie can be produced on demand.

The further down the beach we get, the more numerous the creatures we find. These mid tide pools are out of water for less time and the environments that bit more stable. All the animals on the beach really need to stay wet, Heather explains, apart from the seriously hardcore ones like limpets and barnacles that can stand to remain out all day in the sun.

In the next pools, we – or rather, Heather, who spots things that my eyes are not attuned to – find chitons, living fossils that appear to be part of the rock itself, cushion stars and hermit crabs, large and aptly named strawberry anemones and the Medusa-like snakelocks anemone. You should really come down here at night with an ultraviolet light, she says. The snakelocks anemone, like many other rock pool creatures fluoresces bright green beneath UV, a result of a particular protein in the cell of its tentacles.

Heather makes notes of the rocks beneath which we find the eggs of different fish that breed in the pools and, on hands and knees over one pool, she points out a dark spot attached to the rock. That's a sea hare, she tells me. I consider saying that it looks more like a blob of gunk, though as we watch, the blob stretches its dun-coloured body out and extends the long, distinctive 'ears' from which it derives its common name. They are remarkable creatures, Heather says. When they are disturbed, sea hares, like squid and octopus, can release a cloud of purple ink to provide a smokescreen through which to escape predators.

'For me, this is where my fascination is,' she explains. 'It's the stuff that doesn't really look like much until you get to know it.'

The sea hare is actually a type of sea slug, though unlike most sea slugs, they are herbivores, living on seaweed. Their eggs look like hard pink spaghetti, long tangled threads of spawn and, far from the dull thing we can see on the rocks, when they are submerged they can be bright purples and pinks with weird appendages on their back, horns and strange protuberances. A lot of things in the sea are like that, Heather says. They rely on the sea for their structure. When they are out of water, like the sea hare, they look a little like dull-coloured wine gums, though put them in the water and they come to life.

Heather's son appears with his margarine tub and we peer in to see a Cornish clingfish. Otherwise known as a suckerfish, the clingfish has developed fused pelvic fins, which it uses as a sucker to stick itself to the underside of rocks, and on its back a pair of startling blue or turquoise, iridescent 'eyes' stare upwards to warn off predators.

Aside from Heather's partner and son, who are investigating another patch of the shore, there are few other people on the beach, and we are so engrossed in the pools that I do not notice we are being approached until Heather jumps up and introduces me to fellow rock pooler, Richard Pearce.

Richard has been coming to this beach for even longer than Heather. A former biology teacher, he grew up not far from here and has brought countless students to the isolated cove to study the rock pools, many of whom have gone on to careers in marine biology, though what has kept him coming back again and again is the survey he has been conducting three times a year, every year for over half a century.

Where Heather is effusive, Richard is softly spoken and I have to lean in a little to hear him over the wind. He takes me to see some of the pools he knows well to show me one of his favourite creatures, the St Piran's hermit crab.

Leaning over the pool, Richard picks up a few shells gently and, confirming it rather for me than for himself, tells me that each shell in this pool will have a St Piran's hermit crab in it, a crab that was completely absent from the beach for decades until five years ago.

Whereas Heather's relationship with this beach grew out of countless childhood explorations, Richard can pinpoint the exact moment at which he became particularly interested in this cove. He was on honeymoon on St Martin's in March 1967, just after the Suezmax oil tanker, the *Torrey Canyon*, one of the largest on the water, wrecked on Pollard's Rock on the Seven Stones reef off the Isles of Scilly, causing what is still the UK's largest oil spill, an environmental disaster of enormous proportions in the seas and on the coasts around Scilly, Cornwall and Devon. At just shy of 300 metres long, the *Torrey Canyon* was carrying a full cargo of crude oil from Kuwait to Milford Haven when the captain decided to take a shortcut between Scilly and the notorious Seven Stones reef.

Having heard the news reports, Richard and his wife convinced the helicopter pilot taking them to Scilly to make a detour and they circled the wreck a couple of times to get a good look. Later they stood at the daymark on St Martin's from where they watched the RAF Buccaneers, ordered by then prime minister Harold Wilson, who was also on holiday in Scilly at the time, to drop 41 1,000-pound bombs, 5,200 gallons of petrol and 11 rockets onto the wreck of the tanker. When this proved ineffective, Hawker Hunters and Sea Vixens dropped napalm in an effort to burn off the oil which had created a 35-mile long, 25-mile wide slick. The bombing and burning was largely thought to be a disaster in itself, as the tanker did not sink until the fourth day of the bombardment and many of the bombs missed their target, falling instead straight into the sea.

'When we came back, my father-in-law, who lived in the next cove along from here, was in pieces,' he says. 'It was a lovely, sunny Easter and there were loads of troops down here – clearly on holiday – and they had these drums of highly toxic dispersant, which had been dumped by lorries on the clifftop. They were told to wait until there was a rising tide to pour it on so it would be rinsed out on the sea.

'They were having fun so they kicked holes in some of the cans – there were patches in the grass up there for five or ten years afterwards where nothing would grow. Others they bounced down here and they fell into the pools on the falling tide and just about everything was killed. A few of the big strong limpets survived and some of the brown weeds grew back but it was the equivalent of a ploughed field.'

Some 10,000 tons of detergent were used in the 'clean up' operation, a painful lesson in how not to do it. The rocks were scoured and the molluscs that grazed there were entirely wiped out. Effectively, the operation killed off life in the cove, causing more damage to sea life than the oil spill itself and killing tens of thousands of sea birds. In the documentary, *The Wrecking Season*, Nick Darke, a relative of Richard's, talks about his father, a farmer, wringing the necks of razorbills and guillemots that were drenched in oil from the spill in what he described as a 'dreaded ritual'.

Galvanized by what he saw, Richard got in touch with the naturalist David Bellamy, who came here with some researchers. He asked when the cove might get back to normal and Bellamy replied that no one knew – there was no baseline for an event like this as nothing similar had happened before; nothing so apocalyptic and complete anyway.

It was this experience that prompted Richard to begin his thrice annual survey. Like Heather, he is entirely self-deprecating and describes his method as 'very primitive but unusually continuous'. He identified six survey points and using quadrats started to record the creatures he found there.

What struck him, he says, was how resilient the cove was in the end. After almost entire annihilation, there was some stability in the seaweeds, some of which – estuary wrack, in particular – began to return after about four years. This seaweed gave shelter to the first creatures that then returned to the otherwise razed environment. He found that most creatures that laid eggs in the sea returned within a matter of years, though the main problems were for the creatures that bred by laying their eggs on the rocks. These creatures, like the St Piran's hermit crab, were the slowest to return and are among the animals he has only begun to see again in the past decade.

Fifty-four years into his survey, Richard has begun to write up his findings, transferring the data and his meticulous records of sea snails, limpets, slugs and hermit crabs from his notebooks into a format in which he can send the data to researchers at Plymouth University's Marine Institute.

'What is remarkable is how quickly life returned,' he says.

While the oil spill was catastrophic and the clean-up operation deeply flawed, he is reassured, he says, by the stability of the biological, geological and hydrological system. While so much in the world seems to be in flux – he cites the speed at which people are buying up pieces of Cornwall's coast and developing it, and the huge environmental changes taking place globally – it is reassuring there is some stability down here at least. More than anyone else in the country perhaps, Richard knows the rhythm of the limpets and there is reassurance to be found in seeing them settle each autumn, and in the dispersal of various top shells that were entirely wiped out half-a-century ago that can now be found across the middle of the beach.

'I think over time one gets an intimate knowledge and intimate knowledge is not easily discarded,' he comments.

I ask if there are any creatures he likes to find above all others. He replies, without any hesitation, the Celtic sea slug. Heather, who has joined us again with her son, sends Rockpool Junior off to find us some.

The tide is now at its lowest and Richard, Heather and I make our way down to the rocks that are, for most of the year, covered by water. Down among the gullies of the subtidal zone, we can no longer see the sea, though the booming nearby is a reminder that this whole area will be submerged again in an hour or so. Heather disappears into a crack and emerges again a few minutes later grinning.

'Take a look in here.'

I slide myself in and wait until my eyes become accustomed to the gloom. It takes me a while but eventually I spot them, beautiful starlike brilliances, minuscule gems, bright against the black rock. These, Heather tells me, are scarlet and gold cup corals. They are found in the most inaccessible part of the inlet and are considered both locally and nationally scarce. Where we are standing now is a surge gully, where the water, when the tide returns, will be strong, bringing the corals the nutrients they need.

'I've been coming here my whole life, but I was in my thirties before I found corals here,' Heather says.

I stare at the fiery, orange corals, entranced. They are tiny, about the size of a fingernail, but breathtakingly beautiful, and it feels as though we have stumbled across a secret.

Rockpool Junior reappears to let us know he has found us a herd of Celtic sea slugs on the gully wall not far from where we are. *Onchidella celtica* is a dark greenish blackish slug, somewhat reminiscent of the nobbled rubber fingertips that bank tellers use to count notes. They are, at first glance, almost entirely unremarkable, but mindful of Richard's particular kinship with them I resist the urge to say this.

They remind me a little of the wine gum sea hares and I expect that they are going to transform before our eyes, but it is not for this, he says, that he considers them remarkable creatures. These sea snails are more closely related to land slugs than true sea slugs, though they have adapted to life on the shoreline. They live in the mid-tide area and most of the time are submerged, though they are air breathing animals, taking in oxygen through their mantles. When the tide comes in, they crawl into tiny cracks in the rock and wait it out, holding their breaths (or rather living off the oxygen they stored in their bodies when the tide was out) for hours and hours. They are arch survivalists.

We share slightly nervous glances as the booming of the sea becomes louder. We have just a few minutes left before the gully into which we have crammed ourselves, will be flooded, but Heather, who has disappeared again, has one more thing to show me.

While the others clamber back up towards higher ground, Heather indicates another crevice into which I am to jam myself, though this time, stare as I might, I have no idea what I am looking for and nothing comes into view.

Heather eventually points to something a few centimetres above my head and I make out a slimy drip hanging from the roof of the crevice. It looks as though someone has hocked a loogie with a spitball at its lowest point, poised to fall on the head of the unfortunate who happens to pass beneath it.

'That,' she says, 'is a cowrie.'

I stare at the spitball and eventually I make out the familiar shell within the bulbous part at the bottom of the spitball. The encased cowrie shell looks improbable, like a gross-out magic trick. We back out of the crevice and Heather takes the cowrie gently from its hanging place along with another hanging next to it and places them into an upturned lid filled with water.

'There are both sorts here,' she says, pointing out the differences between the two creatures, one an Arctic cowrie, *Trivia arctica*, the other a European one, *Trivia monacha*. They appear identical, aside from the fact that the latter has three spots on the shell.

As we watch, one of the pale-yellow creatures emerges from its shell. Covered in a slimy mantle and poking out its long orange proboscis, the live cowries are a truly weird sight. Unlike other molluscs, which tend to deposit new shell on the inside (think of the glossy inner shells of oysters) the cowrie, which is a kind of sea snail, wraps its outer shell with its mantle, depositing enamel onto the shell and keeping it shiny and free of parasites or other organisms that might want to live on it. The mantle also contains a gland that produces sulphuric acid, which makes it inedible to pretty much all fish. I stare at it for long enough to lose the context of the lid and the cowries suddenly seem true aliens, strange almost beyond belief.

Later, over sandwiches further up the beach, Heather and Richard share rock pooling gossip. The headlines are that the Latin name of one of the sea snails they have both studied has been changed recently, and on another beach a mile round the corner, a girl found a seahorse a few weeks back. This leads on to discussion of other seahorses that have been found along this coast, their Latin names and habits.

The gentle, beautiful geekery of it reminds me of the conversations between the characters Lance and Andy, played by Toby Jones and Mackenzie Crook, in the BBC series *Detectorists*. Like them, Heather and Richard are – as they tell me several times – both amateurs, though their knowledge of this place and its creatures is extensive. When I ask around later though, I find they are highly respected within the world of marine biology.

The mutual respect and the interest Heather and Richard show in each other's thoughts and findings is touching. I ask when they met and Heather says that though they had both almost certainly been on the small beach at the same time countless times, each with their head down, they had been doing this for years before they got to know one another.

I ask too what they get out of returning to the same place over and over.

'You build up a relationship with these creatures. And you know it's a one-way relationship, obviously, but there's familiarity there,' Richard answers, as we sit on the rocks.

Heather nods. 'I get that feeling with the corals. You see them once and then when you go back and see they're still there, it's a nice feeling. Because so often as a conservationist, you will find you go back to a place and the thing you saw before is no longer there.'

But that familiarity seems to run alongside a constant sense of the unknowability of life in these fringe environments, the draw of the weird, alien nature of the creatures there and the sense of mystery that still surrounds this sometimes land, sometimes sea, place.

'There's something fascinating about the sea as something we can't access for very long periods,' Heather says. 'We can't survive there for long, we can't really understand it. You don't see the land changing so much, but everything about the sea is always in flux. It's that complete otherness of what's going on in these rock pools that is the real pull.'

We walk back up the gullies in which the Celtic sea slugs graze and the cup corals sway, and in which the cowries hang from the rocks in their snotty bundles, are covered again until the next super low tide. The unfathomably large moon will retreat again, and the aliens in their cracks and crevices, in their rock pools and gullies, will go back to being unobserved.

A spring swell on Cornwall's north coast.

Emma Harper / Mischief the mermaid. Photograph by Daan Verhoeven.

4

Depth Plumber

Freediving off the Lizard Peninsula

H ERE'S AN ADMISSION. I'm scared of the sea. There, I said it.

As a species, although our behaviours now have an impact on every ecosystem on Earth, we humans are able to inhabit just 5 per cent of those ecosystems. The other 95 per cent, the oceans, are, for the most part, off limits to us. We are just visitors here.

Far from anyone 'ruling the waves', history has shown us that we are very much at the mercy of the ocean and with predictions of the impacts of rising sea levels coming in thick and fast, that trend looks likely to continue. Despite our desire to be on the sea or beneath the waves, the sea represents terror as well as beauty. Water that might be millpond flat one day, perfect to swim in or to paddle or sail on, is the next day entirely unrecognizable, a pit of churning viciousness that even the foolhardiest thalassophile would avoid.

It is not for no reason that the sea is home to some of our most terrifying monsters of the mind: the leviathan and the kraken; the giant Norse sea serpent Jörmungandr, whose coming signals Ragnarök, the world's end; the humanoid Umibōzu, terror of sailors in Japanese folklore; the finfolk of Celtic mythology; Charybdis and Scylla of Greek mythology; and H.P Lovecraft's terrifying submarine monster, Cthulhu. Incidentally, among Lovecraft's many fears was also a deep-seated terror of the sea and it is difficult not to equate the author with the nameless narrator of his short story 'Dagon', who asserts that he 'cannot think of the deep sea without shuddering at the nameless things that may at this very moment be crawling and floundering on its slimy bed'.

Anyone who has swum in deep water, unless they are entirely devoid of imagination, must recognize the mind's tendency to fill the deep with all manner of horrors. The idea of being lost at sea terrifies us because of the vastness of the oceans, its lack of landmarks bewildering to all but those few true wayfinders, whose skills have fallen out of use and out of fashion in the era of satellite navigation. We lack the shark's sense of electromagnetic field to guide us there, the seabird's too, or if we have these senses we have long since forgotten them. When we play there – and much of what we do there now is play – we are playing with being out of our element, engaged in a game of watery granny's footsteps.

That it is an undeniably risky place to be for any length of time is reflected in the language we use about it. When we are disconsolate, we are all at sea. When we grieve, we are adrift or unmoored. We batten down the hatches and look for a haven in the storm (a safe haven, incidentally, is a pleonasm – the word safe being a redundancy. Havens are safe enough as they are). Of the many phobias from which it is possible to suffer, a whole subset relates specifically to the sea including bathophobia, the fear of the ocean's depths, cymophobia, the fear of giant waves, and Captain Ahab's favourite, cetaphobia, the fear of whales. And when we are struggling – mentally, financially, spiritually – we try to keep our heads above water. We look to dry land, try to remain grounded, and we hope for plain sailing in the days to come.

For centuries, and for millennia perhaps, the seas – from a European perspective anyway – were considered more dangerous than benign. The watery areas on the edge of charts in the Middle Ages demonstrated not just our lack of knowledge of what was there, but our fully justified fear of the sea. On early maps, these areas of *mare incognita* were marked 'Here be dragons', and later they were illustrated with fantastical and awe-inspiring creatures or anthropophagi, or with huge waterfalls that ran off the edge of the world.

An often-repeated piece of popular pub trivia has it that until relatively recently, many British sailors and fishermen did not learn to swim. Aside from the practicalities involved – there were few opportunities for those who enlisted in the navy to learn – in the age of sail, between the mid fifteenth century and the mid nineteenth, it was impractical for a ship to turn around for someone lost overboard and the thought of prolonging the agony of drowning through treading water was not worth considering.

The sea remains as dangerous today. Passengers and crew fall off the back of cruise ships, never to be seen again. Official observers on commercial fishing boats seem to go overboard while undertaking their duties alarmingly often. And fishing itself continues to be one of the most hazardous professions, with fishers more likely to die at work than in any other profession. And though more people can swim now than at any other time in history, drowning remains the second or third most common cause of accidental death in the world, with more than 1,000 people dying this way each day. If we have sense, we respect the sea's great indifference towards us. Anyone who has been caught unintentionally in a rip current and swept away from the beach or knocked off their feet by that fabled larger seventh wave gets a glimpse of it.

So, while we are drawn to it, we treat the sea with the respect due. We take precautions. We check the forecast. We use what water sense we have. We scan from the beach for rips and swim between the red and yellow flags as the lifeguards advise. For me, this respect extends to staying on the sea's surface; as a recent RNLI slogan has it, 'Float to survive'. The idea of heading into the depths has always terrified me. There's a certain deniability about staying on the surface. As long as you don't think too hard about what's going on in the water beneath you, all is well with the world. Leaving the surface behind and descending into the cold, airless, pressurized depths seems to me something only someone with a death wish might want to do.

The seas, like the mountains, attract extremophiles. Watching a surfer take off on a huge wave is as terrifying as watching the climber, Alex Honnold free solo El Capitan. And watching a wetsuit-clad diver take one final deep breath, turn head down and swim 100 metres below the surface, with no oxygen tank, no means of propulsion other than a pair of fins seems, to me at least, the most terrifying of all.

The people who take on these huge waves, huge seas, vast distances and unthinkable heights, have always seemed to me somehow 'other', able to compartmentalize their fear and do it anyway, to weigh the sizeable risk against their skill and experience and think, 'screw it', to push the limits of what was previously thought possible. I am told that competitive freediver Georgina Miller is one of these extraordinary people.

George is a six times UK national record holder in freediving and can hold her breath underwater for over 7 minutes. When we talk on the phone my plan is that she can walk me through her experiences, though she suggests the only way for me to understand it is to experience it for myself. I know this is true. Of course, it is. Yet, it is still unnerving.

In preparation, I watch hours of online footage of world-renowned freedivers performing what seem to me nothing less than minor miracles. In one, a world record attempt, the Slovenian freediver, Alenka Artnik takes a final deep breath at the surface, puts her head in the water and dives as whales dive, her monofin briefly kicking out of the water before she descends. After the first few kicks, propelling her down from the surface, she barely seems to move. Aside from her hands, which she holds by her side and which move slightly as she falls through the water, she is almost entirely still as she glides down and at one point, about 85 metres into the dive, she appears to be asleep. When she reaches the metal plate at the bottom, 120 metres down, and turns to kick back up towards the surface, she raises her hands above her head, and propels herself upwards using her whole body and she appears more cetacean than human. Towards the surface, she stops kicking again, allowing her buoyancy to lift her the last few metres and emerges smiling. It is the most serene feat of endurance I've ever observed. She surfaces at 3 minutes and 28 seconds, the first woman ever to have dived this deep on a single breath.

Unable to get my head around what I have just seen, I watch the film again and attempt to hold my breath as I watch. Although I am alone, it is embarrassing how soon I find I have to breathe – and I am sitting at a computer on dry land, not pushing myself down through the water column. I cannot imagine being able to hold my breath for more than a minute or so, let alone for the times these divers are pulling.

I look up records and stats: the most extreme of the extreme.

The current world record for depth is held by the Russian freediver Alexey Molchanov, who dived to 131 metres on a single breath, using only fins. To put that in context, that's a depth almost one-and-a-half times the height of the Statue of Liberty on a single breath, three times its height when you factor in the journey back up to the surface.

The absolute record for depth is held by Austrian freediver Herbert Nitsch, who dived to 214 metres on a single breath. Nitsch, one of the pioneers of the sport, achieved this in 2007 in the No-Limits discipline of freediving, in which divers use a weighted sled to descend and a balloon to come back up. This discipline has been excluded from competition due to the dangers involved, including lung squeeze, narcosis, blackouts, stroke, entanglement and equipment failure, many of which result in death.

By the time I arrive at Porthkerris on Cornwall's Lizard Peninsula early one Saturday morning, I have prepared myself to meet a group of macho daredevils, people who are there for the high (or rather, for the high of the low).

I am running late as I bring the van to a stop at the bottom of the winding single track road that leads down to the beach where George is waiting for me. As she beams in through the window and tells me to take my time, there's no rush, I realize that she does not fit the image I have built up in my head at all. I park the van and as I approach the tables beneath a canopy just above the beach, where the others are already gathered, I can hear George laughing. It is something I will hear often during my time with her, another incongruence. I had expected, perhaps, a sort of marshal seriousness, in line with the seriousness of the business at hand.

There are four of us on the course and three instructors. We do quick introductions. Sitting to my right, Pete is a quarry diver from the Cotswolds. He barely says a word throughout the course. So far, so much as expected. When the woman to my left, Emma, announces that she is a mermaid, George nods, as though this is an entirely normal thing for someone to say.

'I have ADHD as well,' Emma says. 'I might not shut up until you get me in the water. When I'm in the water, everything's different. I'm a lot calmer, a lot quieter. But until then, you're stuck with this.'

Tracey, who is sitting next to Emma, introduces herself as a mermaid too, though a less experienced one – she only learnt to swim twelve months earlier. She and Emma are taking the course together to learn how to do it 'properly'.

Tracey worked for the health service for thirty years as a senior nurse in an intensive therapy unit and as lead nurse on dementia for the county. It was a high-stress job, she says, and on top of that she was diagnosed with multiple sclerosis a few years ago. As her stress built, so her illnesses became more severe and she became increasingly depressed.

'By the time I saw this group of St Ives swimmers on Facebook, my confidence – my body confidence especially – was zero,' she tells me later. 'I wouldn't even wear a swimsuit in public. I pushed myself to do it and when I parked up in the carpark, I couldn't even get out of the car.'

That was when she met Emma, who befriended Tracey and introduced her to the world of mermaiding.

I wonder whether they are joking, though later Emma takes us to her car to show us one of her tails, which she keeps in the boot. It's huge and heavy, all pinks and purples, a monofin encased in rubber that cost her over £4,000. It is about more than just the tail though, she says. It comes with hair extensions and a diaphanous top and she has a distinct 'mersona', too, a personality she takes on when she is swimming in her mermaid costume. Emma's mersona is called Mischief and she is hired to 'wash up' on the beach at children's parties and charity events. She has also been hired for underwater photoshoots at dive sites in Mexico and Scotland.

'It's like drag queens or men who enjoy dressing up in their wives' clothes,' Emma explains. 'When I put my tail on, I stop being an ageing mother of three, and I become a mysterious creature. It's not about sitting on rocks and looking pretty for me, it's a personal thing.'

The whole experience is beginning to remind me of the time I accidentally wandered into the middle of a live action role play in the woods and found myself surrounded by hobbits and elves, all of whom did their best to ignore me as they went about their Middle Earth lives.

We spend the morning sitting in the shade outside the trailer (itself run by a record-holding freediver, Alice Hickson). George hands us our kit – wetsuit, mask and snorkel, metre-long fins and weight belt – and talks us through the processes the body undergoes when diving on a single breath and the ways in which we can keep each other safe while we are diving. She starts us off with a few fundamentals, momentarily utterly serious. The first is that we need to take the dives at our own pace, to relax into it rather than pushing ourselves too far too quickly, and the second is that we must never freedive alone. George explains to us a phenomenon known as shallow water blackout in which the diver returning to the surface simply passes out. If this happens and there is no one acting as safety diver, death occurs 100 per cent of the time. Understandably, much of what we will learn on the course is how to dive safely and to ensure that our dive buddies are safe too.

The reason we can hold our breath for so long underwater is the mammalian dive reflex. When we put our faces in water, especially cold water, the body reacts by slowing the heart, conserving oxygen. As we descend, where the pressures on the body are higher than at the surface, blood shift occurs. Blood in the extremities is pulled in towards the vital organs and the chest, allowing the body to withstand the great pressures acting on it and, crucially, protecting the lungs from collapse. At greater depth, our spleen contracts, pushing out oxygen-rich blood into the system. It is an astonishing hangover from an earlier time in our evolution and there are a whole range of theories as to why we have this ability.

In 1860, Charles Darwin wrote to his friend Charles Lyell, 'Our ancestor was an animal which breathed water, had a swim bladder, a great swimming tail.' Darwin had it that our distant ancestors came from the sea and that we still retain vestigial traces of this time in the water.

A similar idea resurfaced a century later, in 1960, in the theory of the 'aquatic ape', proposed by Alister Hardy in *New Scientist*. Hardy suggested there may have been an aquatic phase in our evolution, though that idea is much disputed now. It is a tempting theory. Whatever the reason for this ability, human babies, which spend the nine months or so of their gestation swimming in amniotic fluid, are born with a dive reflex and, though it grows weaker as we age, we can still trigger it by immersing ourselves in the water. But whatever the reason, perhaps that's not entirely surprising. For most of Earth's history, all life was in the seas so, in theory at least, each journey to the sea is a return to our original ancestral home. While the effect on us is less dramatic than in sea-dwelling mammals – a grey seal can hold its breath for up to half an hour, and a blue whale for up to 90 minutes – we retain the ability to dive to great depths and hold our breaths beneath the water for far longer than seems probable.

The morning is punctuated by the sound of the compressor firing in a container nearby as divers refill their bottles. George tells us that she started as a diver and dive instructor, though she made the switch to freediving after an experience leading a wreck dive in Thailand. Her group was sitting on the sandy sea floor, 37 metres down when a woman in a monofin appeared at the same depth, with no equipment other than her mask and fin. She seemed entirely at home in the depths without the bulky equipment but improbable alongside the heavily kitted-out divers. The woman waved and disappeared. I suggest it must have been a strange sight, unnatural even.

'When you think about it, which do you think is stranger though,' George asks me, 'breathing underwater like divers do, or holding your breath?'

We practise slowing our breath and observe the impact it has on our heart rate – freedivers' hearts have been known to slow to 11 beats a minute at depth, a speed a doctor friend tells me would almost certainly put them at death's door if this was being observed on land. We practise techniques for equalizing our ears too.

Equalization is a key skill for anyone who wants to plumb the depths, due to the increase in pressure the further down you dive. It's a seemingly simple case of shifting a small amount of air in the ears, though it can have a huge impact on the diver's ability to achieve depth. I find equalizing fairly easy, and I can deal with the theory. Everything is fine, in theory, and the revelation about mermaids has distracted me from the fact that we are going to be putting this theory into practice.

In the afternoon, we head down to the beach to practise breath holds on dry land. One of the instructors, Alex, talks us through what to expect. As carbon dioxide builds up in the lungs, our body will tell us to breathe, he says, though we are safe far beyond that point. Contrary to popular belief, it is the increase in carbon dioxide in our system that makes us want to breathe rather than a lack of oxygen. We may feel a constriction of the throat or the urge to swallow, as well as our inner voices shouting out to us that we ought to be breathing and, later, diaphragm contractions will cause our chest or stomach to convulse, though even then we are still safe to continue holding our breaths. The key is to stay entirely relaxed. Most divers, he says, play games to distract themselves from this discomfort. Alex favours going through the alphabet in his head, thinking of the name of an animal or object for each letter to distract him from the discomfort. Other divers focus on the body, relaxing each muscle in turn.

Alex leads us through three breath holds, encouraging us to push each one just a little further than the last, to sit with the physical sensations that arise without reacting to them, and after the third breath hold, he gives us our times. Emma has managed 3 minutes and 20 seconds and I – to my surprise – made it to 3 minutes and 18 seconds. Perhaps I might be able to do this. I won't need to hold my breath for anything like that length of time in order to get to the 10-metres depth required to pass the qualification.

Before our first water session, we squeeze into two-piece open-celled wetsuits with the aid of a bottle of conditioner and more breath holding. The thick, open pore neoprene wetsuits are stiflingly hot on land and I have a head full of theory, so getting into the water is a welcome cool down.

There are several disciplines in freediving aside from using it simply as a way to explore the coastline in a bit more depth. Static apnea, one of George's specialities, involves lying face down in the water and holding your breath for as long as possible, accompanied by a partner who times the breath hold and checks the breath holder is still conscious by tapping them periodically. From the outside, she admits, this discipline can look a little like someone is timing a floating corpse. Like the breath hold we did earlier, while some of it revolves around physiology – lung capacity and the body's ability to conserve oxygen, most of it is in the mind. Dynamic apnea involves swimming as far as possible horizontally along the seabed or the floor of a swimming pool. The other disciplines are all about achieving depth, following a line that disappears into the blue beneath until the diver reaches a plate set at a specific depth.

We practice static and dynamic apnea just a few metres off-shore along with rescue manoeuvres on a mannequin that has seen better days. I am buoyed by my experiences earlier with the breath holds on land and I am beginning to get excited by the promise of the mammalian dive reflex kicking in. Theoretically at least, when this happens, I should be able to go beyond my land record, though when I try the static breath hold, face down in the water, I barely make it to a minute and a half.

I practise diving and swimming along the seabed, following a rope that Alex has laid, getting used to the metre-long flippers, and it is at this point I begin to feel dizzy. I get out of the water and try to clear the sensation. I am annoyed at myself for getting seasick a few metres offshore.

While I am regaining my balance on land, I ask Alex, who has been guiding me through the exercises, what he gets out of freediving.

'It's the closest you can get to living in that world,' he says, an experience unmediated by the need for the bulky oxygen tanks and respirators used in traditional diving. 'You're there on a level with the other creatures that share the sea.'

As well as that, he tells me, for him it is all about the people, the community. Though you might meet stressed divers, you never meet an agro freediver, he says. It makes sense. Freedivers spend a lot of time considering their breathing, meditating, calming their minds. Stress won't cut it. Stress means you burn more oxygen and limits your dive time.

I nod, though nodding makes me feel sick again, and settle instead for a slightly nauseous smile.

Over lunch, the other divers take my mind off the seasickness with tales of 'shell off' mermaids who swim with no clothes other than their tails, and George tells us about a freediver friend who was hired for a party in the United Arab Emirates in which she swam naked in a huge glass tank while the party went on around her. Emma fetches ginger biscuits which we nibble by her car and she admits to feeling seasick too.

When we get back to the classroom, George's partner, Daan Verhoeven, himself a record-holding no fins freediver, and an underwater photographer who has shot many of the world's best divers, has arrived, along with their two dogs. George and Daan make a formidable couple. Strikingly good looking, they appear relaxed in the way I come to discover most competent freedivers are – comfortable in their own skin.

I tell Daan I have been watching some of the films of freedivers he has posted to YouTube, in which divers appear to fly through vast spaces in the ocean, or snake their way through submerged wrecks. These mesmerizing submarine narratives are the product of days and weeks of careful planning and preparation, and even after watching them several times it is difficult to understand how he films them. As well as the technical issues of shooting divers below the surface, Daan has the added complication of capturing all his footage on one breath. It is precise, complex, subtle stuff, highly demanding, though no matter how artistic the film, the experience of posting to a platform in which everyone can have their say is enough to keep him grounded.

'I get two reactions,' he says. 'One is that this is incredible, amazing. The other is "this is fake" or "this is gay". Sometimes both of those.' He shrugs off these comments.

Daan is already talking about his next challenge, a film shot in a submerged cave in the bay in which he and George live, just a few miles away. The opening to the cave is small and it is pitch dark inside, and there is an additional challenge of a large bull seal that lives in the cave. He plans to take another diver in with a glowing ball, in a watery echo of Plato's allegory of the cave. He suspects though that a proportion of the people who watch this challenging, technical shoot will respond to it in the usual way. While I can't understand the offensive comments, I can understand the disbelief. It looks unlikely that someone might appear so profoundly comfortable when they have been deprived of air.

Later, we swim out into deeper water to practice deeper dives on a line attached at one end to an inflated ring on the surface and to the other a weight. This is our introduction to another set of disciplines in which the diver either pulls themselves head down along the line, or swims alongside the line towards the weight at the bottom. Where we might get stuck at this point, George tells us, is if we are unable to equalize the pressure in our middle ears. We have practised the techniques on land, but there is no telling if we'll be able to do it in the water until we have a go.

The first few metres are, apparently, the hardest. The diver expends the most energy here as they are at their most buoyant close to the surface, so it is here that it is the most difficult to dive. It is the reason for the absurdly long fins. We will need to equalize with every couple of kicks as we descend. Further down, as we are compressed under the increasing pressure, the effort needed to propel us down decreases, until we will no longer need to kick our fins. We will be drawn down into the depths by gravity. Watching this on Daan's films, divers who reach this point look as though they are being dragged towards the Earth's centre. When the divers talk about it, though, they tend to describe this feeling in almost mystical, gnomic terms of communion and connection, of transformation and transcendence.

When I ask George about the experience of diving to greater depths, she talks about a shift in the way the mind works on a dive to 60 or 70 metres, the cessation of the constant voice in her head, the one that says, 'I don't like this' or 'I'm frightened of this', the thinking part, her narrator, she calls it.

'Your narrator gives you edges, if that makes sense?' she says. 'When you are falling, your narrator shuts up and you become less aware. Maybe you can feel the water on your face or the rope in your hand, but at a certain point you don't really have physical or mental edges anymore. It's a strange type of existence.'

Daan nods, 'Exactly. And in losing yourself you feel a sense of connection to everything.'

The journey back up from the plate is different. This is the point at which the diver falls back on their physical conditioning and confidence. The return to the surface is more like a work-out, they tell me. At that point in the dive, there is no other option – the only way out is up. It is clear what you have to do and you have to find your way back to the surface, fighting the gravitational pull and kicking upwards. It is at this point that the build-up of carbon dioxide in the body becomes more apparent, as its effects begin to be felt on the body, and the diver has to rely on their training, though this experience too seems to have a spiritual aspect, a kind of rebirth.

'On the descent,' Daan explains, 'you are almost disappearing or becoming one with an element you love – the water – in which you don't know where you end and where the sea begins. On the way back it is almost like a process of overcoming yourself. You know you can do this. You've done it before, and it's almost like you become a better version of yourself. You lose yourself on the way down and you become a better version of yourself on the way back up.'

I take my first dive, in which I am to pull myself down through the water column using a line attached to a weight, the discipline known as free immersion. The first couple of metres feels okay, though shortly after that my mind kicks in, an insistent voice that tells me, 'You know you couldn't breathe right now if you wanted to and you're going to want to breathe. In fact, you want to breathe right now.' My narrator, far from melting away, is going into overdrive. I try to fight the sensation and keep propelling myself down, though my body revolts and turns itself back up to the surface. I try again, with the same results. The low-volume diving mask, with the glass close to my eyes, starts to feel claustrophobic and I find the murkiness of the water threatening.

On the next buoy along, a few metres from mine, Tracey surfaces after a mammoth 17-metre dive, the first she has attempted, and Emma and Pete seem equally in their element.

The sea is rough – a strong easterly wind is kicking up an uncomfortable swell – and bobbing on the surface, holding on to the bright yellow buoy, trying to calm my mind and my breathing feels impossible. Though I attempt a few dives, there is no way I can relax enough to do everything I need to do. To make things worse, my seasickness kicks back in with a vengeance and, with the world swimming around me, I admit defeat and retreat to the shore. I feel battered and not a little downhearted, though I try to put a positive spin on it: if nothing else, my first encounter with freediving has been a lesson in humility.

On the way to the car, I pass a group of divers sitting on the rocks. They all look as green as I feel. They were fairly deep when they started to get seasick, they tell me. One of them recounts how he had vomited in his regulator, after which he decided the conditions weren't for him either. I begin to feel a little better about having bailed.

When I get over my hurt pride, I am intrigued at my body's response, the involuntary surfacing, the tension, the sense of stress and fear, and the difficulty I had achieving depth where the others seemed to glide down effortlessly, the disparity between my experience of diving and the one George and Daan described.

Shortly after I return from my first freediving experience a fever dream of an article appears in the papers that seems to me somehow like a message. A lobster fisherman, Michael Packard, was swallowed whole by a humpback whale while diving off Cape Cod. My overactive imagination transports the event into my dreams, along with the thought of not being able to breathe while diving. I start to find myself waking in the night to chest convulsions, breathing in deeply and I realize I have been dreaming about diving, holding my breath for long periods of time in my sleep.

At this point, I could stop. I have given it a go. However, there is something about the experience that won't leave me alone, something about the serenity of the freedivers I have met that suggests to me that I have not yet experienced what it is all about. I resolve to put a pause on the theory and concentrate on the practise. I buy a snorkel and low-volume diving mask, rebook my second day of training with George for a few weeks' time and get in touch with Emma and Tracey, who agree to meet me for what they call a 'play dive' to practise before I return to Porthkerris.

The conditions on the south coast beach near Falmouth are the polar opposite to those we experienced at Porthkerris. The sky is cloudless blue and the water millpond flat and clear, though as we swim out off the beach I feel the sense of discomfort rising, a kind of vertiginous feeling, a tightening of the chest. My borrowed weight belt makes me nervous. I try to control my breathing, remind myself that I am supposed to remain completely calm. The mermaids are entirely at home here. They take frequent short dives as we swim out, laugh and joke. I am certain they are doing this in part at least to put me at ease.

The sea floor is dark with seaweed and Emma and Tracey head for what the old Cornish would have called a drethan patch, a sandy area in the centre of the bay (as opposed to a rocky, sea-weedy bed, which has a specific term of its own: *pilly*). There they help me work on my duck dive, the movement that will take me from the surface to diving straight down towards the sea floor. They try not to laugh at my flailing arms and legs, though Emma gently suggests I might want to keep my movements to a minimum, to streamline – you conserve oxygen that way.

On my fifth or sixth dive, for a moment, I get it. The dive feels effortless and when I reach the sea floor, I am surprised, as is the large crab on which I almost land. For the few seconds, among the sea grasses, with the surprised crab and the light filtering down through the water, I get it. This all takes place in less than 30 seconds, after which my sense of discomfort resumes and we head back to shore.

Over coffee and cake at the beach café, Emma tells me, 'For me, it's that all-encompassing feeling of being held by the water. I even love the brain freeze you get in really cold water – the colder it is the more of a reset it is. It's linked to my ADHD – that's why I like it down there. The water has always been a place to shut me up. It's like when you switch the computer off, count to ten and switch it back on again. I like to stay in the water for that count of ten.'

She points out all the sights and sounds that are currently bombarding her senses, from the conversations at the other tables, to flags flapping and dogs barking, to the sunlight and air on her skin and the fact that I keep absentmindedly tapping my pen on the table. I stop. When she gets in the water, she says, it is like putting ear defenders on. There's still noise, but it is dampened. There is still light too, but it is filtered through the water. She is profoundly comfortable in the water, she says – more so than she is on land, perhaps.

I ask her what I am doing wrong.

'It's like you're trying to impose yourself onto the sea – like you're fighting it,' she says after a pause. 'You'll never win that way. You're looking at it as though the water is going to eat you. I think you need to realize that the water is there to support you and that you can relax and ride with its movement and it will hold you. But until you learn to let go and be held by it, it's *interesting* to watch.'

Back at Porthkerris, George explains that freediving is different to other sports, which rely, to an extent, on bloody-mindedness as well as skill.

'In most sports, when you feel uncomfortable with it, you have to dig deeper and push harder. This is the absolute opposite of that,

Emma Harper / Mischief the mermaid.
Photograph by Daan Verhoeven.

mentally and physically. The more you let go of your ambitions and targets and stress and thought processes, the better it works. It's a nebulous thing – the harder you try to grab it the more it wants to drift away.'

Daan agrees. 'One of the cores of freediving is relaxation. I think of relaxation as something passive. You just let your body do as it wants. You let gravity take over. Relaxation is just giving in to gravity. It's a passive kind of thing. We're not used to being passive and letting things happen. In freediving, there's a lot of letting things happen.

'There's no point in fighting the sea. It's complete folly. And there's a joy in that. You give in to something that is much stronger than you and by giving into it, you get accepted and you can fall deeper. The biggest joy of freediving is falling – you're not really in control, gravity takes over and that turns out to be something very pleasant.'

Freediving is still a young sport. When Daan began to free-dive, a few years before George, the world record for depth while freediving with a monofin was 87 metres. The current record for a freediver with no fins – a more physically challenging discipline – is now far greater than that and the current record holders are diving to depths that were only a few years earlier thought to be impossible. The way George and Daan talk about it reminds me of the older surfers close to home who talk about the early days of British surfing, when they were discovering the possibilities of the sport. The early years of any new sport are exciting, with huge leaps in performance taking place each year.

As with any frontier, the sport comes with its requisite pioneers, like Nitsch, who push the boundaries and make the headlines with tales of chest squeezes, paralysis and sometimes death. In this way it resembles an inversion of mountain climbing. So the competitive divers get deeper and deeper, refine their techniques, understand more of the science of what happens to our bodies under pressure and push our understanding of just what we are capable of when we hold our breath and immerse ourselves.

After weeks of high pressure in which the sea is clear and flat, a strong easterly wind blows in again and all diving at the Porthkerris site is cancelled. George calls early in the morning and asks if I can meet her at a flooded quarry inland where it will be safe to get in the water.

We change in the carpark under the watchful eye of the quarry owner's dog, and on the way down to the water, George talks for both of us, about the gently curious geese that will swim around us on the surface and the hundreds of goldfish that will swim around us when we dive, the descendants of a couple of freed pet fish that bred. The water in the quarry is warmer than it is in the sea but here water is almost black, which does nothing for my sense of discomfort. George swims the float out and drops the weighted guide line at the foot of a dark cliff where the water is at its deepest.

My first two dives are short and shallow. I get to 5 metres, though I still can't get my head around turning myself upside down and voluntarily heading away from the surface. I push further, through my nervousness, and add another metre or two to my depth, but the pain in my ears pulls me short this time. I breathe, relax, try to remember what mermaid Emma said about fighting the water.

I breathe in – 2, 3, 4, 5, 6 – and out – 2, 3, 4, 5, 6, 7, 8 – trying to ignore the feeling that without this body of water below me I would fall to the ground.

In – 2, 3, 4, 5, 6 – the vertiginous thought fades and I shift to the sensation of the water, the temperature and the feel of it on my hands.

Freediving with no fins at Swanpool. Photograph by Emma Harper.

Out – 2, 3, 4, 5, 6, 7, 8 – until all the air in my lungs is gone and then a slow fill from the stomach, up through the chest and into the throat.

Then the same again, a complete emptying of my lungs and a complete fill, then hold. I pinch my nose, equalize my ears, tip my face into the water, bend at the waist and drop. I equalize again. Kick. Equalise.

The Japanese have a word for sunlight filtered through trees, *komorebi*. Poet Gerard Manley Hopkins coined something similar – shivelight – which describes the lances of sunlight that shine through the leaves to the forest floor. The light here is something like that. It is dark, with soft beams of sunlight. If we had a word for the light in the first few meters of water it might be grundlight, incorporating the old Norse word for the shallows, a more diffuse, mellower version of shivelight.

A few metres down the water becomes darker, though the white rope is a reassuring presence, a thread that will lead me back out of the labyrinth. George is diving somewhere alongside me: I know that, though I cannot see her. I pass through a temperature wall below which the water becomes suddenly colder. I pass a few goldfish and have the momentarily surreal sensation of being inside a huge goldfish bowl. And then the bottom plate is in sight.

I feel a momentary panic, the urge to turn back to the surface, though I recall something George mentioned about staying with that feeling, acknowledging it and continuing. I pause for a few seconds and concentrate on a speck of dust in the water, channel my interest on that. I equalize my ears again and kick down and I am at the bottom plate. For the few seconds I am there I am completely calm. I can hear my heartbeat and nothing else. I grin, turn and kick my fins and the journey back to the surface takes just seconds. What felt like a great depth on the way down feels entirely different on the way back. Although

I am returning almost exactly the same way I came on the way down, the experience is entirely dissimilar.

When I resurface, George has got there before me. She is beaming. She has introduced me to the first few metres of the world of the deep. And with that, something clicks, some shift in my head that this is something I can do, and I dive again and then again. I take my time, relax, pay attention. I concentrate on the sensation of being held within the water, the quiet that descends as soon as I take the first kick down, the bizarre sight of hundreds of goldfish swimming around me in the darkness. It begins to rain, and we lie on our backs and watch the droplets enter the water from a few centimetres below the surface. George teaches me how to anchor myself to the quarry floor and to blow bubble rings up towards the surface. For the first time, I find myself enjoying the experience.

I am under no illusion of having reached great depths. The plate was set at 12 metres. To put that in context, Alenka Artnik's world record dive was over ten times that depth. The rush of having done it is something else, though.

George asks me if I felt the gravitational pull when I got to the bottom of my deepest dive. I am unsure. Perhaps. For a moment. It is something I want to experience though, something that will bring me back to freediving.

Later, I look up a TED talk by the French freediver, Guillaume Néry. 'I'd like you to know that if one day you try to stop breathing, you'll realize that when you stop breathing, you stop thinking too,' he says to an audience in the darkness beyond the stage.

'It calms your mind. Today, in the twenty-first century, we're under so much pressure. Our minds are overworked, we think at a million miles an hour, we're always stressed. Being able to dive allows you to relax your mind. Holding your breath underwater means giving yourself the chance to experience weightlessness ... This is the plight of the twenty-first century: our back hurts, our neck hurts, everything hurts because we're stressed all the time. When you are in the water, you let yourself float as if you were in space, you let yourself go completely.'

Néry captures something I began to feel when diving in the quarry. The fear I felt when I started is beginning to be replaced by something else entirely, similar perhaps to the way the monsters on the edge of the maps were pushed off in favour of representations with what was found there when we looked and we discovered that we would not be consumed by the sea serpents or go over the edge of some endless waterfall.

The fear is replaced by curiosity, the desire to float in watery space again, to dip beneath the shifting waters of the sea for a while down to the still deep, to be held by the sea and return to the surface changed.

5

Caul Child

Making handplanes & bellyboards in Porthtowan

WHEN SHE WAS BORN to a seafaring community in South Shields on England's north-east coast, the midwife told Fi Francis's mother she would never have to worry about her daughter dying at sea. Her reasoning was that Fi was a caul baby, born with the birth membrane (or caul) attached. For Fi's father, a chief marine engineer, it was a particularly important sign.

The superstition that it is lucky to be born with the caul attached, and particularly that a child born with one would never die at sea, dates back to at least the Middle Ages, when the belief was widespread across Europe. Occurring in about one in every 80,000 births, the rarity of being born with the caul led to a belief that the child would be lucky, that they would achieve greatness and that they – or whoever held the caul – would be safe at sea.

One ancient Nordic belief held that children born with a caul were also born with the ability to navigate between worlds and to peer into the future and, in the days of wooden sailing ships, cauls were known to change hands for significant sums, and ship's masts were often set on top of a caul to protect the ship and its sailors. A sea captain bought the caul with which Lord Byron was born. Although it did not protect the captain

The author's handplane.

from drowning, Byron, who swam the stretch from Venice Lido across the lagoon and up the Grand Canal, as well as being an adventurous sailor, remained safe at sea. The caul-protected Byron, inspired by his support for Greek independence and a preoccupation with Leander of Greek mythology, who would swim the passage nightly 'to woo,— and Lord knows what beside', his lover, Hero, also famously swam the Hellespont, the four-mile stretch of sea between Greece and Turkey, to prove it could be done. Eventually, Byron succumbed to a fever he contracted on dry land, following the Siege of Missolonghi, in 1824.

As with most superstitions, there's a logic to it. The caul is part of the birth membrane and in particularly rare cases babies are born entirely en caul, with the amniotic sack still intact. It makes sense that a child who is, effectively, born swimming might be thought to have some protection from the many risks involved in going to sea: the dangers of being swamped, of sinking in stormy waters; a boat being driven onto rocks and foundering; of being caught in the running gear of a fishing boat and losing limbs or being dragged down into the deep with the net. And even if none of these terrors came to pass, there was always the risk of the fisher coming back with an empty hold after days or weeks at sea, of having survived the storm but leaving their family destitute at the end of it. It is hardly surprising that those who worked the sea, had to travel on it or had a partner who had to, would develop practices that might seem strange on land – an attempt to game the odds, to take any chance over and above that afforded by hard-won skill and experience – so that you might be spared.

The caul superstition is just one of hundreds of sea-related shibboleths. Other include avoiding mention of rabbits and hares (and God forbid you would take one onto your boat), fixing silver coins to the nets on the first day of the year, and keeping a cat on board to bring luck. Throwing a shoe at a fisherman before he left for sea was good luck, as was nailing a horseshoe to the inside of a boat's hull. And nineteenth-century fishermen in Mousehole, Lamorna and Newlyn used to leave a fish from the haul out on the beach on returning to land, an offering for the Bucca, a sea spirit who could be generous or vengeful in equal measure.

To see how deeply this superstition is embedded in maritime culture, look no further than Antonia Barber's perennially popular Cornish children's book, *The Mousehole Cat*, based on the legend of Tom Bawcock. As the story goes, Tom sailed out in a great storm and brought back the catch that saved the village from starvation.

I meet Fi by chance, in the workshop of designer and surfer James Otter, which sits a stone's throw from the cliffs of Cornwall's north coast. I am there to create the simplest of watercraft, a handplane – the smallest of surfboards – a piece of wood about 8 inches long and 6 inches wide which is used to catch a wave while bodysurfing. Fi and her friend, Gary, are there to make bellyboards, the precursor to the more buoyant polyethylene or polypropylene bodyboard, a long tea tray-like wooden surfboard on which the rider slides down the face of a wave.

James meets us at the blue door of his workshop, barefoot and smiling. He has reason to smile. James helps people to craft their own wooden surfboards, a cry back to the days of the long, shaped wooden planks on which the ancient Polynesians and members of Hawaiian royalty rode the waves, though the techniques for building wooden surfboards have come on since then. Similarly to Jof Hicks with his handmade lobster creels, James is attempting to create a connection for the rider with the materials used to surf, as well as with the experience of surfing.

Methods of surfboard production have barely changed at all since the first foam blanks were produced in the late 1940s, providing the cheap, lightweight, buoyant basis for the modern

surfboard. After the surfing boom of the 1960s, in which production rocketed, surfing has continued to grow in popularity. Though
it is difficult to put a figure on it, one estimate has it that somewhere in the region of 20 million surfboards are produced each
year. The problem with these boards is they are polluting in many
ways. In an activity that is so seemingly benign and undestructive,
surfing's polluting by-products jar with many surfers. You only
have to spend some time with a shaper who wears a heavy-duty
filtration mask and relies on industrial extraction units to avoid
the effects of the carcinogens and other toxic chemicals which
form the raw materials of the trade to get a taste of the problem.

While a surfer's mark on the ocean seems incredibly small –
a line carved into the face of a wave that remains in the world
for a fraction of a second before the wave collapses and the
surfer paddles back out – the tools of the trade, the board and
wetsuit, especially when they become waste, are far less benign.
Polyurethane foam from broken and abandoned boards leaches
chemicals into the water and chunks of surfboard add to the
ever-increasing plastic problem in the seas. The fibreglass and
resins used to glass and finish surfboards are also toxic in several
ways. The production process is no better – the foam cut off
surfboard blanks is generally discarded and ends up in landfill.
And each year, tens of thousands of cheap, single use polystyrene
bodyboards are left on beaches around Cornwall as the summer
season draws to a close. Even though shapers are experiment-
ing with environmentally friendly, biodegradable alternatives
like mushroom (or rather mycelium, the stuff of mushrooms),
and wood, and wetsuit makers are increasingly working with
less toxic materials, the eco option is still considered niche in a
multi-million-pound industry. As James describes it, he's very
much on the outskirts of the water sports world.

There is a particular hush in the workshop, a kind of concen-
trated, focused quiet. The room smells of cedar, and light from the
high windows picks out motes of sawdust in the air. A wooden

longboard hangs alongside the tools that line the walls, and at the back of the room there is a rack of different length wooden surfboards. Fi describes the workshop as having 'purposeful calm', which sums it up well. Everything in its place, well-ordered – everything we need right now is here.

At a blackboard, James talks us through the process. He introduces us to the basics of shaping, the dynamics of the board in the wave, the types of rails we might carve and the possible shapes for the nose and tail, the decisions we will need to make in order to shape a board that will work well for us in the sea. Under his supervision, we will design, shape, sand and varnish our watercraft and leave with a new toy that will last us for several years. And even if it is lost at sea, it will biodegrade; the damage it will do is minuscule compared to that of the usual lost surfboard or bodyboard.

We listen intently, slightly nervous about the possibility of screwing up, of making the wrong cut as James introduces us to the Japanese pull saws and rasp saws we will be using, a variety of clamps, and the different grades of sandpaper with which we will perfect the finish on our watercraft.

At our benches, we stare at the plywood blanks James has prepared for us. We try to imagine the shapes they will become before marking pencil on wood and committing to the first cut.

James walks between the benches. He makes the odd suggestion here or there and provides an expert eye to ensure we don't succumb to the temptation to cut too much from our blanks. He has run this workshop countless times. It is based on a well-established process, a set of steps that is the same each time, though within that, there is endless variety.

After our first stint at the workbench, Fi, who until this point has been quiet, speaks up. 'I might need to take regular breaks. I get tired.'

We break for coffee and sit on log ends outside the workshop, talking about what has brought us here. For me, it is easy – I have been waiting until I had the time to create my own board of whatever size for years, having seen James's wooden boards in action at our local beach break.

Fi takes a deep breath and tells us that just a few weeks earlier she was lying in a medically induced coma in King's College Hospital, having suffered a severe brain haemorrhage and heart failure, and that it is a small miracle that she is standing here today.

'Most people don't survive one brain haemorrhage,' she says. 'I'm astounded that I've survived two. And I've not just survived – you can survive a haemorrhage but in a terribly compromised position – I've survived well. I'm what they call physiologically and psychologically intact. I've never thought about the human condition in that way before.'

She describes coming round from the surgery and from the coma as a tentative process. 'You're under immense sedation and your brain doesn't really feel like it's yours. It thinks of things and goes to places that aren't your normal purview. But I knew even then I wanted to let the water take the weight. And I remember thinking I need to find my fingers, I need to find my skills, I need something for the future.

'Recovery from brain injury is a long-term thing, so you need to find reasons to go on. I remember thinking I need to find something that takes me from here to being recovered and for me the bridge for that is the water. As soon as I left the hospital, I knew I had to get into the water.'

I return to my bench sober from Fi's revelation and we get to work shaping the rails, the curves around the edges that will help our boards cut through the water.

Fi's first brain haemorrhage occurred in 1997 on a Sunday morning in October, she tells me later. It came completely out of the blue, an aneurism that may have been sitting there from birth. The aneurism was located on the communicating artery, the major arterial supply to the brain alongside the centres of the brain that control breathing. She described the feeling of the haemorrhage as being like someone shoving a sword through the centre of her head. She was lucky, she tells me. She was taken to King's College Hospital on the understanding they would perform a craniotomy, an invasive procedure she describes as being riddled with risk of what doctors euphemistically describe as collateral damage. As luck would have it, a surgeon who had been in Italy, learning a new technique for treating brain aneurisms, was due back at the hospital on the same day to trial the new process, embolization. Whereas a craniotomy involves exposing the brain by opening a flap in the skull, in an embolization a catheter is introduced through the femoral artery and snakes its way through the heart to the point in the brain where the aneurism sits. The catheter guides a platinum coil which is released into the aneurism, recoils and plugs the leak.

As Fi was being ferried across London in an ambulance, the surgeon was stepping off his plane at Heathrow and the confluence of the two at the hospital led to Fi becoming the first person in the country to undergo the new procedure, the same one that would save her a second time after she was airlifted to King's again in spring 2021.

It seems incredible that she can be standing at a workbench, making a surfboard she plans to use the following day so soon after an injury so huge. Fi still has months, if not years, of recovery ahead of her. She is, she says, still at the stage where she has better hours than others and there are no days when she is free of it. Her lungs were damaged from aspirating and there are still residual blood products hammering around her cerebrospinal fluid. But what she has struggled with most, she says, is moments of joy and connecting fully with the world.

'If you don't know what you're able to do and you're lying there, intubated in the hospital bed and they're bringing you round, and you suddenly realize it's another day, you don't know what the end game is, but you hope, because that is sustaining, that you might have possibility and opportunity. It's lovely to still be here. It's strange that we can lose sight of how precious it is.'

We continue to shape our boards with rasp saws. We make finer and finer adjustments until we are happy with the shapes we have produced. We break for lunch and then turn to sanding, after which we treat them with tung oil, step back and admire them and, standing outside the workshop, pose for a photograph, holding out creations aloft. I am tempted to run straight down to the sea, and it is clear that Fi wants to do the same with hers, but James advises that we treat them with another few coats of oil before testing them out.

The next day, the oil on my handplane is dry enough. Or, rather, it is probably not dry enough at all but my impatience to try it out wins. I bundle the kids into the van and we head to a favourite beach, a small cove nearby that opens out to a vast beach at low tide.

The tide is ebbing when we arrive, exposing the long stretch of sand that runs in front of the cliffs in both directions. It is picture-postcard perfect and the beach almost empty. I take bodyboards for the children, but having seen the handplane, they are desperate to use that instead, so I stand in the surf and watch them taking turns to throw themselves into the waves with it, disappearing in the white water and emerging several metres away, holding the handplane up to demonstrate they haven't lost it yet. They are confident in the water, happy and entirely absorbed in trying to use the wave's energy to propel themselves towards the shore. If good surfing is, as the coach who gave me a few pointers on technique told me, a case of whoever is having a good time, they are the best surfers in the water that morning.

I take my eyes off them for moment and look out towards the horizon to scan for the next set of larger waves rolling through and when I turn back I see we have been joined by a couple. One is holding a wooden bellyboard and it takes me a moment to recognise Fi and her friend, Gary. They don't see me immediately and I watch them push off into waves, as absorbed in it as much as my children are. Out of all the beaches along this coastline and all the times they could come for a surf, out of all the breaks along this long stretch of beach, we have been drawn to the same wave at the same moment. I wave across and Fi waves back and brandishes the bellyboard. They don't stay long, just long enough to get their fix of the sea.

After Alana, Tom and I have dried ourselves by the van, we sit on the step drinking hot chocolate. I think about the way they are starting to paddle out further, to push off into deeper water in order to reach the wave before it starts to break, to extend their ride on it. They are starting to wipe out on larger waves too. They are finding their feet, on their boards and in life too. They no longer want me to push them off into the waves; they want, as I wanted at their age, to make their own mistakes. As a father, it makes me nervous, though I know they need to do this.

The risks of the sea are still there, freak waves and rip tides, strong currents and all the dangers that were ever there when people were drawing monsters on the edge of the maps and some more besides that we've added since then – pollution, toxins, antibiotic-resistant bacteria. It's a risky thing, to go to sea. It's a risky thing to be alive at all, too risky, perhaps not to indulge in the simple pleasure of hurling yourself down the face of a wave on a piece of shaped wood, with or without a caul in your possession.

S/V Linden.

6

Wind Worker

Running away to sea

IN MY GRANDPARENT'S HOUSE in Malvern, the house in which I spent many childhood holidays, among dusty boxes piled high in one of the basement rooms, there was a telescope, a brass sextant and various charts I used to take out and marvel at. Most of the evidence of my grandfather's career at sea was contained in these boxes, a whole swathe of his life about which I knew little aside from the fact he had been in the merchant navy, where he worked his way up to being first mate. Before my father was born, my grandfather had sailed the world and only returned to land to marry and start a family, something he knew he could not do if he was already married to the sea. It was clear, though, that the sea kept a strong hold on him. When he took me and my brother walking on the Malvern Hills as children, he would tell us stories of life on board ships. Not the realities of it, not the horrors of war, nor really of any of the serious things he had done nor experienced, unless it was something light-hearted and trivial – a prank played, or some small adventure, which usually involved him bending the rules. The stories he told us were mainly fantasies of smuggling. He would have smuggled brandy and cigarettes, he said, as a benign, piratical figure and that was how he always seemed to me. He recited poetry sometimes too, in the drawing room. Aside from pretensions to smuggling, one of the legacies of the years he spent on board ships was a prodigious memory for poetry.

When my grandmother died just before the turn of the millennium, my grandfather briefly considered returning to sea. He confided to my father later, he had not done so for fear – or, perhaps, in his grief, for hope – that if he set off alone in a yacht the waves would swallow him whole and we would not see him again. He continued to sail occasionally though, on yachts and tall ships, well into his mid-eighties. On returning from these trips, he would casually drop into conversation that he had climbed to the very top of the rigging, a place where the crew of the ship were generally unwilling to accompany him.

He left for sea in January 1943, aged fifteen, and joined HMS *Conway*. He was sent to the harsh regime of the school ship, with the motto 'Quit ye like men; be strong', by his father to become just that, a man. At some point during his time there, he borrowed an anthology of poems from the ship's library and became so attached to it that he never returned it. He memorized its contents during long night watches, and after a while he could switch the poems on when he was in his bunk and disappear into verse for a while. It was like, he said, turning on a radio and even now, in his late nineties he can still recite scores of poems.

I must go down to the seas again, to the lonely sea and the sky . . .

After I first heard my grandfather recite the lines of John Masefield's most celebrated poem, 'Sea-Fever', they lodged themselves in my head. They took root and never left.

Masefield had trained on the *Conway* too, though he had long since left the navy and was poet laureate by the time my grandfather left home to undertake his training. Masefield had arrived on *Conway* aged thirteen and his experiences there shaped his vision of the sea and of sailing. Later in life, he would write several poems dedicated to his time on her.

A three-masted, wooden, 92-gun battleship, *Conway* was launched in Plymouth in 1839 to a crowd of 50,000, exactly a year after Queen Victoria was crowned. It was a ship of another era entirely. By 1943, the days of sail were long gone and the Second World War, with all its technical advancements both barbaric and miraculous, was in full flow, though the nineteenth-century battleship was still used to train naval recruits.

My grandfather, like Masefield, learnt to navigate by the stars on board the *Conway*, to plot a course and use a sextant. And like Masefield, who credited his time there to his decision to dedicate his life to storytelling, the wooden training ship with its acres of sail was where my grandfather too caught his sea fever.

> *I must go down to the seas again, for the call of the running tide,*
> *Is a wild call and a clear call that may not be denied.*

There is a whiteboard on the fridge at home on which my family conducts its daily affairs. It outlines who is responsible for picking up which child from which club or lesson, doctors' appointments, meal arrangements, the complex, practical wheres and whens of family life. Against the row for Sunday 2 June, my daughter writes, 'Dad to the middle of nowhere'. She knows I am heading north, far, far north, to Svalbard. We have looked at maps and

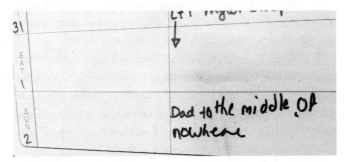

'Dad to the middle of nowhere.'

I have pointed out the archipelago on the edge of the map and, within it, the small town nestled in one of the fjords from which I am going to meet my ship, though all she sees of it is blank space on the map, a child's projection of the pristine, immutable whiteness of the Arctic wilderness, a space suitable only, perhaps, for the drawing of dragons or a man-eating cyclops.

The sea is on my doorstep in Cornwall, and with it some of the best sailing grounds in the world. There are plenty of boats to sail here: dinghies, yachts and ships. It would seem reasonable that I might be satisfied with that, though I am abandoning them all for a while. I am doing something I have dreamt of doing for as long as I can remember, since I first heard my grandfather read Masefield's iconic lines. I am running away to sea, succumbing to wanderlust. I am doing it very politely, though. I have not slipped away in the early hours; nor have I stowed away on a ship leaving Falmouth Docks. Instead, I have asked Emma's permission to abandon home for a while for the lonely sea and the sky, and I have talked my way into a place on the crew of S/V *Linden*, a 100-metre long, three-masted wooden schooner.

If I was not aware before that I am engaged in an extension of what Francis Spufford describes in *I May Be Some Time*, his exploration of Arctic and Antarctic travel, as a kind of hazy love affair between the English and the ice-bound seas of the poles, my daughter's scribbled note brings it into focus. I have only the vaguest of plans. At the point of setting out, I have little more to go on than a time and place to meet my ship. I pack a bag and make my way 2,000 miles north: Newquay to London, London to Oslo, Oslo to Svalbard.

I have plenty of time to consider my daughter's 'middle of nowhere' comment too, since when I arrive at the harbour in Longyearbyen, bag on my back, I find modern yachts, high-powered tourist RIBs, small cruise ships, the *Polarsyssel* – the enormous blue ice breaker that patrols the waters of Svalbard – but nothing that resembles a three-masted tall ship. I am overdressed for the mild Arctic summer and 24 hours overdue a sleep. I make calls and eventually get through to *Linden's* owner, Rasmus. *Linden* is still in Tromsø, he tells me, almost 1,000 kilometres away.

He outlines a litany of disasters that has befallen his ship, a list which will grow over the next few days. Events have conspired to make her four weeks behind schedule: a severe storm has kept her in port; an inexperienced pilot has snapped her bowsprit and she needed repairs; her captain has broken his arm and she needed to turn back and a new captain procured; she had engine troubles and had to return to port again. Worse things happen at sea? Apparently so. In the melee, no one let me know. Tomorrow, I am told. She will arrive tomorrow.

Linden does not arrive the next day, nor the day after that. My hotel is in the former miners' accommodation at the top end of the valley that contains Longyearbyen and I stalk the two-and-a-half miles between hotel and harbour several times a day. I track *Linden's* movements obsessively on marinetraffic.com. The *Linden* I had seen so far only in photographs on my home computer shrinks further still until it is a small, blue arrow on the screen of my phone. After making some good progress initially, she appears to be going nowhere. Headwinds keep her glued to the same spot just south of Svalbard. I distract myself by hiking in a nearby valley and kayaking on the Isfjord, but I want to be sailing.

The ski-resort feel of Longyearbyen, with its adventure companies and bars full of Fjällräven-wearing tourists, jars with the Arctic I had imagined. Beyond the town centre, though, it's a rough around the edges, pitched together frontier kind of town, and that becomes increasingly apparent as the snows melt. The town dump is clearly visible on the shore of the Isfjord, along with scores of abandoned, rusting snowmobiles and the ground is heavily littered. As the permafrost melts, the contents of this dump are pushing themselves off into the water. Nearby, the town's sewage pipe runs straight out into the fjord where, on my second day in town, I watch a pod of eighty or so beluga whales passing through. At the edge of town, a huge coal mountain is a conspicuous sign of the fossil fuel that still powers Longyearbyen. Dreams of doomed explorations leach into what little sleep I manage to get in the 24-hour sunlight, brought on by having studied the stories of the great sea voyages to the far north, and poring over seventeenth-century charts which label the seas around Svalbard as parts unknown or *mare incognitum*. I begin to think that maybe I have made a mistake, I ought to have taken a trip closer to home.

I get used to hearing the question, 'Has your boat arrived yet?' asked, invariably, with some measure of amusement.

'Not yet,' I answer. 'Tomorrow, I hope.'

I am beginning to doubt it, though.

When I visit the North Pole Museum, the smarting sensation that I might return home without having stepped foot on a ship is offset slightly by the feeling of Schadenfreude that comes of reading about others' disasters. You only have to scan the long history of Arctic exploration to understand the sketchiness of plans and the high rate of failure in this most remote part of the world. In the museum, I read about American journalist, Walter Wellman, who mounted several failed attempts to reach the North Pole in the late nineteenth century, first by airship and later by steamer. Each of his time-consuming and cripplingly expensive attempts ended in catastrophe, one – in 1906 – just three hours after the expedition began. Wellman's airship, loaded with $100,000 of equipment came down on the ice just a few miles from where it had taken off.

Some stories are more sobering: accounts of trappers, explorers and tourists mauled to death by bears or trapped by the ice; whole crews frozen because of miscalculation or misplaced confidence, lost in the long Arctic storms and longer winters. It's a reminder that everyone here is a runaway of some sort or other.

Svalbard has no native population and until the early 1900s had no permanent population at all. Before that, the main visitors had been whalers, trappers, hunters and later (mis)adventurers.

While I am waiting in town, I hear other stories from people who have run away for temporary respite from their lives. On one of my trips to Longyearbyen harbour I find a yacht on the pontoon loaded with skis. Sitting on deck is a doppelganger of the author Will Self. I stare just a moment too long, though when he shouts a greeting across the pontoon to me in a broad West Coast American accent that he is 'super stoked' to be here I reassess.

We get talking and fake-Will Self asks me if I've heard about the crater at the North Pole which contains a whole undiscovered civilization and possibly aliens too. The reason we don't know about it, he says, is because of a huge government cover-up. He does not have time to reach the North Pole this summer, he tells me – he's going skiing instead – but he wants to know if I think it is worth him organizing a trip there next year. I consider telling him he is about 200-years late to join the ranks of would-be explorer John Cleves Symmes' hollow-earthers but he has already moved on to outlining his thoughts about running for president, which, he says, may further delay his North Pole plans.

The hollow earth story enjoys brief spells of popularity periodically. It was originally suggested by the astronomer and geophysicist, Edmond Halley in the late 1600s and although the theory was disproved within decades, the idea was resurrected by John Cleves Symmes and the American newspaper editor J.N. Reynolds, in the mid-nineteenth century. It seems to me like a continuation of the drawing of monsters on the edge of maps, a desire to fill in the blank spaces. Fake-Will Self's preoccupation is a minor narrative, though, compared to the other stories that are told of this place. The ones that have endured are those of encounters with the sublime, of the struggle to reach a particular point (the North Pole being the ultimate of these aims) or of struggle, failure and the many predictable and unpredictable deaths available to adventurers in the far reaches. There is a reason these stories stick. They are narrative writ large on a landscape – or rather, a frozen seascape – that seems to invite both our imaginative investment and test our preparedness for the harshest of environments. The furthest reaches north and south are considered by many to be the last true wildernesses.

Then, several days after I had expected to see her, *Linden* arrives. I spot her from half-a-mile up the valley, her three wooden masts towering above the squat warehouses by the harbour and the whaling ships repurposed as tourist vessels. Alongside the yachts and cruise ships, *Linden* is stately, glorious even. She fits exactly the vision of the tall ship I have in mind whenever I recall Masefield's poem. She is not all she seems, though. She sails under a Danish flag, although she was built in 1993 on the Åland Islands in Finland, a replica of the 1920 schooner of the same name. Built for northern waters, she has a steel-strengthened hull, though from the outside she looks like a traditional wooden tall ship.

In contrast to many of the heavyweight adventure outfits I have encountered since I arrived, *Linden* is an experiment in small-scale ecotourism. She will spend her summer taking groups of up to twelve to explore the fjords of Svalbard.

When I come on board, the crew observe me through bleary eyes. It becomes clear that the news of my impending arrival has been lost somewhere in the 570 nautical miles between here and mainland Norway, and that no one on board is expecting me. The crew have each managed only a couple of hours sleep since docking at four that morning and I feel like an intruder on the ship.

Linden's captain, Nikolai is philosophical about it. We talk boats and drink strong coffee and, after what I assume is a gentle vetting, he welcomes me on board. They are currently a member of crew down, he says, so there is a cabin free. I stow my bag and Nikolai agrees to set me to work with the rest of the crew, though I get the impression the crew think I might be more liability than help. One suggests I might re-coil some of the ropes on deck, though when I ask what the rest of the crew is doing, he says they are making up cabins for the first guests of the season. He seems surprised when I suggest I might help with that instead. I am tired and irritable, though, and don't want to be fobbed off with non-jobs.

Over the next few hours we vacuum, polish, make the beds, clean the cabins and the heads, hose and scrub the deck. We rebuild the Zodiac, the ship's tender, piecing it together like Meccano. The crew are exhausted but scrupulously polite. Aside from Nikolai, who is in his forties like me, they are a young crew, most of them in their early twenties and most of them are Danish. It's not unusual, in the Danish education system, to do a year on a training tall ship. It gives you skills for life, they tell me, the ability to work with others, to work together towards some common aim, and it is outward facing. It gets them out of a small country and into the world. As four of us shuffle along the bowsprit to refold the foresails, toeing along a board a couple of inches deep, precipitous above the dark water, my agitation begins to dissipate. By the next morning *Linden* is ready to take on passengers for a weekend expedition into the fjords.

As we leave Longyearbyen there is a sense of a cloud lifting, not just for the guests, some of whom have stayed on in the hope *Linden* would arrive, but for the crew as well. Most of them are new to the Arctic, and they seem as wonderstruck as the guests. For a while, work stops. I sit on the forepeak as we plough through a heaving sea past snow-capped peaks that stretch away as far as I can see, towards Skansebukta, a bay at the foot of a mountain on the outer Billefjord. Gulls, guillemots, puffins and little auks ride alongside us. The strung-out sensation I had when I first stepped on board begins to clear. We sail clear of Longyearbyen across the fjord and anchor in the calm, dark water under the towering cliffs of Skansen, the mountain's distinctive layers of different coloured rock stacked like plates above the vivid green and scree-grey of the lower slopes, industrial Longyearbyen simultaneously only a few hours and a whole world away.

These moments of calm do not last. There are always jobs to do. 'People think that life on a ship will be all setting and trimming the sails,' says Thomas who, besides the captain, is the crew's most experienced sailor, as we wash endless dishes in the galley. 'But more often than that, it's about repainting the hull, stripping rust, doing the dishes.'

Thomas has been crewing on tall ships for several years. It is all he wants to do and he seems entirely at ease on a ship in a way he does not when he is on land. He is right about the dishes. For the crew at least, if not for her guests, life on board is a constant rotation of washing, drying and stowing of glasses and plates, of endless meals to be prepared and presented, of cleaning the saloon, changing bedsheets and washing towels. There is a running series of problems and fixes to make, all dealt with calmly. Holes are drilled, glue applied, ropes respliced, sections of the deck sanded back and revarnished. Though she was built recently and has a steel framed hull to withstand the ice, from the outside *Linden* is still a traditional wooden tall ship, and she needs constant attention to maintain her equilibrium. Life on board is ensuring she stays at anchor through long nights while everyone else sleeps and hosing the decks to keep the boards from drying out. It is countless small tasks of maintenance and upkeep, carpentry and engineering as much as it is anything to do with actually sailing.

There is a joke among the crew.

'When will we stop for dinner?'

The punchline is, 'When the sun sets.'

In the Arctic summer, the sun, of course, does not set. Throughout the summer it tours the horizon and keeps a constant watch, though it never drops out of sight. Though we do stop to eat, and we eat well, the days are long and each night I collapse into my bunk.

During my first 72 hours in Svalbard, waiting in Longyearbyen as *Linden* ploughed inexorably north against headwinds from Tromsø, unsure as to whether or not she would actually arrive and not able to sleep much, my system was out of sync, unable to recognise night in the absence of darkness. In the early hours, I walked the town's empty streets or tried to read but was unable to concentrate.

The ship rebalances me, though, with her routines, with her sway on the water. The work tires me out so much that when I walk across the deck towards my cabin one evening, I find myself thinking, 'Oh, horses, that's nice,' and it takes me a moment to work out there are, in fact, no horses on deck and that the noise is the halyards tapping against the rigging and the spars. When I close the cabin door and lie in my narrow bunk, I am asleep within seconds, and when my alarm wakes me for my anchor watch, I smile to myself, tired but replenished.

Linden's *Arctic guide, Emil, scans the shore.*

For the first few days, in most of my tasks, I am doubling up on someone else's work. I share an anchor watch with another member of crew and I am watched, albeit at a distance, in whatever job I have been given. As neither fully crew nor fully guest, my work is subtly checked by another crew member, though one morning Nikolai hands me the ship's wheel and tells me he is going to get what he describes as 'coffee lunch' and that he may be gone for a couple of hours. He checks that I can set a course, nods his approval and disappears, leaving me alone at the wheel of a three-masted tall ship, navigating Forlandssund, 78 degrees north. I check the course again through the shrouds, the distant dark peak towards which Nikolai has asked me to steer. This, I realize, is what I had hoped for. I would have come here for this specific moment alone.

Eventually, the constant light of the Arctic summer will be replaced by 24-hour darkness. To sail in the high Arctic is to be reminded that the diurnal patterns we think of as a constant are not the only patterns; they are constructs that are useful only in a limited sphere. It is to be reminded of the narrowness of my worldview, just as when we shut off the engines and sail it reminds me of the noise we have created in order to propel our lives forward. Perspective is everything, and the far north illuminates this better than anywhere else I've visited. In my time off, I take to climbing the rigging and sitting on one of the crosstrees, high above the deck. The scale of the landscape, the mountains and glaciers, the sheer abundance of life here is hard to grasp. It is a painfully beautiful sight, which, to paraphrase Seamus Heaney's poem 'Postscript', catches me off guard and blows my heart open.

At Pyramiden, a former Russian mining town abandoned at the shortest of notice in 1996 due to shrinking coal supplies and a lack of political support, we spot a polar bear on the sea ice. Before I came here, I had always pictured polar bears walking on pristine snow. There is something touching and disturbing about watching one stalking the ice in front of abandoned Komatsu diggers and buildings daubed with Cyrillic lettering. We watch the bear from a distance in almost total silence. Emil, our Arctic guide, talks in hushed tones about the distances at which we must observe them if we are to observe them at all, the necessity of leaving them in peace.

Some tour operators have evolved crafty methods of circum-navigating restrictions on getting too close to the polar bears and walrus. Guides and guests will overstep the mark, he says, and disturb bears with cubs. The same happens with the large haul-outs of walruses with calves, the intruding photographers causing deadly stampedes as the walruses rush for the safety of the water. The boat (though not the operator) will be banned from the area for the next year, so the operator takes that boat to a different location and replaces it with another from their fleet, and the cycle begins again.

A polar bear on the sea ice at Pyramiden.

We abandon our plans to head to shore, rerouting towards Nordenskiöldbreen, where Nikolai and I watch through the rigging as the walls of one of Svalbard's largest glaciers resolve themselves into vast and complex masses of peaks, valleys and crevasses. Approaching the glacier at boat speed, looking out from the bridge across the wooden deckhouses, this feels as though it could be any time during the past few hundred years. As with our encounter with the bear, a hush falls across the ship. It's not hard to imagine a similar sort of silence falling across the deck of an expeditionary ship in the mid-1700s.

I learnt to sail in the boat my grandfather built in the late 1960s, a Mirror dinghy. Like many men who returned from sea and wanted to keep their love of the sea and of sailing alive, he was precisely the target market for Jack Holt's self-assembly dinghy that could be carried on a roof rack for a visit to the sea. It was the boat in which he had taught my father to sail and, in turn, the boat in which my father taught me to sail.

In my mid-twenties, I graduated from the practical but slow Mirror to fast catamarans and the first test of my relationship with Emma was whether we could share a boat, an 18-foot Dart catamaran, designed just a few miles from where we now live in Cornwall. On a catamaran, the sense of bringing near what is remote at speed is one of the thrills of it – the sense of movement across the waves and the moments of weightlessness when one of the hulls lifts out of the water and, suspended on the trapeze above the white caps and with the wind full in your face, it almost feels like flight.

Linden moves slowly. She does not fly so much as she glides, implacable and stateswoman-like, but she wields her own magic. She is solid and graceful. Nikolai refers to her affectionately as the 'grande dame'. She requires a lot of attention, he says, and she goes nowhere quickly, but she does so with style.

'Sailing has its own pace,' Nikolai says. 'It has its own time and space. It makes you appreciate the distances you travel better. And it's not often you can really get away from the sounds of cars, airplanes, motors, people.'

Each morning, as I trace her path on the chart I have drawn in my notebook, although it feels as though we are covering huge distances, I realize we are crossing and recrossing a small area within a vast archipelago. The pace of sailing seems to open out time for reflection that is rare in an age when it is possible to cross an ocean in a matter of hours.

Early mornings on board are one of my favourite times of the day, the times at which I take anchor watch and when the ship is silent except for the generator hum. I share anchor watch with Emil and one morning, just after six, as we watch the approach of the sea ice that might encase the ship, he tells me how he came to be on board. He was drinking in a bar in Longyearbyen, bemoaning his imminent departure from Svalbard after losing his previous job, when he met the ship's owner, Rasmus. When he woke up the next morning, he was in a cabin on *Linden*, the willing victim of a kind of benevolent press-ganging. He has lived on board ever since. He was a bit wild, before, he tells me (and there is certainly something of the polar bear about him, especially when he is losing at cards). Life on board a ship has stabilized him, though.

'Which one of us is going to wake Shackleton, then?' Emil says and nods towards the gangway beneath which Nikolai is asleep in the captain's cabin. The ice, which looks thin as a windowpane, is actually several metres thick and there is now a real danger that we'll get encased.

There are increasing stretches of companionable silence between me and the rest of the crew, and increasing periods of time in which I am left at the helm with my own thoughts and a course to steer. The crew stop talking so much in English and switch back to Danish – most of them are Danes – which I take as a sign they are letting go of the impeccable politeness with which they've treated me so far, a sign they are comfortable enough to continue as they were. Once we know each other a little, they are mostly quiet while we sail, self-contained and happy in their own thoughts.

There is another kind of quiet that comes when we hoist the sails and turn the engine and generator off, when we shift to true boat speed, when the background noise of machine-driven life is replaced by a true calm; and another particular variety of quietness that falls across the deck when pods of whales converge on the ship and we gather on the forepeak to listen to the deep breathing and blows, no one wanting to interrupt the moment with any noise of their own.

'It is peaceful in your head out here.' It is gone midnight and Nikolai is addressing the empty saloon as much as he is talking to me, I feel. Like Thomas, Nikolai is entirely at home on ships. He has spent most of his life afloat, sailing yachts and Ro-Ro ferries and later as a sailor in the British Navy where he learnt English. Nikolai's first captain was Irish and while his Norwegian accent is barely perceptible when he talks, he has inherited an Irish lilt.

At the end of the first trip, I have resigned myself to my curtailed stay following *Linden's* late arrival, until Nikolai and Emil sound me out about staying on for a longer voyage the following week. They are still a crew member short. It seems I have been accepted. After a flurry of phone calls, to Emma and to the university where I teach two days a week, I arrange to extend my time as a runaway at sea. We strip the beds, hose and scrub the decks, vacuum, polish, make beds, make ready for the next guests. The crew teach me the hand signals necessary on a ship of *Linden's* length, when communicating between the bow and stern, and Nikolai shows me how to use the bow thrusters for manoeuvring her into position to anchor.

Small things hold the crew together: long sessions of the card game Casino that last into the early hours; the Danish children's board game Partners; there are rope puzzles learnt on training ships, in which two sailors must attempt to disentangle themselves from a series of deceptively simple knots and which often end up more like wrestling matches on deck. Late in the evening we swim, climbing down a rope ladder or jumping from the deck, diving and backflipping into terrifyingly cold water surrounded by sea ice, controlling our gasps for breath. When we emerge, we retreat to the sauna (all Finnish ships are furnished with a sauna). Sometimes we cast spinners over the side of the ship and fish. One evening, an hour or so into a fishing session, Thomas appears beside me on the deck.

'There are no fish here, you know?' he says. 'We just do it for the hygge.' He laughs loudly into the silent fjord and I continue to fish, though, as Thomas predicts, I catch nothing.

Three of Linden's *crew play rope games during a break.*

The time I spend on *Linden* is dreamlike. Here, I find something of the life at sea I realize I was hoping for as we plough through heaving seas and still, as we drop anchor beneath towering glaciers and in front of abandoned trappers' huts, or within sight of colonies of walruses, as we swim in achingly cold waters late at night. On watch, I see huge pods of belugas, minkes and fin whales too. They are gathered in the fjords for the outpouring of nutrients from the feet of rolling glaciers, which feed the plankton and krill in these waters.

As we pass close to towering cliffs, we watch clouds of smoke resolve themselves into flocks of little auks in numbers I have never seen before, observe their complex interweavings, their pulling apart and drawing close. I watch the arrival of the Arctic terns too as they return from their long journey up from the Antarctic. Their patterns too are difficult to comprehend, impossible perhaps. Theirs are narratives that remain unknown, unknowable. They are light, they are steel. Conversely, the whales that are so abundant here and which are so incomprehensibly large, seem fragile, like the glaciers we encounter, immense and delicate and in retreat.

A fulmar, seen through the rigging.

Standing at the wheel for increasing periods alone, I am sometimes aware of another presence, a small movement in my peripheral vision. A northern fulmar, cadging a ride on *Linden's* updraught, eyeballing me over a stiff wing. I turn back to the wheel and when I look again it is still there. It reminds me of another Masefield poem, 'The Conway Gulls', written about the tradition on the school ship that gulls were to be held in great reverence as the spirits of former former pupils who had crossed the line and returned to their ship. The fulmar banks away to skim over water that is as still as glass. It tips onto its side and sketches the surface with its wingtips, leaving a thin, impermanent line before tipping onto its other side. These traces last seconds, if that, and are gone, just as the fulmar itself has now disappeared. It would be the easiest thing, out here, to become animistic, to imbue the terns and the fulmars, the bears, the whales, the walrus and the sad, squat reindeer that eat stones on the hillsides, with a spiritual meaning, to find messages in their appearances and disappearances, in the brief moments our paths cross with theirs.

In one quiet moment, standing at the ship's wheel with Nikolai, an enormous, lone blue whale breaches. Framed in the gap between the deck and the foresail, it lifts its tail into the sky and scythes back into the sea. The rest of the crew and guests are at breakfast and Nikolai suggests we should keep our sighting to ourselves as we are unlikely to see it again. Months later, the image of the whale is still etched onto my mind clearer than any photograph I could have taken.

As we approach the Russian mining town of Barentsburg, we get a rare moment of mobile signal, and across the ship, phones beep with a 'Welcome to Russia' message. I receive a flurry of messages and photographs – my son, Tom, in his new cricket shirt, Alana dressed up for Flora Day.

We walk up into the mining town, past the statue of Lenin, his head a patchwork of guano, past the tiny ornate Russian Orthodox church. One of the guests drags us to a bar decorated with snowmobile chassis, where there is a lot of beer and vodka and singing and a hangover at the end of it. We are, I realize later, behaving exactly as you would expect a crew on shore leave to act.

On deck and over meals, we discuss incessantly the changes taking place both here in front of us and further afield, the impact we are having on our planet, whether or not we should actually be here in this most delicate of environments. When conditions allow, we set a trawl from the boom, part of a larger scientific study to measure the distribution of oceanic plastic. There is less here than in the Pacific, but still there is plenty of microplastic to be found in the sunlight zone. There is much talk about the role of tourism in the Arctic. One member of the crew suggests that now we understand so much about the fragility of this landscape, we should leave Svalbard to the scientists.

The archipelago of Svalbard is one of the fastest warming places on earth and a coal producer. Against that backdrop, the town-organized clean ups and the rise of small-scale, wind-driven ships for tourism seems weak at best. It is at once both a centre for research into climate change and also the home of the exclusive Svalbarði water, collected from a glacier, augmented with minerals to give it a taste (since glacier water does not taste of anything much), a sign of conspicuous wealth and disregard for the planet. One of the most expensive bottled waters in the world, Svalbarði ships it to smart hotels across the globe, and of course Harrods, where in 2017 it was selling for £80 a bottle, a symbolic flicking of the Vs to those worried about climate change.

As we return to Longyearbyen, we find an enormous cruise ship in the harbour. She is *Mein Schiff 4*. At nearly 300-metres long, and carrying 2,700 passengers and over 1,000 crew, she is monstrous. When her passengers disembark, each of them in search of his or her personal experience of the sublime, she more than doubles the population of the town. They stagger off the ship, zombie-like, and head for the gift shop on the edge of town where it is possible to buy plush polar bears, Svalbard shot glasses and Arctic-themed tea towels.

In a bar, I was told the locals are extra careful in town when the big tour ships disembark, as the passengers often have little idea of where they are, nor what time of day or night it is, nor even that the roads have cars on them. They arrive in town and demand to see polar bears in the three or four hours in which they have been allotted to explore. Many of them are disappointed to discover it is a rarity to see one and I am told the tour operating community is having serious discussions about commissioning a mechanical polar bear that can be used in lieu of the less predictable and somewhat more shy real deal. Welcome to Arctic Land.

We drop anchor in the fjord and wave our seven guests off on the Zodiac. Later, when *Mein Schiff* has weighed anchor and is ploughing through the Barents Sea towards mainland Norway and then on to Germany, for more whistle-stop tours of the sublime, we watch from the bridge as a bonfire is built on the shore. I ask Emil what is being celebrated. 'It's a local tradition,' he says. 'Each time one of those cruise ships leaves, the town holds a party.'

It's like a relief valve, the town's population coming together to see off a terrifying spirit that has arrived on its doorstep, to expunge it, at least until the next one arrives.

Human impact here is nothing new. The whaling stations, the remains of which litter Svalbard's beaches, are long gone, and so are most of the coal mines. The huge structures built by pioneers like the American journalist and explorer Walter Wellman, hangars for the airships he used for his repeated attempts on the North Pole, are now little more than driftwood. Tourism has stepped into the breach.

I am torn between my desire to experience this place (a desire, I realized, neither more nor less valid than that of those who arrive on ships such as *Mein Schiff*), and a competing desire to leave it as it is.

After the guests have left and we have hosed the deck, stripped the beds and cleaned the cabins in anticipation of the next guests, we play games. My flight is not until three in the morning and the crew says they will stay up with me until I leave. In my last few moments on board, I stand on the bridge, looking out, away from Longyearbyen towards the mountains on the opposite side of the fjord and the closing lines from another poem from my grandfather's anthology, Gerard Manley Hopkins's 'Inversnaid', run through my head as though I have switched on a radio and found it playing there:

> 'What would the world be, once bereft,
> Of wet and of wilderness? Let them be left,
> O let them be left, wildness and wet;
> Long live the weeds and the wilderness yet.'

Cowries.

7

Memory Keeper

Searching for cowrie shells

A T THE FAR END of the island of St Agnes there is a one-armed bandit or, rather, a lucky dip. Six hundred years ago, a cargo ship carrying Venetian glass beads wrecked off the far eastern point of the island, at Wingletang Down, dispersing its cargo onto the seabed where the beads scattered, jewels among the jewel-like stones of the sea floor. They began to wash onto the shore after storms, sometimes in large numbers and then, as they became collectors' items, increasingly desirable and increasingly sought after, less and less often. I have seen them in the museum on St Mary's alongside the intricate and incredibly beautiful brooches found at the Romano-British shrine on Nornour. They are the sort of thing you cannot really ever imagine finding for yourself, though every time I visit Scilly, I try my hand, a half-an-hour lucky dip at Beady Pool. Allegedly, they still turn up, though they are few and far between. They have been there for so long now and sought by so many that the odds are stacked against the player.

One afternoon in early summer, I borrowed a kayak from the campsite at Troytown where I was staying in a coffin-like one man tent and paddled along the edge of the island until I came to its far end. It was warm when I arrived at the small beach and as there was no one else about I stripped off and dove straight into the water. The summer's warmth not yet having penetrated the surface of the water, it was shockingly cold. It seemed, to me, colder even than the glacial waters of Svalbard, though in reality it was a result of the difference between the air temperature and that of the water.

I always forget that the water around Scilly is that much colder than the water round Cornwall. Despite there being just 28-miles between the mainland and the islands, Scillonian waters often feel a good few degrees colder. I climbed out shivering and when I had dressed and warmed up, I walked over the seagrass spit to Beady Pool where I sifted for beads as three oystercatchers stood sentry on the rocks to my right. I found no beads there. I never do. It doesn't help at all that they are the same reddish-brown colour as one of the types of stones found on the same beach. Instead, I found the usual collection of battered fragments of plastics, which went into my bag, and then, just as I was about to leave, tucked into a patch of seaweed, the bleached vertebra of a dolphin. For a minute, holding it, I built out the rest of the animal in my mind, spinning and twisting in the water, and my disappointment at not finding one of the Venetian beads was forgotten.

Whenever I am on a beach, if I'm not looking for wreck, or for fragments of pottery with words, letters or numbers on them, more often than not I am looking for cowries. And even when I am not looking for them consciously, I always have half an eye out for one and half an ear out for anyone who might have found one, though most people who look for them keep the best locations for cowries a closely guarded secret.

Some days now it feels that the internet has blown apart the idea of secrets, in particular when it comes to the 'hidden' places on the coast. In the summer, inspired by blogposts and videos, by guidebooks to 'secret' Cornwall, the small coves, even the ones that you have to trek to get to, are most often busy now. It seems right, though, that some things should remain secret. It seems right that some things ought to be discovered by experience rather than read about in a book or passed down by word of mouth rather than recorded and shared online. Whether it is the best beach for driftwood or rock pools, for waves or caves, for diving or swimming, for wreck or serpentine pebbles, the best rocks from which to fish for mackerel or the best spots in which to dive for lobster, the hunt is everything. Make it too easy and the joy attached to finding the thing you were looking for fades. Shout about it too loudly and you lose the very thing you been so pleased to find in the first place.

I come across one promising sounding patch after a chance encounter with a woman in her sixties who is walking along the strandline on a beach I have never visited before in Scilly. I can tell just by the way she is looking at the strandline that she is looking for cowries too – there is definitely something in the look, in the hunter's pace, the way the walker dips and then stands when she realizes what she has found is just another stone or the wrong kind of shell.

When I ask if she has found any, she takes out a small handful from her pocket and we admire them together. She has found more than me. We get to talking, and when she finds out I am a writer, she tells me that her husband writes too. She points him out, some way off in the bay. The best cowries, she confides in me, are further out there, beyond where he is walking. It is our last day on the islands though and the tide is coming in, so I file the location and make a note to return.

It is another year before we are back. We hustle for the first boat to leave St Mary's to time our arrival to coincide with the final hour of the falling tide. At the top of the beach, swallows swoop and dive and further down there are small huddles of sanderlings on the shore, scurrying ahead of tiny waves that ripple in and chase them out again. We take off our shoes, tie them to our backpacks, roll up our shorts and step into the water. It is startlingly clear. We are heading for a sandbar that has opened around a rock some way offshore. It still seems improbable that we will be able to walk from here to there across an open stretch of water, an act of faith, and Alana and Tom do not seem convinced either. I am sure that at any moment the seabed will start to drop away and that we will be forced to swim if we are to go any further out. I do not mention this to the children but I am glad when the water gets no deeper than my thighs. I pause to investigate seaweeds, crabs that seem as confused that I am here as I am, snakelocks anemones too, their tentacles waving in the current. About halfway across I pause as a school of wrasse swims around me and I feel momentarily like a pedestrian on a traffic island in the middle of a busy road.

The island on which we haul out is occupied by a lone cormorant on a rock. Judging by the rock's covering of guano, it is her regular spot. The bird seems unconcerned by our arrival, though as I make my way round the edge and come closer, it lifts off and flies heavily, almost dismissively, away. The shells here are arranged in concentric circles around the island, and it brings to mind something Jane Darke told me about the way the sea sorts things: to each item its own place, left-footed boots washed up on one beach, right-footed boots on another. Here, the limpet shells occupy one layer, top shells another, sea snail shells of different types in one, delicate shards of sea potatoes in another.

The children demand food and we have an early lunch on the rocks. They wade in the shallow water with their sandwiches, involved in some complex game the rules to which Emma and I are not party. We are joined by a woman with an anorak and a waterproof bag. I don't notice her immediately; I've been distracted by shells and when I look up, I am surprised to see someone else there. It is a small enough patch of rock and sand to make it impossible that our paths will not cross.

'Any luck?' I ask.

She taps her pocket.

'Two. You?'

I shake my head.

She smiles and we wish each other luck and turn our eyes back to the sand.

The island yields nothing more for any of us, though when I look up next, I notice another sand bar has opened up further into the bay and we move on, rolling up our trouser legs again and splashing through the shallow sea.

In some parts of the world, shell collecting is a commercial business and cowries in particular have a history not just in jewellery and in rituals, but as gambling dice, as trading items and as currency in countries as far apart as Egypt and North America, Fiji and Benin, the Maldives and Greece. In Dar es Salaam and Zanzibar some types of cowrie shells, collected mainly for the tourist market now, are now only rarely seen, especially *Cypraea tigris*, the highly polished, spotted tiger cowrie which has been collected since at least Roman times. They have been hunted almost to the point of depletion. Combine this over-collecting with dynamite fishing and with more general habitat loss of the coral reefs where they live, and these cowries are now considered endangered in many parts of the world. While shell money was superseded by coins, and the last vestiges of their use as money is now only seen in parts of the Solomon Islands and sometimes in East New Britain in Papua New Guinea, the legacy of the cowrie as currency can still be seen in the naming of the Ghanaian Cedi and engraved on some of Ghanaian coins, and in the Literary Chinese character for money, a stylized drawing of a cowrie shell.

The cowries we are looking for are not showy like the highly polished, mottled shell of *Cypraea tigris*. They are not the shells from which the term porcelain derives – an old Italian term for the cowrie shell – nor are they the same type of cowrie shells once used as currency across Ghana, India and China. They are not commercially valuable at all, though they are collected in Shetland, where they are known as grotie buckles and in Cornwall where they were traditionally known as guinea pigs or blackamoor's teeth. Robert Morton Nance, the arch collector of Cornish sea words, suggested that Cornish sailors or wreckers came into contact with the money cowrie either through travel or through finds from wrecked ships, and applied their term for it to the less flamboyant version that washed up on their shores. In Scilly, Nance wrote, they were known as moneypennies.

There are two types of cowrie found here, the three-spotted cowrie and the no spot, *Trivia monacha* and *Trivia arctica*, distant relations to their showier cowrie cousins, the two types Heather Buttivant found for me in the storm gully on the low spring tide some months earlier. They are elliptical and range from light pink to white in colour, the smallest about 7 millimetres in length and the longest about 2 centimetres. Against the sand and hidden among rocks, they are near on invisible.

We wade across to the second island, 200 metres or so further on from the last, though this next temporary island holds nothing for us either. There are plenty of pretty shells but none of the type we were looking for. We stay long enough for our shorts to dry and when they do, we are left with tidemarks of salt.

After half an hour of staring at the ground, I need a change of perspective and look up to see sails on the horizon, tall, dark and crisp against the white sky. The boats are too far out to see anything clearly, but we watch them for a while anyway. Though we are sheltered here, the water further out looks ruffled and ploughed by the wind. The yachts are moving at a pace. Later, when we get back to our apartment, I discover they are racing

Bishop Rock Lighthouse.

yachts taking part in the Fastnet Race. One of the best-known ocean races, the 695-mile Fastnet Race begins at Cowes on the Isle of Wight and takes the racing crews west, where they skirt the Bishop Rock Lighthouse just off the Isles of Scilly, on to the Fastnet Lighthouse, the most southerly point of Ireland, and then the long leg towards the finish line at Cherbourg in France.

The sails we can see include those of some of the fastest racing yachts on the planet. They include the giant 38-metre ClubSwan 125 *Skorpios*, the largest yacht ever to sail in the race, and 32-metre Ultime trimarans, fully foiling IMOCA yachts that compete in the hellishly tough Vendée Globe; boats that are the equivalent of Formula 1 cars. At the other end of the racing spectrum is an 11-metre wooden yacht from 1962, *Le Loup Rouge of CMN* and *L'Albatros*, a yacht less then 10-metres long.

Some of my sailing heroes, including Dee Caffari, the first woman to sail single-handedly round the world going against the prevailing winds and currents, and double Olympic gold medallist Shirley Robertson, are among the 337 skippers who started the race, though I have no way of knowing if theirs are among the boats I have seen. From this far out, it is impossible to judge even their speed, though one report has *Maxi Edmond de Rothschild* hitting 40 knots as it passed Bishop Rock. While *Maxi Edmond de Rothschild* crosses the line in just over 33 hours, it takes *Le Loup Rouge* 8 days and 6 hours. For most crews, this is a slog of several days hard racing and of the 337 yachts that started the race, fewer than half finish.

Many sailors I have met quote Arthur Ransome as an influence on them wanting to sail. Somewhere in the back of their minds, there is an image of *Swallows and Amazons*, of a small band of children sailing to an uninhabited island to camp.

Despite having learnt to sail on lakes in the north of England, when I dream of sailing, it is not of the enclosed waters of the Lakes nor being a part of the Walker and Blackett children; it is almost always of sailing the seas of the Inner Reach in Ursula Le Guin's *Earthsea* novels or heading west to the edge of Le Guin's fantasy archipelago to Selidor or to the place on the wide waters where the raft people gather, where they live their lives entirely at sea. I read *Earthsea* about the age of ten and since then I've always connected magic and sailing. It does feel like a kind of magic, using the wind to power your adventures. Rereading the books this year with my daughter, I saw how clearly Le Guin had made the parallel too between fantasy magic and that connected to sailing. In the third book in the Earthsea cycle, *The Farthest Shore*, she writes about how similar the art of the mage is to that of the sailor. Both, she writes, command the powers of the seas, the skies and the wind, and both are capable of bringing close what is far away.

I had not thought about *Earthsea* for years until I first visited Scilly. From the helicopter, as the archipelago came into view it looked to me exactly as the islands on the map at the beginning of Le Guin's *A Wizard of Earthsea* had looked to my child's mind – the connection was visceral and immediate. In Scilly, I had rediscovered a small corner of the Earthsea which I had, until that point, forgotten.

Standing on the edge of the tiny islet, I feel the pull of these fast yachts, though for now it is enough just to see these racing hulls flying over the sea. I shift perspective back again, swap the macro for the micro again, the long view for the immediate, to what is right beneath my eyes.

The cowrie hunters I encounter inevitably have their own theories on how best to find the elusive shells. One tells me, authoritatively, that cowrie shells with their rounded shape float as air gets trapped inside the shells, so are left at the highest point of the tide. An eight-year-old I meet on a rock pooling day tells me they can be found in the darker bands left by the falling tide, small shelves on which the shells are stranded. She doesn't know why this is the case, but she swears by it and her mother confirms that she has a startlingly good record. Some pass their hands lightly over the sand, as though they are divining for them; others dig holes, sure they sense them beneath the surface.

One of the many superstitions to which I cling is that if I am searching for cowries, I must not pick up any other type of shell (with one exception, wentletraps, which are sometimes found alongside cowries). There is something intensely pleasing about finding the shell you are looking for, and it seems worth the trade-off, to forego any other for the promise of finding the one you want.

It is approaching low tide and the island we are aiming for now has appeared. It is further out than the other two, improbably so, a long spit of sand with a fist of rocks at its extremity. The sand spit looks like the back of a huge eel and it will be covered again in an hour or so.

We wade across, find our spots, and settle in. Alana finds her first cowrie within minutes. She shouts and holds it up as though she has discovered the grail. Tom looks for about a minute and then lies on his back staring up at the sky like an upturned beetle, and complains about not being able to find anything, though he is laughing while he is doing it. Emma is sitting on top of the ridge, her knees beneath her chin, and has found several already. She has a better eye for them than me – she has the cowrie eye. For every shell I find, Emma will have found three or four or, if she is having a good day, ten. I am sitting on the leeward side of the sandbank when I find my first, the tiny smiling mouth in among the small stones. Once I have spotted one, a second appears quickly. It often happens this way. Success begets success. Having seen one, more come into focus. Emma says it is all about attitude. If you approach the beach having tricked yourself into believing you have already found one, then you are more likely to be successful. Like wrecking, cowrie hunting is the sort of activity that invites superstitions.

In my family at least, the experience is a codified affair. Each person chooses their patch and a hunter's patch is sacred. If one person has chosen well and finds cowries there, it is not an invitation for someone else to invade that patch, regardless of whether or not they are a spouse or child. Further, not all cowries are equal; a broken cowrie must be cast away immediately, preferably lobbed over the shoulder like spilled salt.

I talk to friends and discover they have family rituals about the shells too. My friend Kat tells me in her family they called them wishing shells. At the end of a day in which they had found some, she and her parents and brothers would sit by the water and cast each shell back in, making a wish on each one.

I sift through the line of shells I have chosen as my patch. I take off my glasses, make good use of my myopia, get close to the ground. Everything around disappears for a few minutes. Like many of the other activities we engage in by the sea, this one is about flow. There is a dropping away of the world around, a shift of focus to a patch of ground inches below the eyes to the exclusion of everything else. When I look up, the sand bank is disappearing. The wind is up and there are kite surfers in the bay now and for a moment I entertain the idea that we might ask one of them for a lift back to the main island, though we agree to wring the most out of our time there and to risk being stranded for a while longer.

One of Cornwall's current collectors, though not of cowries particularly, is Tracey Williams, who I came across first on Twitter. On her @LegoLostAtSea account she documents her finds of sea-washed LEGO from a container spill in the 1990s. We met on an outgoing tide at one end of a long stretch of beach and walked east while she told me she traced her collecting habit to her childhood. Tracey is from a military family and as a child, in the house in which they lived on the Royal Airforce base near Lyneham, close to the home of fossil-hunter Mary Anning, she used to hunt for fossils in the garden with her father. He would save all the treasures he found while digging the garden and Tracey would wash them and try to identify what had been unearthed. She would regularly find fossilized corals and fish and other treasures closer to home: china chicken eggs, old bottles, tiny irons for ironing lace collars, children's toys.

Tracey's fascination with finding things in the ground continued into adolescence with her first jobs, picking potatoes on farms, and later when she began to volunteer on archaeological digs. By the time the *Tokio Express* cargo ship, heading for New York, spilled 62 containers including one that contained over 5 million pieces of LEGO 20 miles off Land's End on 13 February 1997, she was bringing her own children for their first holidays in Devon. The ship had been hit by a rogue wave, which swept the containers off the ship's deck.

Shortly after, pieces of LEGO began to wash up on beaches around Cornwall, much of it sea-themed. Tracey recalled finding flippers and life-preservers on the strandline, though over the years, less and less washed up and she forgot it entirely. In 2010, when the family moved to Cornwall, the first place Tracey headed was the beach, and on her first walk there she found a piece of LEGO and her interest was reignited.

Tracey began to walk the beach four times a day, arranging her work around the tides so she could make it onto the beach for low tide, collecting LEGO that washed in and that was excavated from the sand dunes after storms. She set up a Facebook page to track who else was finding it and where, mapping and recording its spread.

It seemed to me entirely unlikely that we would find anything on this huge stretch of beach, so when Tracey stopped and suggested that I look closely at the patch of sand beneath the dunes, the red LEGO speargun, among the nurdles and fragments of seaweed was a strange sight. On a beach which was now huge at low tide, it seemed inconceivable that we could have found the one tiny thing for which we were looking. From the reports on Tracey's Facebook group, others have had similar reactions. One person told her that she almost fainted when she found a piece, and like detectorists some finders of the *Tokio* LEGO send in videos of them doing a happy dance having found a scuba tank or a life vest. They could easily afford to go out and buy a set of LEGO, she said, though they are in it for the thrill of finding it in the wild, so to speak. By virtue of it having been lost, it has become treasure.

People seek Tracey out with their finds now, and not always LEGO. One of the most valuable pieces of treasure that can be collected on the beach is ambergris, produced by sperm whales and used in medicines and some perfumes. She recalled a man getting in contact with her several years ago thinking he had found some. He was so convinced that he had given up his job. If it was, it would have been worth a fortune. In February 2021, some Yemeni fishermen found 127 kilograms of ambergris and sold it for over £1million. However, Tracey's contact was not so lucky. I pictured the scene in which he sheepishly asked for his old job back and hoped he had not burned too many bridges on his way out.

Although we have a large bag of LEGO at home that the children seem now to have forgotten, I treasure my red speargun. I put it in a small jar on the dresser. It is treasure and deserves to be treated as such.

For me the experience of collecting is more about the searching than the finding. It is the experience of sitting on the beach, sifting sand and small stones, the surprise at actually being able to pick a light grey-pink shell out of a mass of light grey stones and shells and pieces of beach detritus.

We have looked for cowries on countless beaches. We've gathered intel on areas where others have found them, secrets passed on in whispers. On our secret and rapidly disappearing beach in Scilly, we regroup after having mined our respective patches and show each other our finds.

A LEGO speargun from the Tokio Express *container spill in 1997.*

The kids have found a lobster claw, some urchins, sea glass, and a lump of quartz. Some of these will make their way home and sit on a shelf on the dresser or they will be arranged in a loose menagerie of the sea. These incidental arrangements, the ones that come about by way of coat pockets and the side pockets of backpacks, of delicate things transported in Tupperware from which the sandwiches have been eaten, remind me of another such collection I have seen, that of the pioneer of landscape theatre and one of Cornwall's great collectors, Bill Mitchell who, along with Nick Darke, was one of the largest figures of Cornish cultural life in the past forty years.

I only met Bill briefly, shortly before he died, though he left a strong impression on me. Even though he was seriously ill, he was an imposing figure, tall, sharp-eyed and full of charisma, charm and presence, aided in no small part by a gold tooth that shone out when he grinned and which gave him the look of a genuine pirate.

Two years after Bill died, his widow, the artist Sue Hill invited me to undertake a residency in the attic of the house they had shared in Redruth, just a few miles from where I live. This was the space in which Bill did his thinking, where he developed the ideas for his theatrical extravaganzas. I had heard from friends who worked with Bill about his creative method before, the narrative boxes he made from antique and junk items, though it was not until I visited the attic for the first time that I understood the scale of the operation.

Climbing the steep stairs at the top of Sue's Edwardian house, the attic was a kind of sensory overload. Every corner, wall, roof space, shelf and tabletop was crammed with stuff. Not an inch was free. At first, I felt overwhelmed by the sheer volume and variety of ephemera in the room. Virgin Marys jostled with saints and doll's houses, bird cages, model ships, birds' skulls, and feathers. I couldn't imagine being able to create anything in here. My own writing space is uncluttered and any bits and pieces, aside from the storm glass and a soapstone elephant, are confined to the drawers in my desk.

Once I got over the sensory overload, the urge to play overtook me, and I began to walk around the room, which felt like a cross between an overcrowded, chaotic museum and an overcrowded, chaotic antique shop. I began to pick items up and weigh them in my mind. Was this more interesting than that? After a few days I had got into the swing of it and was beginning to put bits and pieces together, trying things in combination. Sue was away for much of the time I was there and as I could not work out how the heating system operated, I sat in my thermals, coat, hat and gloves at a desk untouched since Bill last used it. Through the Velux window, I could see the sea. I discovered among the many things he collected were jazz and classical CDs and I spent days going through the collection and playing Thelonious Monk and Bill Evans, Debussy and Mahler.

The taxonomist, Carl Linnaeus would have had a heart attack on seeing the way Bill organized the boxes which line the shelves from floor to ceiling. One was labelled RED, another TEETH and yet another HATE, all written in chalk capitals. Others still bore the labels SHATTERED GLASS, WEST and FUTURISTIC. The cases and boxes were filled with items Bill had collected, organized by colour or theme, to a scheme of classification only he understood.

Sue told me that when they first met in Peterborough in 1976, it was their shared love of collecting that sealed the deal for her. Both of them, she discovered, collected snow domes and Ladybird and Observer books. They would go to flea markets together, and later car boot sales, collecting things that were beautiful and tactile, and when they moved to Cornwall together, a decade later, and bought a tiny end of terrace cottage that Sue described as smelling terribly of damp and having doorways so low Bill had to stoop to walk between rooms, the shed there was soon filled with the products of Bill's developing collecting habit.

Bill Mitchell's boxes.

It was in this shed, inspired by New York artist Joseph Cornell's boxed assemblages, he began to make his own narrative boxes, assembling scenes from his found and bought items. It was, Sue told me, a way of him manipulating his ideas, a distraction activity you do while your mind is doing other work.

'The boot sale thing had become a real drug by then,' she said. He would scour antique stalls and flea markets and return home with headless dolls, with toy cars, postcards, newspaper clippings. He made friends with people who worked at the local dump (later, the recycling centre) and they would set aside interesting things for him. There were certain things he was drawn to, Sue said: the statues of the Virgin Mary I had noticed when I first entered the attic, clowns, globes, cuckoo clocks, early bagatelle machines, of which he had a huge collection. He would come home with one and then a few days later another would appear, and another, and each collection grew, different branches of the same tree.

He would then bring some of these items together in smaller collections, things that made sense to him, and arrange them in sandboxes or shoeboxes. In one of these boxes, a model of a legless, armless and headless, naked Greek hero stands supported on crutches, with a dried starfish in the place where his head should be. In another, a dismembered Action Man with the head of a bull sits on a tall stool with his head in his hands. These boxes were Bill's thinking in action.

In a parallel with the development of his landscape theatre epics for Kneehigh Theatre and later with his own company, Wildworks, Bill's boxes were never static. Until the last two weeks of his life, none of them were pinned down, everything was always in a state of flux. He would mix and remix, play and reshape them, add and take away, and he continued to do this until his last week, when he began to fix some of them down. It was creative play and a way of allowing images to arrive. In both the boxes and Bill's sketchbooks, the same images occur over again, suitcases and boats, wings, things with wings, images of the lion tamer, beauty and the beast, the minotaur, the moment a child becomes an adult.

One of Bill Mitchell's assemblages.

Many of the items in the attic were mid century toys and advertisements, or packaging with people and animals on it, echoes of Bill's childhood. Whereas Sue was brought up in Redruth in Cornwall, Bill grew up in Dartford, his environment entirely urban. Bill's father was a turner and fitter at the engineering firm, Vickers Armstrongs, and his mother a council cleaner, and there was little money around. As a child, Bill had loved Dinky Toys and he recalled having to save for six weeks to buy a single toy, and he kept them in their boxes, pristine and untouched. Even at an early age, things were precious to him and one of the most desolate moments of his young adult life was returning home and seeing all his toy cars being run up and down the street, his mother having given them away to other children in the neighbourhood.

Sue's childhood, on the other hand, was entirely different. Growing up a few miles from the sea in Cornwall, their father would take Sue and her sister, Di, sailing, over to Scilly or to France in a clinker-built ship's lifeboat converted into a gaff cutter, called *Ella Speed*. She remembers, even aged thirteen, having to take her turn at the helm on long journeys. Her watch shift would be six until eight in the morning, when her father would get some much-needed sleep in the cuddy. She showed me photographs of the young her grinning back to the camera beneath the foresail from the bow, a huge container ship passing by in the background. It was a heavy responsibility, she said, being a child in control of a 32-foot boat on the open sea, with no land in sight. They were often sailing in the shipping lanes, so she had to keep an eye out for cargo ships like the one in the photograph as well as keeping an eye on the course. When you look at Scilly on a map, it is easy to understand why it might make her nervous; a slight miscalculation and you could miss the islands entirely and end up sailing into that huge blank space of blue beyond.

'It would probably be classed as a form of child abuse now,' she said, 'though looking back, it was the greatest gift that we got to do that as children.'

When Sue's father died, the family painted his coffin trompe l'oeil to look like *Ella Speed*. They rigged it with a mast and sails in the crematorium in a funeral orchestrated by Bill. She recalled the boat-coffin was too large for what she called 'the horrid, curtained slot in the crematorium'. When Bill died at the age of 65, ever theatrical, ever the designer-director, he orchestrated his own funeral too, following which a huge wake was held for him at the spot on the beach at Gwithian, where the Kneehigh crew had camped throughout the run of *Ghost Nets* over 30 years before.

The few other visitors have retreated and we are alone on what remains of our temporary island now. The shore looks as though it is now a fair distance and I wonder if we have pushed our luck too far, though on the wade back the water again reaches no higher than our thighs.

While the finding of cowries is an individual pursuit, the keeping of them is not. We admire each other's finds and then pool them. At home, we have a glass jar on a shelf on the French dresser to which we add our cowries. It is a small collection and though it has no particular value, I realize of all the things we own, after making sure Emma and the children were alright and that my guitar was out of reach of the flames, I would save the jar of cowries in the event of a house fire. They are a family archive of time spent together on beaches across Cornwall and Scilly, and on the Brittany coast. They are heavy with memory, of the sensation of the sun on my back, the squelch of bladder-wrack and kelp beneath my feet, of the sound of the children laughing together. If, at some point, in years far off, I descend into dementia, I hope to carry these memories with me. While the image of the tail of the blue whale in Svalbard is etched into my mind – a glorious thrill of a memory – the cowries are the agglomoration of smaller memories, pearls.

Searching for cowries is not really about cowries at all. It is about the accumulation of family capital or of time spent in quiet contemplation. Later, at the flat we are staying in on St Mary's, we will tease each other over our success or lack of success as we pool the shells we have found and, when we return home, we will add them to the small jar on the dresser, tiny fragments of time folded in on itself and tucked into a smile.

Cowries and wentletraps.

Surfers at the Chapel in Cornwall's Badlands.

8

Wave Rider

Surfing Cornwall's Badlands

I HAVE WATCHED the surfers here ever since we arrived. I have watched them from the shoreline as the sun dipped into the sea behind small, perfectly formed peelers and from up on the cliffs on winter days when the waves were like steam trains at full tilt, the white smoke of their chimneys whipping back as they powered towards the land, the riders on them all but invisible aside from the lines they carved on the wave face.

I have spent hours watching shortboarders trammelling down the line, all speed and power, exploding off the lip or switching back at the peak, throwing up a ring of spray against which they were momentarily silhouetted, and bodyboarders slotting into low, green, barrelling waves. And in the summer, I've watched hordes of beginners with their unplanned yelps of delight as they found their feet on a wave for the first time, a wave that I imagined followed them home and saw them through some dark hour in the office in the winter months.

One Saturday this summer, while I was drying on the sand after an hour's plunge in the foam, I watched a friend on his longboard. The waves were perhaps 4 or 5 feet, the breeze blowing gently offshore and all the day's colours were bleached out by the high sun. It was the sort of day that deserved its own soundtrack; something soulful with a clean, jangling guitar line, a Hammond organ, a harmonica and drums driving the whole thing.

Despite a crowded line-up, it was easy enough to pick him out: he has a distinct silhouette. Even sitting on his board, he was tall, a head above most of the other surfers bobbing on their boards out beyond the breaking waves, which arrived in lines perpendicular to the shore, peeling off to the right as they approached the beach. He paddled into one and, in the glare, I lost him for a moment. When I saw him next, he was on his feet and had picked up speed. From where I was sitting, he appeared to float on the wave. On land, he is all skinniness and angles, but on the water, he is pure grace. He held his shoulders low and his hands loose by his side as he shifted his balance now forward now back, as he worked with the wave, as it broke more quickly, as it slowed, as it surged forward, deep blue crested with white. As I watched, he adjusted his trim and cross-stepped to the front of the board, his hands raised to just below chest level, as though he was performing a well-rehearsed dance step. He balanced, toes on the board's nose, first one foot, then two, knees slightly bent, chest back, perfectly balanced, the board locked into the wave, and I could almost hear the soundtrack swell above the hush of the breakers.

Off the water, he was going through a hard time, this particular surfer. His father, who lives a few hours' drive away, was seriously ill and he was spending most of his time, when he was not working or looking after his children, on the A30, driving up and back, up and back, shuttling between fatherhood and childhood, balancing the challenging demands of both, and the challenges of work too. For these few seconds, though, on the wave, he appeared to be weightless, a featherlight figure who had perfected the trick of walking on water. The whole event, though it lasted just seconds, seemed to bend time slightly, and it appeared to me rendered in slight slow motion. Like the surfer who slips into the green room of a barrelling wave and emerges, as though spat out by the spray created in the hollow tube, what he was doing – hanging ten – represents, in surfing terms, a pinnacle moment, an expression of years of hard-earned skill and practise, of balance, timing, wave reading and wave riding.

It's easy to think of surfing in terms of the pinnacle moments achieved by these who have dedicated a good part of their lives to the waves. The initiated often talk about these moments in semi-religious terms. It's hard to describe the ineffable.

It is all but guaranteed that if the surf is up here, whatever time of year, there will already be riders on the wave before you get there, no matter how early. This is Badlands – deep surfing country.

Serious surf is reserved for early risers and for the most committed who sleep on thin mattresses amid their boards in their vans within earshot of the waves. It is reserved for those who can calculate the length of the fetch, the wave period and height, those who can accurately predict where the best waves will be found. In his surf memoir, *Barbarian Days*, William Finnegan points out that there is no agreed standard measure for wave height among the surfing community. Novice surfers, he writes, tend to vastly overestimate the height of the wave, while veterans downplay it. Finnegan cites the wife of a big wave surfer who claimed she could accurately calculate the height of a wave in refrigerators, which seems to me as good a measure as any.

The serious surfers attempt to predict the effects of a hurricane on the American eastern seaboard or a depression in the mid-Atlantic on a reef or a beach break several hundred miles east, the way a particular wave is likely to react to a particular profile of beach. They are the most genned-up of amateur meteorologists. When it is *on*, messages are exchanged on WhatsApp and locations agreed, and those in the know converge, having concluded that this particular place at this particular time might offer the best of the day's waves.

When a builder we employed shortly after we moved here disappeared a week into the job, we assumed another urgent job had come up or perhaps a family emergency. It transpired there was a forecast that the wave at Thurso, on Scotland's north coast, was about to go off and he had dropped everything for it. He had jumped in his van and headed north for the 820-mile drive. If the prediction was correct, the wave at the out-of-the-way reef break would be worth it. The wave at Thurso East is generally known to be one of the finest right-handers in Europe, a large barrelling wave that – aside from the frigid conditions – would not be out of place on the Hawaiian coast. It is not as though there are no ridable waves on our doorstep here; it is more that the temptation is undeniable for some surfers. It is not unusual for a builder, a plumber, an electrician, a decorator or postman here to travel with a board and wetsuit in the van, just in case. When the surf is good, it is surprising how no one seems to have that much urgent work to do (well, if you are surfer, really not that surprising at all). It's one of the prices and privileges of living here, an unwritten addendum to pretty much any contract on the north coast.

If the surf is good, I'll be late.

If it's really good, I'll see you once the swell has passed.

As the Cornish are fond of saying, *I'll be with you dreckly*.

We didn't know when we moved into our house that the area was known locally as Badlands. It is not a name that appears on any map but ask any surfer in Cornwall and they will know the stretch on the north coast, between Portreath and St Agnes.

When I first heard the name, I looked it up: it didn't tally with what I thought badlands were. To me, it seems to speak of the Wild West, of godforsaken scrubland and desert like the Big Muddy Badlands of Saskatchewan, which were known as a

Wave riders in the heart of Badlands.

hiding place for outlaws in the nineteenth century. It brought to mind the yellowed and sepia tones of Sunday afternoon westerns I dozed through as a child. Yet this green and blue, granite and gorse stretch of coastline appears on countless posters, postcards and adverts declaring the beauty of the county and, at a glance, it is difficult to see why it deserves the name.

Spend some time here though and it becomes clear the beauty of the place can mask the dangers. The beaches along this stretch of coast are often not the easiest on which to surf. Facing out towards the west they are open to the full force of the Atlantic. My local beach break is at the end of a long valley down which the Coastguard helicopter thunders to rescue those who have been unlucky or who have got it wrong, swimmers unaware of the power of the rip, surfers who underestimate the power of the waves, those who paddle out on days when there is too much moving water. At night, when the helicopter goes over, I count from my bed the minutes between it passing down the valley and its return.

Badlands graffiti.

The Badlands' moniker is a thing of the past for the most part now, though the branding rears its head again every now and then, a name that crops up in graffiti on mine shafts and abandoned buildings. The most common explanation given is that it came about due to the aggressive localism that was rife in the 1980s, as surfing became more popular and local surfers felt their waves were getting crowded out. A friend who has spent most of his life here tells me the localism here was less a reality and more a legend built up to scare off tourists wielding boards that spend fifty weeks of the year gathering dust in a garage. It was, he explains, a kind of self-fulfilling prophecy in which the reputation of the place preceded it rather than a result of any actual threat. It's our wave, the locals were saying. Show some respect if you want to surf here.

The way St Agnes surfer, Minnow Green, tells it, Badlands was established by a group of local surfers who bought themselves black shorts in an echo of the Hui O He'e Nalu (the Club of Wave Riders), the gang that enforced their own law at Mākaha Beach in Oahu, Hawaii. Da Hui were also known as Black Shorts, after the uniform they wore that marked them out as enforcers. They saw themselves as protectors of the wave, a marginalized group who were defending an activity that defined them as opposed to *haole*, or white colonialist surfers, who increasingly wanted access to waves they viewed as theirs. The Black Shorts were notorious for their violence against visiting surfers, though in Minnow's recollection, the worst that ever happened in Badlands were a few wax-daubed windscreens and visitors' tyres let down in the carpark.

This chimes with champion longboarder and filmmaker Sam Bleakley's research into the history of British surfing. In the 1960s, he told me, Californian surfers took their lead from more established Hawaiian surf culture, importing the good, the bad and the ugly, wholesale. The British surf pioneers, deeply influenced by the Californians, picked up the same traits. So, heavy localism passed along the chain, along with surfing styles and slang, and was reinforced by surf films such as the *Gidget* series, *The Endless Summer* and – in the early 1990s – *Point Break*, which displayed it as an ultra-macho, often gang-related pastime.

That culture, when combined with a particular topography of coastline, he explained, can lead to a phenomenon like Badlands. On some longer, more open surf breaks, some sections are more challenging, more technical – this is where the more competent or adventurous surfers will head – whereas other sections that are more mellow and less challenging are better suited for beginners. On other, smaller breaks, like the ones here, the same wave has to be shared by everyone using it, which brings with it more potential for clashes.

By the time Sam and his generation of surfers came through the ranks, having been taught by their pioneer parents, attitudes had begun to change. This generation wanted to open the sport up and, in terms of technique, surfing had come on a long way since their parents started to surf. The next generation out-surfed and outshone their parents and though it was not always an easy change, a shift of power began to take place, a challenge to the way things had worked on the waves so far.

The older generation of surfers are still paddling out here though. They recall the early days of Badlands with wry smiles.

Chris Hines is a fixture in Badlands. He has surfed here since he first moved to the valley forty years ago. He is easy to spot on the beach with his wild shock of grey hair and infectious smile, and he seems to know everyone. It is midweek in late summer and most of the tourists have headed back up country. The beaches and roads are emptier than they have been in months. Across the whole of the demi island of Cornwall and on Scilly too, there has been, in the last few days, a collective exhalation.

There is an offshore breeze and the waves are small, a couple of feet high at most (certainly not fridge height). There are several surfers out on the usual assortment of longboards, shortboards, twin fins and bodyboards. Chris has a wooden bellyboard and I have my handplane.

Riding an empty right at Porthtowan.

'Surfing was still a minority sport when I started out,' he says at the water's edge. 'Now it's mainstream. It's coming up to the end of September and there are at least 45 surfers just in the small patch of sea in front of us. There would have been three or four of us out there back then. On a crowded day there would be maybe 25 people in the water. Few people surfed year-round and very few in the winter, so you knew everybody and you would know people from the next beaches as well. If you saw someone over the age of 40 surfing that was rare. Now maybe 50 per cent of people in the water are older.'

It is great that there are so many people interested in surfing, he says, though it brings with it challenges about showing respect for each other and giving each other space. Respect is a big thing in surfing. Respect for the water. Respect for the other surfers around you and for the informal code of conduct that helps surfers to avoid the worst accidents, most of the time anyway.

Chris was born in Devon and moved to Cornwall when he was nineteen. Cornwall was a lot poorer back then, he says, or rather coastal areas around the county were poorer. Now, a lot of people have adapted their lives to be able to live, work and surf here. Most surfers here in the 1980s would have one board and one wetsuit as opposed to the quiver of boards many now own, along with wetsuits for each season, allowing surfers to stay in for longer, year-round.

'I used to surf team Marigold. Flock-lined if I was feeling flush,' he says, and it takes me a moment to work out he is talking about washing-up gloves, worn to surf in winter to stop your hands freezing. 'The standard of surfing has improved,' he continues. 'It was pretty awful, looking back.' Whereas now, on a big day it is not unusual to see the more experienced surfers pulling into a barrel, it was almost unheard of when he started out. The boards were more basic and the wetsuits too.

'When I started here, you knew everyone in the carpark. We all talked to each other. As a result of that we had conversations and things happened. That's how SAS came about.'

The story goes that a few of the surfers each threw a tenner on the table and called a public meeting which resulted in the birth of SAS, Surfers Against Sewage, in 1990. They thought it would not make it beyond the first summer, though by the following spring what started off as a conversation in a pub had grown to become a campaigning group ready to lobby Parliament to stem the flow of raw sewage into the sea. He describes it as a frontier movement, run out of a caravan in his garden, rallying a hundred surfers in wetsuits to descend on Parliament Square.

'When we put our heads above the parapet, people all around the country started to get involved,' Chris says, describing the road trips he used to take to other surfing communities. 'Each of the tribes was quite small and it had all the novelty of being a bunch of surfers, so it was very much a David and Goliath thing. We were taking the sea into the corridors of power. They were never going to come here.'

As we stand on the beach in our wetsuits, Chris suggests the real Badlands was in the poor state of the waters here in the 1970s and 1980s. This beach was widely dubbed Porthtampon by the local crew, he tells me, as you might paddle out the day after a rainstorm and come up from a duck dive with a sanitary towel on your head.

'Just along the coast from here there were two raw outfalls.' He gestures to out towards the cliffs to the west of the beach. 'Two million gallons of crude sewage and not even a sieve in place. All the sewage from Camborne, Redruth and Pool used to come out here. As the tide came in, the shit would come in with it. It was like surfing in the toilet of the largest conurbation in Cornwall. That was the Badlands.'

Only a few days before, I had been in the water at dawn

with James Otter and his team of surfboard shapers as part
of their surf-whatever-the-weather group, Monday Morning
Surf Club. There had been heavy rain the night before and the
sea was thick with debris, washed out of the overflows and
churned up by the heavy weather. When I returned home,
I checked the app created by SAS, which monitors the state
of rivers and seas around the UK, and there were twenty separate pollution alerts around the coast of Cornwall alone that
morning, big red crosses against sites all around the coast. A
couple of months later, the charity would campaign against the
government's plan to block amendments to the Environment
Act 2021 that would force water companies to deal with the
effluent they pour into the seas, on the grounds that it would
be too expensive to solve the problem. Their campaign would
press the government to put a legal duty on water companies
to reduce the amount of sewage they can pour into the sea.
They are still fighting the same battle as in the early days:
profit versus planet.

As Chris and I paddle out, the chimney of an engine house
comes into view. Badlands sits at the heart of tin and copper
mining country. Out of shot of the postcard *Poldark* images,
the coast here is scarred by huge spoil heaps on which nothing
will grow, and there is arsenic in the water that runs through
the countless mineshaft and adits that stretch out for miles
beneath mid-Cornwall, like a series of massive rabbit warrens.
And further out we can see the large white dome of Nancekuke,
a forbidding military site with a huge golf ball listening post that
sits high on the cliffs.

We paddle past a surfer who is coming to the end of a ride.
Chris waves and shouts across, 'How's the knee?'

'It's all good, you know,' the surfer replies. 'How's the hip?'

'They cancelled me.'

'Bad luck.'

'I get to be in here, though, so . . .'

Throwing up an arc.

Chris had been due to have his hip replaced, though with the local hospital at capacity, his surgery had been bumped and instead he has come out surfing. When I ask him if he feels any bitterness about having had to abandon his shortboard for a bellyboard, he is sanguine, telling me there's a certain circularity about being back on a bellyboard.

'Surfing has been the dominant factor in my life,' he says. 'I had my first bellyboard when I was about five and I learnt to surf when I was eleven or twelve, around Widemouth Bay and Sennen. I would hassle my parents and they would drive me to the beach. Now, however many years later, I'm back on one. When you're on a bellyboard, everything's overhead. I've been having loads of fun on it.'

Chris and I don't paddle out to the main break but choose a smaller, uncrowded wave, closer in to shore. We stop talking and concentrate instead on the incoming waves.

There is always something thrilling about propelling yourself down the face of a wave with just a pair of swim fins and a small piece of wood to give you traction on the wave and I come up grinning again and again in the white water. Take away the politics and you're left with something approaching pure joy. We accept that, jammed into our wetsuits, most of us look more like overweight seals than sea gods. The wrong side of forty, most of us fall off more waves than we catch and if we are mindful of it, we laugh at our own ridiculousness and at the unadulterated pleasure of sliding down the few we manage to ride.

Chris catches wave after wave and on one I hear him whooping back on the breeze. Back on the beach, we watch the next generation of surfers ripping on the wave further out. 'As you get older, your relationship with the sea and the waves changes and your expectation changes,' he comments later.

'When you're young, you always want bigger and better. Then, when you get a bit older you get more relaxed about it. Now, I'm happy if I get two or three good waves in a session. I'm not really looking to perform. The experience is more for me than for someone watching now. This morning, I got one wave which was really long and steep, where I was in the pocket. That was all I needed.'

Back on the shore, we watch the surfers for a while; the waves pulse through in clean sets. The localism of the early days of Badlands continues in places, too, driven by competition on the wave and frustration at the pricing out of locals from their favourite surf spots. Surfing continues to act as a microcosm of society, an activity in which a resource must be negotiated by those who want to use it. The water companies continue to pump sewage into the seas and waterways and the campaigners at SAS continue to challenge them. The older surfers continue to paddle out once they have recovered from their hip operations and the next generation continue to discover the waves afresh and outshine the generations that went before. They define Badlands for themselves.

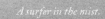

A surfer in the mist.

A walrus diving in the waters off Svalbard.

9

Ocean Wanderer

Watching a walrus in St Mary's

FOR MONTHS after I returned home from the Arctic, every time I closed my eyes, I found myself on *Linden's* long deck with my back against one of the masts, the cold sun on my face. At home in bed, I could still feel the gentle roll of the ship on a glassy sea. Even so, there is something distinctly surreal about reading a report of a walrus just 50 miles from where I live, as though a part of the Arctic has literally followed me home.

The quay at Hugh Town, the tiny capital of the Isles of Scilly – usually busy only when the boats are loading or disembarking – is packed. Everyone wants to see the walrus. A tripper boat pulls away with a boatload of tourists heading for one of the off islands. It makes a loop so as to bring the boat alongside the bright yellow *Star of Life* ambulance boat on the back of which the walrus is currently perched, making him the focus of a broadside of lenses. As the tripper boat moves off, an overloaded inflatable tender – a family with two young children, shuttling between yacht and quay – moves in for a closer look. Seen side by side, the sight of the walrus and the tender serves to show just how large the out-of-place animal is. The family in the inflatable look tiny, though they do not seem to be aware of the danger posed by the several tons of walrus whose space they are currently invading.

It seems that everyone on the quay is a walrus expert. Certainly, everyone has an opinion. I find myself trying to recall what little I know about them. While I was waiting for the arrival of *Linden*, I joined a small group of tourists to kayak in Borebukta, one of the wide bays off Isfjorden. While we were out on the water, beneath the huge cliffs of the glacier at the head of the bay, we were cut off from our boat by sea ice. Our guide, a young man who had until this point referred to everything in the fjord as 'rad', seemed nervous when he saw four walruses on the ice between us and our boat.

'We're fine as long as they're out of the water,' he murmured. 'While they're on the ice, we're faster than they are. When they're in the water, it's a different matter.'

Gone was the faux Californian surf slang, replaced with a very earnest Home Counties accent. It would not be rad to be in the water with inquisitive walrus. They like to test things with their tusks. In fact, a walrus testing a kayak in the freezing waters of the fjord would not be worth thinking about. It wouldn't attack us in our kayaks, our guide said, but it might feel very much like that if it took an interest. We took it in turns to head count the walruses on the ice though, and to keep an eye out for any others that might be in the water as the rest of the group tried to find an open lead, a clear passage back to the boat. It turned out the walruses were not interested in us at all. And, luckily for the family in the tender in St Mary's harbour, the walrus there does not seem to be interested in them either. He raises his head though, and snorts.

The big draw for wildlife watchers in Scilly is usually birds – puffins, little auks, guillemots and rarer visitors using the island as a stop-off on a long migration – though all lenses are on the walrus. Even the huge Egyptian vulture that appeared on the islands a few weeks before the walrus arrived, the first that had been spotted here in over 150 years, is now old news.

The walrus on the Scillonian ambulance boat, Star of Life.
Photograph by Charlie Elder.

In the café, where I stop for coffee most mornings, they are selling stickers that show a walrus wearing a hoodie with the logo for the St Mary's Boatmen Association. Nicknamed, somewhat unimaginatively, Wally, he has become a temporary mascot and remains so in the other places he took in on his journey south. In Tenby, where the walrus stayed for a while, he features on postcards, prints and paintings, cushions, bunting and greetings cards in the Nook craft café. Somewhat more bizarrely, he was also made into a matryoshka doll, a walrus within a walrus within a walrus. For the tourist destination looking for an edge in the game, it appears that a walrus will do it.

I take my coffee out to the end of the quay where a journalist with a long lens camera is taking shots of the walrus for one of the regional Cornish newspapers. It's big news. On the way back, I run a gauntlet of broadcast crews reporting on the arrival and get collared for a mumbled and somewhat stuttering soundbite for the ITN news.

Depending on who you talk to he is either fascinating (to the holidaymakers busy filling memory cards with snaps of him) or a menace (to several of the local fishermen, two of whose boats he has sunk, swamping them as he attempted to haul out).

There are various theories about how the walrus found his way to Scilly. They range from the somewhat ridiculous idea that he fell asleep on an iceberg to the theory he is following feeding grounds or seeking a mate, that he was displaced by older bull walruses and fled or had a navigation problem and was blown wildly off course before landing in an archipelago 26 miles off the coast of Cornwall. Others suggest he is a refugee of climate change, driven by the melting ice. He wouldn't be the first climate refugee from the Arctic. In 2011, a polar bear was recorded having swum for nine days straight, a distance of 426 miles, in the Beaufort Sea where the sea ice is in rapid retreat. She was accompanied by her cub, who died on the journey.

This walrus was first spotted in March on Valentia Island off the south coast of Ireland, and then again in Wales, where he stayed a while, first in Broad Haven and then in Tenby, where he was filmed in a stand-off with one of the coastguards, who was attempting to encourage him off the lifeboat slipway with a foghorn, and then off the coast of Cornwall, before heading down the coast of France and Spain. He landed in Scilly in mid-June. Walruses, though not entirely unknown, are a rare sight in waters this far south, a fact attested to by the walruses' status as a 'visiting vagrant' species in the Wildlife and Countryside Act.

We have history with the walrus. In the 1700s and 1800s, we hunted the Atlantic walrus almost to extinction, for their oil, which was used for lighting, their meat, in particular their flippers, which were considered a delicacy, their intestines, which were used to make waterproof jackets, and their tusks for ivory. It is illegal in most parts of the world now to hunt walruses, though they, like so many other species in the Arctic, still face threats from increased shipping and icebreakers and from living in environments that are suffering the retreat of the sea ice and other effects of climate change.

Some of the islanders have a WhatsApp group in which they share sightings and photographs of him sitting on the back of various boats in the harbour or having climbed onto a RIB or a fishing boat. In the Co-op, I overhear one of the checkout staff suggesting he ought to be shot and, in the mid-afternoon, I eavesdrop into the conversation of two islanders in The Mermaid.

'I've been on the phone to the insurance. They're not sure that we're covered against walruses. They're going to get back to me. Think of it – he could do millions of pounds of damage and we might not even be insured.'

'They should tranquilize him. With a dart gun, like they do with elephants.'

A man from one of the other tables leans over and joins the conversation, 'They've thought of that. Apparently, he'd roll off whatever boat he was on and then he'd sink and drown.'

The two men make noises of equivocation into their pints as though this wouldn't be the worst thing in the world. The visiting vagrant walrus is both welcome and unwelcome. He is a tourist and a menace. He is a symbol of climate change.

'He's a bloody nuisance,' a woman says loudly into her mobile phone on the *Sea King* as though she wants to advertise her stance on the situation to the hundred or so people on the boat. 'Sitting there right in the middle of the harbour. They should drive him out and keep him out.' She keeps up the one-sided conversation all the way across to St Martin's and she is still complaining about him as she stalks off up the path, her husband in tow.

Who 'they' are is uncertain, though it's likely that one of them is the one person I meet in the harbour who has the best claim I've seen so far to be an expert. A marine mammal medic volunteering for the catchily titled British Divers Marine Life Rescue, Lizzi Larbalestier has travelled across from Cornwall, tasked with monitoring and protecting the walrus while he is here. Lizzi's entire life revolves around the sea, from her conservation work to the seal hospital she ran from her house during the Covid pandemic, when the other facilities had to close – over the course of a year, she and the other medics helped to nurse 130 seals back to health – to her work with the marine rescue team, to her eco-centric, blue health coaching business in which she works with clients on the beach to resolve issues personal and professional.

I put some of the theories about how the walrus came to be here to Lizzi, as well as some of the solutions I have heard proposed in the bars and shops.

Walruses do not react well to being tranquillized and there is a possibility they will die under anaesthesia, she tells me when I recount the conversation from The Mermaid. And even if he was successfully tranquillized, she says, what then? There is nowhere to take him. There is no facility in the UK equipped to deal with an animal as huge as a walrus, even on the mainland. And while seals are rescued regularly by members of the BDMLR (whose acronym is no catchier than their full title), there has never been much of a call for a rescue centre for walruses. Though he's only a juvenile, about four-years-old, he weighs in at about 800 kilograms and is still a large marine mammal. They can encourage him to avoid hauling out onto boats and sinking them, but there is little they can do to stop him if that is what he chooses to do. And, the question remains, even if there was a deterrent that would work, should it be used?

Lizzi waves to the pilot of another tripper boat which is taking a detour to bring them in close to the *Star of Life*.

'They know better than that,' she says. 'and to be fair the more professional boatmen are adapting well and giving the *Star of Life* a wide berth.'

The pilot spots her and waves back somewhat sheepishly before steering his boat away. The boatmen all know Lizzi well by now, the harbour authorities and the fishermen too. She has been listening to their stories and concerns, though she is quick to point out she is there to ensure the welfare of the walrus, not to safeguard property. The two here seem to go hand in hand, though.

Following a series of tense meetings of all the parties involved, including the local council, the Isles of Scilly Wildlife Trust and the harbour authorities, the Cornwall and Devon Police and the boatmen's association, Lizzi is in the process of creating a specially built pontoon onto which the walrus can haul out to avoid him pulling himself up on yachts and dinghies in the harbour, which he has been doing since he arrived. She hopes he will find it, use it and stop damaging boats. More importantly, she hopes it will help him to regain his strength for the journey home which, if he is one of the Svalbard walruses as Lori Quakenbush of the Marine Mammal Program in Alaska suggests, is just shy of 2,000 miles even if he heads straight back with no detours. The more he is disturbed, she says, the less likely it is he will be able to hunt and rest effectively and build up the energy reserves he needs to make the trip back to the Arctic.

Disturbance occurs when people encroach on wild animals.
Photograph by Charlie Elder.

'Disturbance occurs partly because we're massively curious about the natural world,' Lizzi explains. 'Then right at the other end of the scale, there's the sense some people have of entitlement and somewhere in between that, there's an obliviousness to what we mean by disturbance. People might think that a walrus lifting his head isn't disturbance but he has been disturbed. His whole nervous system has had to go into alert, in order for him to do that. Even if he's not jumping, he's saying, "I see you, you could be a threat."' Some days, she says, she has noticed him being disturbed every 3 minutes by people in tenders, on paddleboards and kayaks, often getting within a few feet of where he is hauled out.

Lizzi is concerned yet confident, calm and clearly at ease here. When I ask her about it, she tells me that she always felt safest by the sea and in particular on the beach. All the holidays she took during a childhood she describes as 'sketchy' were at Treyarnon Bay near Padstow and she traces her interest in the sea back to those early days.

'My mother was a troubled soul who liked a drink and my dad's coping mechanism, I think, was to come and fly at St Merryn Airfield. My sister and I would get to play on Treyarnon Beach. He would leave us with a piece of tarpaulin and some bamboo and make us a little tent. We were completely feral. We would walk over to Constantine, run down the dunes and disturb the birds. Of course, you don't register that you're damaging the coastal environment when you're kids. We would lose ourselves in nature because we were noticing everything else outside our chaotic home life. Every positive experience I remember from childhood was coastal.'

She describes to me the same sort of physical need to be beside the sea that has cropped up time and time again with the people I talk to around the coast, the connection they feel that becomes gravitational somehow, undeniable. I ask her to explain the feeling to me and she looks around from where we are talking some months later, sitting on a huge stretch of beach in Cornwall.

'Look around,' she says. 'We're sitting in the middle of the beach and yet this feels like a really private conversation. We're in the wide open. It gives you everything – space, big sky, creativity.'

In his book, *Blue Mind*, Wallace J. Nichols suggests the theory that we are predisposed to feel at home by the sea. Like the grasslands where we evolved, the coast gives us long, uninterrupted views. From the beach we can see danger coming from a long way off. It assuages some of our primeval anxiety that we have not managed to shift, despite the actual threats to us coming from entirely different quarters now. Listening to Lizzi describe the analogue qualities of the beach, the subtle elements of it that make it an immersive place to be – the sound of the sea, for example, the white noise of water on sand, or of stones being rolled up and back in the waves – a place that encourages us to be present, it sounds like each journey there is a kind of coming home.

It seems somehow appropriate that someone who finds so much solace, peace and safety in being on the beach now devotes a large proportion of her time to ensuring that it is a safe place for the animals that call it home too. We return to the places where we feel safest.

Marine disturbance, the issue Lizzi is concerned with when it comes to the walrus, is a growing problem according to the Cornwall Wildlife Trust. Since the charity started to collect records in 2014 of incidents of people on jet skis, motorboats and walkers on the coast disturbing marine life, the incidence of marine disturbance has more than tripled. In Cornwall, it tends to peak in July and August, coinciding with the huge influx of visitors, many of whom want to get up close to seals, sea birds, whales, dolphins and porpoises. It shows in the propellor marks on the porpoise I found washed up on the beach in the storms earlier in the year, though it's also evident in more nebulous ways.

One day in July, jet skiers were filmed chasing a pod of 20 dolphins with calves near Newquay, riding the jet skis over the backs of the dolphin calves and pursuing them when they attempted to leave. The same month, a jet ski rider was seen chasing a seal off Looe Island, a protected nature reserve and paddleboarders made their way across from the mainland to another protected marine reserve island and disturbed the seal colony there.

Seals are pupping at this time of year on remote beaches around Cornwall, just as the tourist season really gets going. Seeing or hearing people causes them to abandon their safe beaches, putting the seal pups in danger. Grey seals, unlike walruses, are not protected in the same way by law.

In a bar in the Russian mining town, Barentsburg, I met a filmmaker who proudly showed me his footage of a polar bear rearing up in the snow as he brought his drone in low over its head. He was thrilled with the shot and seemed entirely unaware of any sense that his drone had disturbed the bear. The guide on our ship, Emil, told me this is not unusual. Everyone wants to get their shot of the bear or the walrus. He told me about one particular problem with photographers on snowmobiles getting so close to the bears with young cubs that the cubs would chase the snowmobiles. It made for stunning photographs, he said, though when cubs chase people, they often repeat the behaviour as adults. These are the bears who end up coming into the town or attacking skiers, and therefore the ones that end up being shot. Disturbance takes a high price, almost always on the animals.

On the whole, the animals involved do not have the means with which to protest or to alter the situation – the power dynamic is entirely unequal – though there are a few recent examples of animals demonstrating their frustration. In 2020, a new aggressive behaviour was noted in orcas, which have begun to target yachts around Spain, Morocco and the Strait of Gibraltar. Over two months in 2021, 53 incidences of killer whales barging yachts in the area were recorded. The group of orcas, thought to be from the same pod, started to attack the rudders of yachts passing through their grounds, in some cases knocking out the steering capacity of the boats and in others, biting chunks off the rudders. Dr Ruth Esteban, who has been studying the interactions between people and killer whales – which are toothed whales, the largest animal in the dolphin family – says she is not sure why this is happening. However, she notes that young orcas have, in the past, been injured and killed when they have come into contact with fishermen, with whom the orcas compete for the Strait of Gibraltar's declining populations of bluefin tuna.

It is often reported in stories in which animals and humans clash that the animal is at fault, where it is almost always our own ignorance or sense of entitlement that is to blame. Earlier in the year, when the Colombian singer Shakira had her bag taken by wild boars in a park in Barcelona, the *Guardian* reported that, 'Boars have become a widespread nuisance in cities, as urban environments have increasingly expanded.' That suggests the boars are the problem rather than the spread of people into their environments, that we are the ones who are inconvenienced and not the animals whose habitats are denuded, deforested, polluted. We are, the boars and orcas seem to be saying, unwanted visitors in their habitat, and though the news reports the orcas as targeting the yachts, there is some ring of truth about what Starbuck says to Captain Ahab in Melville's epic novel: 'Moby Dick seeks thee not. It is thou, thou, that madly seekest him!'

In a twist I had not expected, while snorkelling off Flushing beach with two marine biologists, I had my own experience of something similar. A crow took the trousers I had left in a bag on the quay, extracted my wallet from the back pocket, flew it up to a perch in a nearby oak tree, some 40 feet off the ground and proceeded to take out my cards and money. I stood and watched in my wetsuit from the quay as it scattered the cards into the impenetrable bramble bushes below and eventually as it made off with my National Trust card, my driver's licence and £20 in cash, flying lazily back over the beach and out of sight. The oak tree was in the grounds of a large house and when I knocked on the door the woman who answered, once she had got her head round the story, said, 'Oh, that'll be Janis's crow.'

The bird, it turns out, had form, following one of the villagers whenever she left her house, though she had no idea why it would pick on her in particular. At the top of the tree, I expected to find a whole trove of stolen items, though all that was there were the remains of my wallet and a few stamps. Staring down from the crow's nest in the heights, it occurred to me that all the crow had been doing was wrecking, taking something that had washed up on the tideline, that, by the common law, now belonged to it as much as it did to me. As any wrecker knows, anything found on the foreshore is fair game. I had visions of the crow treating itself to a beer and a slice of quiche with the stolen National Trust card and the £20 (using the driving licence as proof of age) and it made for amusing articles at my expense in the *Falmouth Packet*, the *Metro* and the Russian daily newspaper, *Lenta*, where, apparently, crow stories are all the rage.

We are so used to seeing ourselves as the primary species – adopting an anthropocentric rather than a biocentric approach to the world – and this approach, it is clear, time and time again, does not work.

Take a step back and there is something incredibly moving about seeing a walrus in a crowded harbour. It is unusual to see walruses on their own. They are social creatures. They seek each other out and haul out together in great numbers, often close enough to touch fins. The pinniped experts suggest the walrus in Scilly favours the busy harbour as a way of finding company, even if it is with people, despite the fact he is being disturbed continually.

The author's stolen wallet in the crow's nest at Flushing.

The walrus is a keystone species. The health of the walrus is used to determine the broader health of the seas. There are just under 4,000 walruses left in Svalbard, a healthier number than the 100 recorded in 1952 when the walrus became a protected species, although it is still considered a vulnerable species and remains on the International Union for Conservation of Nature's red list.

Decade on decade, the Arctic is experiencing a 13 per cent loss in the summer sea ice on which walruses rely for their haul outs. The warming world is literally melting their homes from beneath them. Lizzi favours the theory that the cause of the walruses' displacement is climate change. His appearance here, she says, is part of a broader pattern of animals leaving their normal routines and finding themselves in environments in which they are more vulnerable.

As a species, we made similar leaps about 180,000 years ago. We left the plains and spread out across the globe and there are few environments in which we found we could not live, the sea, a much, much earlier home, being one of them. In this way, the sea is Edenic to us, tantalizing and 'other', a garden to which we cannot return, though, for better or for worse, we appear to have inherited a stewardship of this garden. We know, clearly, that it is our behaviours and actions that are shaping it and changing it, and in many cases making it uninhabitable for the animals and plants that live there, and it is only our actions (or inaction in terms of what we might leave alone) that will improve its health.

The Isles of Scilly are a marker of sorts too, of rising sea levels. The islands are very slowly sinking and are in a state of what is euphemistically being called 'managed retreat' which, though not imminent, is a very real state of affairs. It is nothing when compared to some of the world's islands like the low-lying Maldives and the Marshall Islands in the Pacific Ocean, where the threat is much more immediate.

The International Panel on Climate Change reports that by the end of this century sea levels could rise between up to 83 centimetres, depending on the amount of carbon dioxide released into the atmosphere, and the combination of the vulnerable animal on a vulnerable island makes the whole thing feel precarious. According to the US Geological Survey, by 2035 some of the Marshall Islands may be entirely submerged and others left with no fresh water as a result of the aquifers being contaminated by salt water. On Tuvalu, part of the archipelago, which is spread out across a million square kilometres of ocean, the groundwater is already contaminated, and earth is too salty to grow most foods. The islanders now rely on rainwater.

When I return to Scilly a few weeks later, the walrus has just left. There was a heavy storm, which Lizzi believes unsettled him. Either that or he was displaced by the solitary bottlenose dolphin that had arrived in the harbour and which I see briefly, milky white, swimming beneath the tripper boats.

Shortly after I return to the islands, the walrus is spotted off County Waterford in Ireland. He goes off the radar for a while then, though in late September he is sighted again off the coast of Iceland, 560 miles from where he was last seen in West Cork, suggesting he is, perhaps, heading back towards Svalbard to continue to grow and, eventually, to find a mate. As islanders and experts alike have shown, it is difficult not to anthropomorphize. I find myself doing it, casting the walrus as one of the young Romantic poets, engaged on a grand tour before he returns to the cold north to settle down (or to write epic poetry), though animals do not see the world in this way as far as we know.

As far as we do know, though, this story has a happy enough ending. Listening to the arguments about minimizing the impact the walrus has on the human life around it, it feels as though we need to shift the conversation from the anthropocentric to a more biocentric viewpoint. The first seems to require all other life to accommodate us, though, as the Covid pandemic suggested, when we encroach too far into habitats that are not ours to move in on, bringing us into close contact with animals in a way we have never been before, there are unforeseen effects for us too. The second approach requires more of us. It requires that we respect the right of animals to their habitats, that we learn to share the spaces in which we come into contact with marine mammals, for example, in the shallows around our islands. While the first approach is acquisitive, the second is collaborative. The walrus on Scilly brings into sharp relief the broader issue of the way in which we interact with the other creatures with whom we share the planet.

We are drawn to the sea for pleasure, for food, for business and trade, and the more we are drawn there, the more we come into contact with, and conflict with, the other animals that share that space. We have always sought to profit from the sea, from its fish and mammals, from its corals and shells, its beauty and restorative powers, its hidden reserves of minerals and oils and now, increasingly, for its ability to sequester the carbon we are releasing into the atmosphere and that we so badly need to lock away. All the conservationists and marine biologists I spoke to have stressed the need for us to negotiate these spaces better, to protect the environments of the animals that live there, to become shepherds of the sea, supporting the life within it, the common message that the health of the sea and the creatures in it is essentially the health on which we, eventually, rely too.

I can understand the interest everyone had in Scilly's walrus visitor. While it may well be yet another sign that all is not well with the world, there is something glorious too about seeing this grand mammalian wanderer in Scilly, the sheer joy brought on by knowing that we live in a world in which there are also polar bears, walruses and whales. The sight of the wild northern seas brought close inspires more than just walrus tea towels and stickers: it inspires wonder.

Photographer Nick Pumphrey in the blue hour.

10

Dawn Patroller

Swimming in St Ives

A FEW YEARS AGO, I joined an online writing group set up by an author friend, the aim of which was to write intensively from four each morning until the children woke up. I love the idea of getting up early and I was full of enthusiasm to become someone who is – Benjamin Franklin-like – early to bed and early to rise (and consequently healthy, wealthy and wise). It turns out I liked the idea more than the practice. I made it to just one session of the early morning writers' group. Or rather, during the one session I attended, I made coffee, stared at my screen for a while, drank the coffee and went back to bed, too tired to type.

Similarly, when I saw St Ives photographer, Nick Pumphrey's #Dawndays photographs on Instagram, I admired his idea of getting up before sunrise each day and taking shots of the blue hour from the sea, of starting the day intentionally. From afar. I admired it from the comfort of my kitchen table, usually about mid-morning but the thought of actually doing it didn't appeal much at all, though I knew if he agreed to talk it would, in all likelihood, involve an early start. And sure enough when we talk on the phone, he suggests we meet before dawn at a small beach on St Ives Head on Cornwall's north coast.

I am sorely tempted to hit snooze when the alarm goes, though I drag myself out of bed and I am standing by the van just before five. The barn owls and tawny owls have quit their night conversations and the huge wasps' nest in the stand of trees opposite is quiet too. There is a thick fog lying on the valley as I head out towards the A30 and from there on to St Ives. I had intended to have an early night, though the evening before there had been a thin glaze of water across the beach and in the post sunset there was little to tell the land from the sky aside from the line of the waves, and I had stood watching the night fall for longer than I had planned, caught between the land and the sky.

Today is the equinox that marks the end of summer, the point at which day and night are equal, one aspect of the world momentarily in balance. Cornwall is starting to feel more balanced again too after a summer of marked imbalance. The huge influx of tourists has started to die down; the caravans, camper vans, motorhomes, 4x4s loaded with roof boxes and second homers head east again, and the county seems to breathe a little easier. There are certain places I tend to avoid entirely during the summer because of the crowds, St Ives being one, and this summer in particular I have given it a wide berth. The pandemic has put extra pressure on the county and with foreign travel off the cards, Cornwall has even more visitors than usual. A quick look in the estate agents reveals a three-bed terraced house in St Ives might now set you back upwards of a million pounds and a one bed flat more than £630,000. The draw of the sea has brought with it a corresponding increase in the price of houses in the area one friend calls 'the frosting' around the edge of Cornwall.

Just after surfing at my local beach, early one evening over the summer, I eavesdropped into a conversation taking place between a group of younger surfers. There were raised voices and I thought they might be discussing a run-in on the water, but it turned out they were talking about the impossibility of any of them being able to afford to stay in the area in which they had grown up. They traded stories of houses in the village going for £100,000 over the asking price and discussed ingenious plans for getting onto the housing ladder. One was writing letters to every landowner in the area who had an abandoned building in one of their fields, offering to rebuild it in return for reasonable rent. Some were planning on moving into vans or caravans and trying to get a spot in a farmer's yard or moving between lay-bys. They snorted at the idea of affordable housing – there is none round here.

Attempts to reverse this trend have had mixed results. In 2016, the residents of St Ives, one of the most popular tourist destinations in Cornwall, voted to ban the sale of new houses as second homes. Three years on, a study by the London School of Economics suggested the move had backfired, with developers backing out of building new houses and the price of the existing housing stock there rocketing, meaning that all existing houses that went on the market inevitably went to buyers from up country.

The desperation of the young surfers recalled another conversation too, one I had with a fisherman in another of Cornwall's picture postcard villages a few years before. He laughed bitterly when I asked which of the houses was his as we stood by the boat with which he makes his living.

'I grew up here.' He pointed out for me the cottage in which he was born. 'But you won't find a fisherman in one of these now. We all live in the new estate out the back of Penzance. These are all empty.' He sounded resigned to it. It's the same story in villages all around Cornwall.

Once he had packed up and headed off in his van towards Penzance, I walked through the village in which almost every other house was either a holiday home or a second home, long since packed up for the winter. The whole place felt like a ghost village in which the locals had been priced out.

As I walked through empty streets, past empty pubs in coastal villages throughout the winter, I was struck by the idea that these places now had the feel of theme parks: Coast Land, reserved for a couple of weeks summer holiday for a certain sort of visitor. Many of my friends locally let out their houses over the summer and move into their vans or into tents, aware of the premium their beachfront houses attract during the holidays, while others who rent find their letting agreements cancelled as their landlords can make so much more from short-term holiday lets. The online forums are full of pleas from families who want to stay in the area but who can find nothing to rent. At a time in which all many well-paid professionals need in order to do their job is a laptop and a wi-fi connection, it seems to be coming to a head, with an exodus of the cities that began during the Covid pandemic.

This is nothing new. It is a continuation of a trend that started when the railways first arrived, opening out an inaccessible corner of the South West to tourists across the country. Shortly after the release of her novel, *Jamaica Inn*, in 1936, Daphne du Maurier noted that the Cornwall she described in that novel was very much a thing of the past. The inn she remembered from her first visits had already become a tourist destination. One of the breakout Cornish films of recent years, the deeply atmospheric *Bait*, brings out these tensions beautifully. In one scene, a furious tourist flies out of his cottage on the harbour clad only in a dressing gown and demands the local fishermen stop making so much noise loading their boat as they are disturbing his holiday peace. When I asked director, Mark Jenkin, about it he confirmed that scene was taken from a memory of the village in which he grew up, a recreation rather than simply a wry comedic set piece.

The Cornwall seen by tourists often belies the vast disparities in wealth in the county. It can be difficult to see, as much of the poverty isn't apparent unless you look for it, or head inland. The homelessness here is often not obvious, it is hidden in caravans and transit vans, in barns and on sofas, an uncomfortable and inconvenient truth about the draw of the sea.

Bluetits sea swimmers at Perranporth.

This morning the roads are almost empty and the only people I see as I navigate the narrow streets of St Ives in the pre-dawn dark are laundry vans and bakers making deliveries.

When I arrive, the beach is empty. I change into my wetsuit beneath the wooden duckboards of the beach café and put on my fins. I will wait for Nick here. I have always admired those who swim on their own, especially at night – my friend, Helen, whose full moon swims are so much a part of the pattern of her life that it seems unthinkable that she might not swim; the women who swim year-round from the town beach at Falmouth and the hardy crew who swim out off Battery Rocks at Penzance – but I've always felt nervous to try a swim in the dark on my own. Down by the water, I'm surprised by the pull I feel from it to get in. Standing on the dark edge, it is more inviting than terrifying, so I slip into the sea and swim out on my own.

Coinciding with the equinox, at this time of year the air temperature and sea temperature are almost in balance. The water is warm, silky even. St Ives Head behind me is a black wedge, punctuated by a string of lights above the café and above that there is a full and bright harvest moon. I paddle on my back, otter-like, staring back at the moon and when I turn onto my front again St Ives Bay opens up in front of me. In leaving the valley, I have left behind the mist and the sky is clear, the water still. This bay is protected from the easterly wind by the land to my left and although I hadn't expected to at all, I feel entirely at ease. It feels intimate, somehow, floating with my head at sea level in the dark. It feels like a little win.

Sea swimming, already popular around the Cornish coast, experienced a particular boom during the pandemic. Though there have always been sea swimmers and the New Years' dip is a long-established tradition in coves around Cornwall, the pandemic prompted a somewhat feverish dash for the water. The small, disparate groups of – mainly women – swimmers coalesced under the name Bluetits, their numbers swelling as more and more people looked for an outlet during lockdown.

In between lockdowns, all across Cornwall and Scilly I meet people who are immersing themselves, people who have lost friends and family to the Covid virus, people struggling with loneliness, with anxiety and depression, with the stresses of balancing work and family, with fears for the present and future. On St Mary's, I swam with a doctor and a teacher in water cold enough to take my breath away, and on Bryher with a farmer. On a visit to Scilly in early July, I met six women, doctors from Treliske Hospital in Truro, on the quay at St Mary's who had just swum the 28 miles from the mainland, raising money for Surfers Against Sewage. Some of the swimmers I met were evangelical in their enthusiasm, keen to spread the good word about the healing properties of the sea. Others were taciturn, getting in alone, head down into the waves, ploughing their lane as though their lives depended on it and others seemed to swim more for the chat afterwards, for the chance to talk and to connect.

Countless articles about the benefits of sea swimming appeared online, as well as guides to the best spots in which to take a dip. About the same time, branded 'wild swimming', hoodies and caps started to appear and in November 2020, the term 'dryrobe wankers' made it into the pages of the *Guardian* in a discussion about swimming off Dublin's iconic Forty Foot promontory, where some felt the influx of new swimmers, many clad in said warm, towelling jackets, was not welcome. For months, my social feeds were full of images of healthy-looking souls demonstrating they had taken a cold dip. It is the latest revival in a long line that stretches back hundreds of years to the Ancient Greeks.

One of the biggest of these revivals occurred in the early eighteenth century, when several treatises on the benefits of cold water immersion were published, along with theories about hydrotherapy. This was the point at which some of our grandest spas and public baths were built or, in some cases, revived and rebuilt. By the late eighteenth century, the gentry were carving stone baths around the Cornish coast and enjoying the fashion for 'taking the water', as it was known. On Cornwall's north coast at Portreath, there are no fewer than seven stone baths carved at different points of the tide in the 1780s. Known as Lady Basset's pools, they were the creation of Lord and Lady Basset, the owners of a large estate and family home at nearby Tehidy.

With the arrival of the railways in the mid-1800s, the Cornish tourism industry really got started though, bringing the masses to the sea, establishing a stream of visitors from the middle classes who came to take the waters for themselves. It is a continuum that leads right up to the packed beaches of the summer just gone, and the sky-high price of property in towns like St Ives.

A figure appears on the beach. Nick Pumphrey is tall, thin, long-haired, with an impressive beard. In his wetsuit, in the dark, silhouetted by the lights of beach café, he looks the way I imagined Tolkien's ents might look when I was a child. He is holding a camera in a waterproof housing at the end of one of his long entish arms. By the time he swims out to me, I am still grinning widely with the thrill of it and he nods to me. He can see, I think, that I get it.

Nick's Dawn Days photographs show the dark sea in all its different moods. In some, the water is silk smooth and almost gossamer-like, picking up long reflections of the rising sun, the setting moon or the lights from the Porthgwidden café as Nick shoots back towards the shore. The delicate tips of breaking waves are rendered in exquisite detail, the infinite moods of the clouds and the water. In others, spindrift whips up off the peaks of waves upon which each individual ripple is picked out in the dawn glow, and in others still the sea is a whirling mass, an angry vortex, or the lighthouse tower at the end of the pier in the harbour rises up out of the mist, as though it is floating, a buoy rather than something fixed to rock. The blurred lines of lights on shore streak across surreal seascapes taken with a long exposure. In some the light is flat and sluggish, the photographs grainy and the line between the sea and the horizon indistinct, while in others it is crystalline sharp. Though they are stills, there is motion in each of these images and none of them looks the same as the next. It is impossible to take a photograph of the same sea twice.

The thing that strikes me most about these photographs, though, seeing them laid out side by side, is the sheer range of colour in the water and the sky that he captures, the sky's shifting palette as the ocean tilts towards the sun. I am lucky enough to have seen the Northern Lights, late one night in a garden in Durham, though the colours of dawn here are easily an equal to those swirling rivers of colour in the sky that appear on bucket lists all over the world.

When you spend enough time around the sea it can become difficult to find the right words to describe the exact feature you are looking at, in standard English in any case. In Cornish dialect, there are words for things for which we have no equivalent in English, and I return to Robert Morton Nance's *A Glossary of Cornish Sea-Words*. Anyone who has swum through a glowing, shimmering sea at night, for example, will be familiar with the difficulty of describing the experience. So, *bremming* describes phosphorescence in the sea, in particular the gleam given off by a school of mackerel at night when swimming through the phosphorescence, *glan* its general glow, and *prinkle* the sparkling of the phosphorescence itself. As a fisher or sailor, it would have been important to be able to accurately and quickly convey specific features in the sea. *Cowsherny* describes a murky, muddled sea, *foxy* the lull between a storm and *seech* the foaming edge of a wave as it runs up onto the land. *Guskins* are a sheltered part of the sea in the lee of the land, such as the patch of sea in which we are swimming, and *lew* describes the mist that hangs in the valleys, such as the one in which I had woken that morning.

Dig deep into many languages and there are words that have mostly fallen out of use to describe specifics of the sea where we might now fall back on approximations. So, on another part of the Atlantic coast, along the Irish coastline, *stranach* is the murmuring of water rushing away from the shore, *tuaimneacha* the loud noise made by the sea when powerful waves continually batter the shore, *gleo* the sound the sea makes when bad weather is incoming, and *dumha thuama* is the sound of the sea against sand dunes. There are words for different qualities of waves, for specific types of landscapes or seascapes, words to describe the experience of being at sea in different conditions and our responses to them. One of my favourites is the phrase *uaigneas an chladaigh*, which describes a sense of loneliness felt on the shore and the haunting presence of those who lived and died there long ago. It speaks to a layered landscape and constant change, a simultaneously frightening and comforting peek beyond the map to the landscape beyond. It hints at the reality that we too will one day be those haunting presences for others who stand on the shore in some distant future.

We don't often stop for long enough to observe how mutable the world is. Repeated activity, or the development of a practice, is often seen as being unfashionable or pretentious. Looking through Nick's photographs, though, reminds me of stumbling across the Irish artist Gary Coyle in a pub somewhere on the south coast years ago. As he clicked through a series of photographs of a frigid Irish Sea projected onto the pub wall, he talked about his practice of travelling by bike through the streets of Dublin down to the Forty Foot promontory at Sandycove and swimming there, day in, day out, first as a bit of a joke aimed at the art establishment and then later, as the Forty Foot got to him, in earnest.

The Forty Foot is an iconic piece of Irish coastal history, formerly the location of men-only swimming club, who would dip naked in a patch of water described so perfectly in James Joyce's *Ulysses* by Buck Mulligan as, 'The snotgreen sea. The scrotum-tightening sea.' Coyle, incidentally, seemed conflicted as to the rolling out of this quote whenever he talked about the project. It

Warbey captures a fishing boat leaving St Ives.

is taken from the opening chapter of the modernist masterpiece, which is set in the Forty Foot and which, Coyle said, brings out 'all the eejits' to the swimming spot on Bloomsday, the annual commemoration of Joyce's life in which fans dress in Edwardian costumes and carry around the weighty tome.

Coyle was softly spoken and soberly dressed, an unlikely sea swimmer, I thought at the time, though almost every day for a year starting in June 1999, he had cycled to Sandy Cove, taking a different route each time. He showed us a map of Dublin overlaid with the routes he had taken, transforming the city into a blur of blue Biro, which looked to me similar to the time-lapse photographs of starlings at dusk I admire. There, at the Forty Foot, he stripped off and swam in Dublin Bay. Coyle had seen, he said, in the naked bodies who lowered themselves into the water that drops as low as 3-degrees Celsius in the winter, unknowing performance artists, repeating their movements and practice day after day.

In his talk, he compared the Forty Foot swimmers he had observed to Alfred Wallis, the Cornish fisherman and self-taught artist, known for his naïve paintings of St Ives fishing boats and his seascapes which propelled him to posthumous fame. He saw in their personal rituals and habits – the following of the same route each day, the parking of their car in the same spot, the entry ritual of standing for a while before immersion, or gradually lowering themselves into the water, or throwing water on their hands and face before entering from the same rock each day and swimming the same distance daily – all the elements of the performance artist.

He was drawn to the way the Forty Footers, most of them from predominantly Catholic Dublin, were wont to describe their dips in terms of penance, pilgrimage or baptism. It fascinated him so much that he decided to 'tether himself' to the Forty Foot for the year and what started as a parody of performance art became a practice that was into its second decade by the time

I saw him. He bought himself a waterproof camera and snapped the seascape each day from the level of the water. By the time I saw Coyle he had swum there almost 3,000 times and taken over 10,000 photographs, documenting the seas in all its shades and moods. He diarized his swims and read from the entries of encounters with the characters he met there. It became a ritual and an obsession for him, and the progression of the photographs took on a hypnotic quality and the pub was silent aside from his narrative and the click of the slide deck.

Nick's approach is, like Coyle's, a whatever-the-conditions one. It is not often, he says, that he decides not to get into the water. He has been bodyboarding, surfing and swimming from this beach since he was a child and he knows it intimately. When I ask him if he has ever felt he should not swim, he tells me about one occasion on which he swam out on a rising tide beneath the cliffs closer to Godrevy on the far side of the wide bay. He swam out in a thick mist and a few metres in he lost sight of the land and when he swam back in an hour or so later, all he could see was the cliff face rising in front of him, no beach and no exit point. The tide had swept him along the coast without him realizing and the high tide meant there was no beach there for him to haul out. He managed to swim back up to his entry point but described the experience as unnerving, to come back in and find the coastline in a totally different state to the one in which he had set out. He would be warier of it next time.

It is a similar story to ones I heard all round the coast. Even experienced swimmers, surfers, sailors and divers underestimate the sea from time to time. Most people I talk to have a story of a near miss, whether they have drifted off from a marker buoy when diving or swum out in conditions beyond their abilities. And there are few surfers I have talked to who have not at some point ignored the common piece of advice, 'if in doubt, don't paddle out'.

Philosophical sea swimmers, like Nick, tend to describe the sea as being a great teacher. Every day in the water is one in which you learn, both about the sea and about yourself. The more prosaic say, 'every once in a while, you're going to get your arse handed to you'. It has happened to me several times. On one occasion, when I was in my early twenties, cut off by the incoming tide, a girlfriend and I spent a few cold and increasingly argument-filled hours on a rock about the size of my desk waiting for the waters to recede after my plan for a picnic turned out to have been less than well thought out. Somewhat unsurprisingly, that relationship did not last much longer.

Not long after moving to Cornwall, walking between two beaches which open out onto one long stretch of sand at low tide, I misjudged my timings and ended up having to wade around the rocks and, eventually, to swim, fully clothed, holding my bag above my head, the last 200 metres or so in a choppy sea, where the tide had completely cut me off from reaching the beach. Although the distance I had to swim was short, I have a clear memory of understanding just the sort of danger I was in. It was mid-winter and the beach onto which I was swimming was rippy at the best of times and the chances of me being pushed out instead of back in were fairly high. I dragged myself out of the water, sopping and cold, and an older man, the only other person on the beach, tutted at me audibly as I passed. I don't blame him. It is the sort of thing at which I now tut when I read that the RNLI have had to be called out yet again to swimmers or walkers who have got themselves into trouble.

I experienced it more recently too, over summer, helping out with a group of ten- and eleven-year-old children at the surf lifesaving club when a rip opened right where we were swimming. It happened so quickly there was no time to react and before we knew it we had been pushed perhaps a hundred metres out to sea. There were other swimmers caught out in the rip too, all swimming as advised between the red and yellow flags, some of whom were now struggling and were swept up by the lifeguards in the high-powered RIB that appeared within seconds. Unlike some of the other swimmers, the children I was with remained calm. They had practised for this. They floated until a lifeguard appeared on one of the brightly coloured surf lifesaving boards. The lifeguard greeted us as though we had met taking a walk on the coast path and suggested we might want to take hold of the loops on the board as waves came crashing in over the children's heads. The group's instructor, having checked everyone was okay, suggested the stronger swimmers should swim back into shore rather than waiting for the RIB. They gain confidence that way, she said. Trouble is almost guaranteed if you spend long enough around the sea, and if you know you are capable of getting yourself out of that trouble, you are more likely to be able to deal with it when it appears.

Although his parents moved to St Ives before Nick turned one and he spent his whole childhood and youth here, he only returned to Cornwall at the beginning of the 2020 Covid pandemic after several years of travel and photography. It was a dark time, he says, and he was in a bad place mentally.

'I like to think I'm pretty cool and calm, but in March last year, I was struggling,' Nick tells me. 'I was worried for my parents and by the bombardment in the media. There was a real atmosphere of fear. I couldn't sleep. I had all these mad scenarios going through my head. But at the same time, I could see there were people doing interesting, creative, generous things, and I wanted to work out what I could do with photography.'

This was where the idea behind Dawn Days of May came from, a simple idea to get up in the dark and swim out into the bay at St Ives with his camera every morning for a month.

'I decided I would get into the sea during the blue hour, be present, learn to be in the moment and document what I see,' he says.

Each day, Nick posted ten photographs to Instagram with the hope that they might bring comfort to anyone who saw them, though aside from that, he had no real objective. His idea was to arrive with no expectations of anything in particular happening, though he found the practice of immersion meant more often than not the day tended to get off to a good start. The insomnia with which he had been struggling improved, and the routine, at a time when many of the routines on which he'd previously relied had collapsed, helped to steady his mind.

An unexpected side effect was the interest other people showed, especially other photographers. After he discussed his plans for his month of dawn days with fellow photographer Mike Guest in Scotland, Mike decided he would do the same, though at Portobello Beach, just outside Edinburgh, and over the month more and more people started to post their photographs of the dawn from the sea. Other St Ives photographers started to join Nick on his dawn patrol and as word got around photographers from further afield joined in, from the west coast of Ireland to Shetland, to Australia and New Zealand, sharing their photographs under hashtag #dawndaysofmay.

The dawn days experiment wasn't without its hiccups. Midway through May, Nick began to feel stressed again. Posting ten photographs a day to his feeds, he found himself shifting towards a mindset in which he felt he needed to get better photographs, to show different aspects of the sea each day, and it took his father to remind him of his original purpose, to get into the sea simply to be there; watch without expectation. It works best when you don't try to control what is going to happen but accept that the morning will unfold as it will, he tells me.

Nick duck dives beneath the surface and when he comes back up he breathes in deeply, then takes a mouthful of sea water and gargles with it. He encourages me to do the same. It is all part of the practice. Shortly after he arrives, we are joined in the water by another photographer, James Warbey. He hugs Nick and after they exchange a brief, 'You okay?', 'Yeah, you okay?', Warbey nods before swimming some way off. He floats. It's touching to see this check-in happen.

'He might not want to talk,' Nick says. 'He's working through some things at the moment.'

It sounds like the nicest of self-help support groups, I suggest. Nick nods. Something like that.

The light shifts. The sky is bluing and although it is clear overhead, there are heavy clouds on the other side of the bay. The beach at Porthgwidden looks east across the bay towards the lighthouse at Godrevy. It is a view Virginia Woolf fictionalized in *To The Lighthouse*, when Mrs Ramsey exclaims:

'"Oh, how beautiful!" For the great plateful of blue water was before her; the hoary Lighthouse, distant, austere, in the midst; and on the right, as far as the eye could see, fading and falling, in soft low pleats, the green sand dunes with the wild flowing grasses on them, which always seemed to be running away into some moon country, uninhabited of men.'

The view we have across to the lighthouse from sea level was similar to the one Woolf would have had from the house she took in St Ives, though this morning the sweeping sand dunes that cradle the bay are still in darkness.

In the distance, the thick cumulonimbus over the hills on the other side of the bay gives way to lighter, wispy clouds above. As the light grows, the rising sun creates a halo around the low, bulging clouds, and the lining is gold rather than silver here. As it grows lighter still, the mist through which I drove when I left home becomes visible, sitting thick and heavy in the estuary mouth at Hayle where the nature writer and conservationist Roger Deakin met Bill Mitchell while he was engaged in his swim around Britain in 1996. Deakin had just swum in the polluted waters of the Red River at Godrevy, named informally after the colour of the mining waste that flowed down through it to the sea, when he stumbled across the Kneehigh cast rehearsing for their landscape theatre show, *Ghost Nets*. Bill, the show's director, made a strong impression on Deakin, enough that he devoted a few pages to the anarchic theatre company, who are now a much-missed part of Cornish life. He seemed impressed, too, with the show, in which all the actors ended up in the water beneath the skeletal structures of the set, draped in fishing nets, the props created from rubbish found on the beach.

The small peaks that rise out of the clouds make it seem for a while as though we are looking on a mountain range from a great distance. The colours in the dawning sky shift continually. This is the time of maximum potentiality, the point at which the world is deciding what it is going to be today. And there is something about seeing those tentative, unstable colours reflected in the water that intensifies the whole experience. From the level of the water it feels as though I am in the middle of it, a part of the dawn.

Small fishing boats, the St Ives fleet, head out from the harbour in a sporadic convoy in the slowly growing light. Gulls fly silently overhead, and gannets too. Three cormorants, sweeping low over the water, pass over our heads and the three of us whoop at the encounter. A few minutes later, a seal surfaces, its dark head not far from us and it watches us in the half-light for a while before ducking back under and disappearing again.

I don't want to interrupt his thoughts while he is in the water, though later Warbey tells me about his journey back to the sea. He grew up in south-west London, though all his holidays from a young age were to St Ives. As a child, he would spend every hour he could in the sea, but when he turned eighteen, he stopped coming and did not set foot in the sea again until May 2020.

'Life got in the way,' he tells me. 'Something in me said I can't do it. The mind is a powerful thing. A lot of it is about body confidence and self-confidence.'

He describes himself as being self-destructive by nature.

'I go into my crab shell, and then it spirals from there,' he says. 'It just gets worse when you're alone with your thoughts.'

Though he continued to live in London, Warbey became a surf photographer, and though he had always wanted to swim with a camera and shoot the action up close, he had stopped feeling comfortable in the water. At the time he met Nick, who he refers to as Pumps, he was storm chasing, shooting surfers on the reef at Porthleven, and ended up getting stuck in Cornwall during the first national lockdown.

'I used to say to Pumps, "I'm going to come with you," and I never did. I made these new year's resolutions in which I'd say, "I'm going to get a shot published from the water," but then another year went by and I still hadn't done it. Then when lockdown happened, I had a panic attack. It was the worst three days I've ever had. I needed to do something about it.'

When he heard Nick was swimming at dawn, he resolved to give it a go and they arranged to meet.

'I ended up swimming at the Black Cliffs that morning.' Nick is referring to another beach some miles further east. 'And [Warbey] got up, looked in the sea and he's wondering where's Nick? He's got his wetsuit on. But in his mind, he's saying to himself, I can go back home now. Same old story. I can run away. It's 5.30 and there's no one else around to see. I can get back to bed.'

Get in the sea? Or go back to bed?

'When I got back in,' Nick says, 'I had a message from Warbey saying, "I got in. I couldn't feel more alive."'

'I went and jumped in and floated and everything changed,' Warbey says. 'It was like a rocket ship started to go up from that moment. I had to make that decision for myself. It would have been a disaster if I hadn't gone in. It was on me. I had to choose. It was something I didn't know I needed. And when I did, I thought, "holy shit", I need this. It was like coming home. I have a very busy mind and it's a complete reset. Without it, I would spiral. It wipes the slate clean every morning. You're not thinking of anything when you're out there and that's what I need.

'I lost my dad a few months ago and it was horrible. He had Alzheimer's. Swimming saved me from that too. The more I do it, the more I need it. I find it such a release and a freedom. When I don't do it, that London side comes out again. I lash out and that doesn't help me.'

When I talk the Dawn Days over with Nick and Warbey, what they describe is on the one hand simple – it is about getting into the water each morning, that's it – and on the other hand there is much more to it. There is the intentionality of getting up early, the element of conscious practice of it. There's the camera, which makes the whole endeavour a creative one, the sensation of being held by the sea itself, of being taken out of the daily grind and suspended for a while, as well as the companionship of others who are working through their own thoughts and struggles. Then there are the well-documented benefits of immersion in cold water on mood and inflammation, not to mention the light. Some recent studies have suggested that the wavelengths at sunrise and sunset help to regulate our circadian rhythms and elevate mood. The intimate encounter with nature is also proved over and again to promote wellbeing. As many of the swimmers I spoke to said, the encounters they have with birds, seals and fish give them a sense of connectedness. And perhaps there is something in there about seeing out the darkest hour, the coming of the dawn as a reminder that the sun also rises.

If nothing else, Nick says, it is a better start than beginning the day by scrolling, comparing his life to everyone else's, or floating around online and getting involved in something he did not want to get involved with in the first place.

Warbey ended up joining Nick each morning for the rest of the dawn days of May and then again when he decided to do a longer stint of 111 consecutive dawn days the following winter, in part to check in on each other through the darkest days. It's still working, he says, this conscious practice of being in the water as the earth turns towards the sun.

Like Nick, Warbey was surprised at the response from others when he shared his photographs. He received messages from other people who were struggling with lockdown, or with the stress of working in the health service at a time it was stretched far beyond capacity, from people who loved the sea but could not get down to Cornwall because of the lockdown. He has been surprised that talking about his own mental health and body confidence has inspired others to open up too.

'Down here, everyone's got an amazing rig – they're all hugely fit – and I think a lot of that is why I swim at dawn,' he said. 'I don't swim during the day often. You won't see me on the beach with my shirt off. But as soon as you start talking about it, other people open up.'

Back on the water, Nick is shooting on a long exposure, spinning the camera and playing with the shapes and lines of the lights on shore and those reflected in the water. With his long hair and beard, he now resembles less an ent and more a camera-toting mystic. If you spend long enough doing this, the experience will do this to you. Warbey, who is almost entirely still in the water, absorbed, has a long lens and is shooting the fishing boats on the horizon and the birds as they pass overhead. I have a small waterproof camera that looks vaguely ridiculous compared to their professional set-ups in their waterproof housings. Later, I will find that I have got the settings on my camera wrong and have been shooting continuously the whole time we have been out, over a thousand photographs, and though most of them are terrible, they show the dramatic shifts in light towards the coming of the dawn. I can see in these imperfect images just how wildly the sea changes second on second, the interplay between the water, the light, the clouds and the sky. Compared to the rich experience of being there, with the sound of the water and the sea birds, the sharp, briny smell of it that lingers in my nostrils long after I have got out, the photographs I take are a pale replica, though the camera has forced me look at the sea closely, to pay attention.

Many commentators have suggested that there is something special about the light in St Ives, a quality that has drawn artists from all over the world to paint here, from J.M.W. Turner's tour of Cornwall in 1811 through to the art movement that developed towards the end of the nineteenth century with the arrival of the railway and the first visits by Whistler, when St Ives and Newlyn began to receive regular visits by artists. They were drawn, as much as anything, by the quality of the light.

The prominent artist of the Newlyn School, Norman Garstin, is quoted as having said of St Ives, '[The] sun comes gleaming over the water in the morning on the one hand and sinks gleaming into it on the other hand in the evening; big waves come tumbling over white sands, and the foam is dyed in turns with all the colours of the spectrum; out of the windows of their foam-spattered studios the St Ives artists can watch the sea pranking itself in all the many tinted garments of the day and evening, and so they become impressionistic and sensuous in colour.'

Scrolling through the photographs, I see what D.H. Lawrence meant when he talked about the 'infinite Atlantic, all peacock-mingled colour' and what the visual artist, Mel Gooding, described as the peninsular light's 'crystalline brilliance'.

There is no crystalline brilliance yet this morning. The dawning has been mellow and slow to arrive. There is no piercing gleam of light over the hills, but instead a kind of swelling. With all the cloud on the horizon, I am not sure we will see a sunrise at all. The sky shifts itself through innumerable permutations of blue above us and the rising sun picks out the outlines of the clouds. Then, just before we head back to shore, a broad, intense column of bright gold appears on the horizon above the hills of mid Cornwall, like a blazing waterfall emerging from within the cloud. It is spectacular and we watch, silent and still, as a fishing boat passes in front of the dazzling light on the sea and is, for a moment, framed in the golden light.

Byron was once quoted as having said, 'I delight in the sea and come out with a buoyancy of spirits I never feel on any other occasion,' but I like the way Nick puts it better: 'It's never a bad idea to do a dawny. There's strength in getting in.'

I emerge from the water with a buzz that stays with me for the rest of the day. Not enough to convince me to do the same the next morning, but enough to know I will be back in in a week or so, once I've caught up on my sleep.

A fishing boat in Mount's Bay.

11

Oar Raiser

Pilot gig rowing in Mount's Bay

A SKEIN OF GEESE passes overhead in a broad V as I get out of the car on the hillside above Newlyn. They are flying in imperfect formation, three of the geese slightly out of sync with the rest. They are more beautiful for the imperfection. The air is still and the birds are so low I can feel the whoomph of their broad, powerful wingbeats. From up on the hill I look out over Mount's Bay across the masts and fishing boat derricks of Newlyn Harbour towards St Michael's Mount. I can see two gig boats are out on the water already.

I walk down the hill past Penlee Lifeboat Station, past a concrete field that has sprouted towers of crates and that offers some idea of the scale of the fishing industry here. The hard, industrial walls of the fish market are softened by paintings of fishermen, boats, nets, a nod towards Newlyn's artistic heritage. Alongside the older buildings on the harbour, modern structures are rising, all glass and grey wood. These new arrivals have yet to bed into the town. For now, they look just a little too clean, their lines too sharp, though it seems likely that Newlyn will knock their edges off. It is a town that feels as though it is doing its best to resist the sharp elbowing in of gentrification.

The Pendeen crew raise their oars.

I am looking for the familiar figure of Anna Maria Murphy on the harbour. I have known Anna since I arrived in Cornwall. She is a poet and storyteller and, as she says herself, an unlikely pilot gig rower. I spot the Pendeen training gigs nestled among the fishing boats before I see her. If they look as much a part of this busy fishing harbour as the fishing smacks with their derricks and wheelhouses, it is because they are as iconic an image of the county as is the silhouette of an engine house. Most weekends, all around the coast, and around the coast of Scilly too, the air rings with the call of the cox and the plash of oars in the water. There are other fixed seat boats used for similar racing in the UK – the Welsh Celtic longboat, the Thames skiff and the Thames Waterman Cutter to name but three – though the largest of the racing communities by far is that of the pilot gigs. About thirty clubs operate in Cornwall alone and though it is a particularly Cornish and Scillonian sport, there are clubs in neighbouring Devon and in London and as far afield as Faroe, Bermuda and Australia.

Modern pilot gigs are all built to the same design, based on a boat called Treffry, which was built by St Mawes boat builder, William Peters, in 1838. However, the Pendeen training boats are made of fibreglass instead of the traditional narrow leaf elm. The fibreglass boats are heavier but more practical for training. The club's two wooden boats are only brought out for regattas and races and, in an extreme combination of Cornishness, the wooden boats are housed in one of the storage sheds at the nearby Geevor Tin Mine.

At most other clubs, the gigs are kept in boat sheds from where the crews must carry them down to the water. Pendeen is unusual in that their boats have a permanent mooring in the harbour. They are a fixture here, part of the community, their presence a statement.

And although the Pendeen crews only usually row to train or to race, they have a ceremonial function too. At weddings of gig rowers, tradition holds that the married couple walk out of the church beneath an arch of oars held by their crew. When local vicar Julyan Drew, who had blessed the club's new boat, died in 2019, the Pendeen crews rowed out and raised their oars for him. They did the same for a Newlyn boy with a terminal illness who was walking the coast path to raise money for charity. The day I go out on the water with them coincides with a global day of action for the climate, mid-way through the COP26 talks in Glasgow. The Pendeen crews are rowing out to show their support for the climate change protesters.

The blue-and-white boat we row out on is has *Silent Mountain* inscribed on the side. It is named after a former member of the men's crew, Chris Cox, who died, aged twenty-nine of a condition called sudden adult death syndrome.

'We called it *Silent Mountain* after him, as he was this mountain of a young man and he rarely spoke,' Anna tells me.

Getting the boat out of the harbour is a delicate manoeuvre. The six rowers and the cox, Anna, have to back the boat out from the pontoon and navigate between the fishing boats and through a small gap in the harbour wall. At times, as they move silently between the boats, Anna says, she imagines they are free traders, slipping out of the harbour with a consignment of brandy. Some of the boats in the harbour look as though they are rusting into the water, while others gleam. Many of the boats are busy, with crews hosing down the decks or working on machinery.

Gig crews have been doing the same since the late eighteenth century, when the fastest gig out of the harbour and the first to the incoming ships would secure the commission to pilot the ship in, as well as ferrying goods from the shore to boats. They were the power boats of their day, designed to cut through the waves. The Cornish and Scillonian coasts were difficult territory for sailors reliant on the wind and tides, and intimate local knowledge of the waters was in high demand by captains keen to keep their cargo and crew safe. Later, the pilot gigs were also used as an early form of lifeboat for ships in distress. The gig crews would go out in the heaviest seas to rescue sailors and, aside from the gig boats themselves, their legacy can still be seen in the Cornish knit frocks, which were worn by rowing crews. In case of a rower drowning, it was easier to identify a body if they were wearing the distinctive knit pattern of Sennen or Mousehole, for example. Pilot gigs had other, less regulated uses, too. They were swift and low in the water, with a shallow draft, easy to manoeuvre in the tight coves of Cornwall and Scilly and were perfect for smuggling.

There was strong rivalry between gig crews and, as with the working boats in Falmouth, the competition led eventually to racing as a way of keeping the crews fit and the one-upmanship between them fierce.

Each of the boats has history, whether *Slippen* from St Agnes which rowed out to rescue the survivors and collect the bodies from the wreck of the *Thomas Lawson*, or the *Ann Glanville* raced by Caradon Gig Club, named after the formidable Saltash woman who led an all-women gig crew in the 1800s after her husband, who came from a long line of watermen, died. She became famous, beating men's crews at several regattas and continuing the business her husband had begun.

We are met at the harbour mouth by two swans paddling on the dark water. Standing on the harbour wall of the South Pier, looking down as we approach, are eight women in yellow cagoules, the synchronized swimmers we are here to see and to whom we will raise our oars.

The six women on the pier are sea swimmers from Penzance who decided to challenge themselves to become a synchronized swimming team in time for the day of protest to demonstrate the human capacity for change. It is, as one spectator later puts it, 'typically Penzance', a blend of the slightly bizarre and inspirational.

The six swimmers are at the beginning of what they are

calling their land swim from the Tidal Observatory at Newlyn, the most important of the UK sea level stations, round to the open air pool on the other side of the bay. Until 1983, the tidal observatory was the site from which the UK's mean sea level was determined, the last word in the height of the seas around our island. The Newlyn tide gauge is housed in a small hut on the end of the South Pier beyond the door we can see behind the swimmers. It is an entirely unassuming place and the technology it is based on is equally unassuming – a hole in the floor of the observatory drops down to the low tide mark, a float, attached to the tide gauge, which was measured automatically and by hand for accuracy. Along the route, which follows the sweep of the bay, the swimmers will mark, in chalk paint, the point high water could reach should climate change not be averted and they will perform their land swim in places on land that will be underwater by 2050 should the current projections prove correct.

The laughter and jostling on the boats fall to silence and Anna calls for oars up. For a minute or so I look up from where I sit in the bow to a sky made up of a sea of oars. The swimmers look down on us in silence too until we drop the oars. We shout up encouragement to them and they shout it back as we pull away into Mount's Bay.

As we hit open water, Anna calls for the crew to show what they are made of and the boat surges forward. Behind us, the All Weather Severn Class lifeboat, the *Ivan Ellen*, emerges from the harbour we have just left, bright orange against dark cliffs and for a few seconds we share the same water, the earliest form of lifeboat and the most recent.

Just shy of 40 years ago, the boat leaving the Penlee lifeboat station would have been the *Solomon Browne*, the wooden, 14-metre lifeboat that launched into a hurricane force 12 storm to reach the *Union Star*, which had suffered engines failure off Mousehole. This event was the last time the RNLI lost an entire crew. It is remembered each year on 19 December in Mousehole with the dimming of the lights and this year, the fortieth anniversary, the Pendeen crews will row out and raise their oars as part of the memorial. The disaster is very much a part of living memory here. The *Ivan Ellen* opens her engines and is gone within seconds and *Silent Mountain* powers on in the direction of Penzance.

When I ask one of the Pendeen rowers how long she has lived here, she replies by saying, 'Well, I remember Penlee.' It is one of those events that if you lived here you remember where you were. It is imprinted on Cornwall, and on Newlyn and Mousehole in particular, just as the events surrounding the *Thomas Lawson* are on the Agnes community.

The rowers in *Silent Mountain* are working up a sweat. They are an eclectic bunch. Paramedics sit alongside nurses, social workers, ex-fishermen, farmers and, in the cox's seat, Anna, who worked for years with Bill Mitchell on shows for Kneehigh, the man she credits with giving her first job in writing. The rowers are not entirely in unison and the boat is full of jokes and laughter. I listen as they rib each other for small things, and as they tell me stories of blisters and the notorious 'gig arse' that fixed seat rowers get from being too long in their seat. The rower two seats in front of me has a shock of pink hair and Anna, at the stern, occasionally comes into view between the two columns of rowers or, more accurately, her floppy artist's hat comes into view.

Anna has been rowing with the Pendeen gig for eighteen years, though she describes herself as unsporty, asthmatic and uncompetitive, an unlikely candidate for gig rowing. Like many of the women in her crew, she had never been a member of a club before.

'People think that sport is over for them when they hit 40 maybe, but most of us are in our 50s and 60s,' one member of crew shouts back at me over her shoulder.

While some gig crews are almost professional outfits, athletes who train throughout the year and put in gym sessions and land sessions in addition to their time on the water, the Pendeen B crew, with whom Anna rows, tend to be, by their own admission, underdogs at regattas. Several members of the crew tell me how they have been improving in recent years, though.

'We're more care in the community,' Anna says jokingly, though there is a serious side to this statement. Some doctors in Cornwall are beginning to prescribe gig rowing on social prescription. Anna estimates that almost half the people in her club do it for their mental health, herself included.

'It clears your mind,' she says. 'When you're rowing your mind has to be on that one thing. Sometimes, everyone is totally silent in the boat, everyone is entirely in the moment. And at those times, you're not really thinking anything, you're just there. Those moments of not thinking are beautiful. It's a relief from yourself.'

It's not all happy families though. There are fallings out, arguments and small feuds which can simmer beneath the surface or which flare up sporadically. The same is true of any family – no one can get along with everyone all the time. And this is what it feels like, from the outside at least, a wonderfully dysfunctionally functional family. In this club, everyone is accepted for who they are.

The Pendeen Gig Club crew in Mount's Bay.

Sitting at the front of the gig, facing back, I recall the closest experience I have had to this kind of community family. It is one Emma and I left behind when we moved away from London to start our own family. For a few years, we had been members of a small sailing club on the Thames. When I came down from the north to join Emma in London, she was already a member. I was new to the city and suffering the lack of balance that comes with uprooting yourself and landing in a place where you feel like an outsider. For someone brought up in a small community, the sailing club, with all its quirks, its shabby chairs and stained mugs, felt to me like an oasis in the capital, a small community to which I could belong among the thousands of others that abut and bleed into one another in such a vast place.

At the club, we didn't talk so much about what was going on at home. I suspect that many of the members used it as an opportunity to find some space away from home. Instead, we discussed the merits of different boats for river racing, the tactics we might use for different courses and how to avoid a biased start line, which was all but impossible on this stretch of river. The rivalry was gentle, though it was not uncommon to arrive to find another member measuring the distance between the shrouds and the prow on your boat, especially if you had beaten the person in question in a race the previous week on a similar dinghy. It was one of the few places I came across in the city where I saw people well into their eighties teaching children and teenagers, passing on tips for sailing in the fickle winds that swung round the buildings on either side of the river, or explaining how to deal with the flow of water at different points of tide and it being the most normal thing in the world.

In many ways, the sailing was secondary to the community it enabled; there is only so much sailing you can do on the Thames and often races were called off or abandoned due to lack of wind, though when that happened no one left, since we were there for each other's company as much as if not more than the sailing itself. We hung around the club house or fine-tuned our boats in the yard, helped one of the other members to fix their boat, or at least offered helpful or unhelpful suggestions while they worked. There were members I don't think I ever saw on the water and it didn't matter in the slightest. At the time, I complained about the committee meetings and the working groups, the endless discussions about rules and regulations and how best to set a course, though when I left, I missed it in the way I miss the squabbling among my own extended family after Christmas is done and dusted and we've arrived home.

The Pendeen women's crew of which Anna is a member have seen each other through depression and anxiety, illness, cancer, births and deaths. When one of the crew has been ill, often to the point at which they did not think they would row again, they will sit in the seat I have been given when they are on their feet again, observers, though still part of the crew. Over time, they are brought back into the boat and when they begin to row again, the rest of the crew welcomes them onto the gig by the raising of the oars. It is, Anna tells me, a way of marking the time they have been away and a recognition that they are going to be okay again. This mutual support system is the thing Anna seems proudest of, even more so than she is of their victories, which are few and far between.

One of the rowers, Caz, tells me she takes her frustrations out on the water.

'When you're going hard, when you're really tired, you think about something that really pisses you off and dig deep,' she says. 'You take it out on the oar. We're a noisy crew when we get going.'

She describes the grunts and growls each member of the crew makes when they are all pulling hard. One of the crew, she says, makes a noise like an injured seagull. Others join in, giving impressions of their crewmates' noises of exertion.

'When everyone's hurting you can tell by the noise,' she continues. 'You get caught up in it, especially when you're getting towards the end and you're trying to rinse the end out.'

The physical aspect of rowing, Anna says, helps with her anxiety, though there's also something about leaving the land behind that helps too.

'You're not on a mobile phone out here,' she says. 'And that's a rare thing now. Sometimes, we row out and stop the oars and remind ourselves how lucky we are to be able to do this.'

The boat is flying now and as I have no role in the rowing I look across to the open sea and listen to the dull thud of the oars' leathers on the wooden thole pins. There is a complex sky, layer upon layer of clouds of different formation which makes a pink-toned city on the horizon. A fishing boat, heading back in, appears to float some way above the surface of the sea, the effect of a superior mirage.

Rowing is a way of getting to know the sea's moods, Anna tells me, its atmospheres and ways. You get to know where the submerged rocks are, the places to avoid. Sometimes, she says, it's a case of the change in the smell on the water and you know you should get back to the protection of the harbour walls. Depending on the wind and tides, the gig crew pulls towards St Michael's Mount on the opposite side of the bay, the rowers ploughing through the water just metres above the ancient, petrified forest buried in the sand beneath. As we head towards Penzance, following the path of the swimmers, we pass the point at which the Scillonian ferry departs. In six months, many of these rowers will be on the ferry, heading for the world championships. It is the biggest event of the racing year and the one the rowers talk about most, the first bank holiday weekend in May when the islands are overrun by gig rowers. 150 crews travel out to the islands to compete, most of them from Cornwall, though crews from Holland, America and Ireland are also represented.

'There are something like 1,000 women on the start line for the very first race, of all different conditions. When the start whistle goes off you get the noise of the oars hitting the water all together and all the puffins rise from the rocks,' Anna says. 'After that first race, you're put into grades and right at the end, the lowest graded boats come in first and as you come in, you moor up and you wait for the other boats to come in. When the final boats come in you all put your oars up and there's a forest of oars. I can't explain the exhilaration.'

We have lost sight of the swimmers now and when we look for them, they are nowhere to be seen, but the three gigs pause again in the water, line up, raise the oars once more and, job done, head back to the harbour. The tide, which is now at its lowest, prevents us from getting back to the pontoon from which we launched and we leave the gig moored between two fishing boats. Later, Anna sends me a text to let me know they got in trouble from the harbourmaster, having taken the space that had been reserved for a large catamaran arriving from France. Being part of the community has its downsides. It means you are always a known element and can't get away with anything.

When we are back on land, I catch up with the synchronized swimmers. Following the climate march making its way towards Battery Rocks, Penzance's answer to the Forty Foot, and the Jubilee Pool where they are due to perform, they are easier to find on land than they were to follow on the water. Penzance's whitewashed Art Deco sea pool, the largest in the UK, juts out into the sea, a wedge of style in the town that is at the far end of the line.

The gallery of the lido is busy when I arrive, festival-like. A young woman, Louise Batty, who is half-Cornish, half-Tuvaluan, talks to the crowd through a microphone. Her heritage straddles two parts of the world and one of them, the atoll country of Tuvalu, is already sinking under rising waters. She talks about the regular inundation of the islands by king tides, the highest tides that flood the lowest lying areas, which destroy homes, salinate the fresh water supplies and destroy crops. It is a reminder that though climate change will affect everyone, it will affect some more than others. As a phrase that did the rounds during the Covid pandemic had it, we are all in the same storm, though we are not all in the same boat.

A harsh late autumn sun shines on the lido and I have to shield my eyes to watch the swimmers as they emerge from the poolside changing rooms. They dive, kick, form circles and lines to a Queen song that blazes out over the speaker system. At one point, as the swimmers fan out in a broad V, two of the swimmers are slightly out of formation. Six weeks earlier, none of them had ever done synchronized swimming. They decided to take on the challenge to demonstrate people's ability to change their behaviour and to achieve something amazing together, to show what we are capable of when we commit to it. The fact that they are slightly out of formation just makes the scene all the more beautiful.

Synchronised swimmers at Penzance's Jubilee Pool.

Bawden Rocks, off St Agnes Head.

12

Horizon Scanner

Wildlife watching at St Agnes Head

LOOKING AT IT through the binoculars, the sea soon became an abstract thing. The scene brought close to me had become a blur of blues and whites and I realized I had drifted. I was not thinking about the task at hand. Cocooned in hats, gloves and a heavy coat against the wind, I was daydreaming again, the seascape bringing back memories within memories like matryoshka dolls, each thought revealing another within.

I was standing high on the cliffs not far from St Agnes Head, taking part in a wildlife survey with Abby Crosby, who is part of the Living Seas Team at the Cornwall Wildlife Trust. We had already recorded the wind strength and direction, cloud cover and visibility, after which Abby asked me to choose a patch of sea on which to concentrate. Now I was supposed to be scanning the sea in segments as Abby had taught me, taking in one small square at a time, moving the binoculars slowly, not trying to cover too much ground.

As we set up the equipment, I had asked Abby what we might expect to see. It had been a good year for spotting marine mega-fauna, she said. Shoals of huge bluefin tuna had been spotted and whales too. She conjured up for me a picture of the pod of inshore bottlenose dolphins that hunt in the shallow waters, travelling

up and down the coast as far as Kent and back, a feeding frenzy
of larger common dolphins further out to sea, sunfish which act
as rafts for seabirds, porpoises and fin whales, which she had
observed with a group at St Ives and which they had watched
breach and blow for half an hour. I asked her which she liked to
see most of all and she told me for her there was no one species
she liked more than the others.

'It's the whole thing,' she said. 'I see the ocean as being like
a body, or a being, one huge organism. It's bigger than we can
comprehend. The whole ocean is one huge living thing and I feel
the need to be part of a network of people who are standing up
for it and speaking on its behalf.'

Abby had a high powered monocular on a stand and I had the
binoculars through which I had watched whales in the Arctic.
She asked me to note any life I saw in the patch of sea she had
roughly delineated with a pointed finger. In my mind, though,
after a few minutes looking through the binoculars, I was 30
miles south, at Cadgwith Cove, where some time before I had
lain on my side on the empty beach, the cold radiating through
my body as it rested on the stones.

This close to the ground I could see that the dark matter
between the stones consisted of grains of plastic and ring pulls,
strands of seaweed and shards of glass. The corner of a crisp packet
poked up, like a weed fighting its way into the light. The smell
of diesel rose from the ground and with it childhood memories
of cross-Channel ferry trips and sitting in the lee of the wind
at the ship's stern, eating squashed sandwiches. I had a visceral
recollection of sheltering behind the ship's great funnels, feeling
the pitch and roll, the long swell, and watching as the slow curve
of the wake stretched out behind.

I lifted my eyes from the beach. Beyond, the sea was so calm
it was hard to imagine that somewhere out there towering waves
raced across oceans, tossing about huge containers fallen from
cargo ships; waves that drown and terrify. From here it was hard

to see where the water ended and where the sky began. Looking for the horizon became painful.

That memory was of February and the beach was Cadgwith Cove on the Lizard Peninsula, where I was researching a novel I was writing. If you had caught me a few weeks earlier or later it could have been Polperro, Mousehole, Mevagissey – or any number of other coastal villages.

While I was there, I was building a coastline in my head, stitching it together as I toured these tiny places that clung onto the land, though I was also creating it from memories, fishing villages I had visited in Northumberland, on the west coast of Ireland, the Hebrides and the east coast of Scotland – small details gleaned and appropriated from each. In Falmouth, I watched as the boats sheltering close to the shore were obliterated by the incoming storm, walls of water battering the shore. In Newlyn, I was eyed suspiciously by fishermen as I wandered between their boats in the harbour, nervous of overstaying my welcome. On the outskirts of St Agnes, near where I stood scanning for

The fishermen's store at Cadgwith Cove.

wildlife with Abby, on a day when the wind had blown the sea white, I sat on the edge of the cliffs above the village and looked out over the waves. I barely saw another person all afternoon.

I was surprised that I had never bumped into Abby before. It turns out we run along the same section of coast path, where she also walks her dogs, though often I am not paying attention to other people when I am there. When I am on the coast, I give myself licence to drift in a way I rarely do when I am out of sight of the sea. I allow myself to recall incidents and accidents that occurred, some recent, some from way back, fragments of events that rise of their own accord from the ocean of memory. I recall scraps of discussions and dreams, and tuck small details from them away for later use: the dew on a stack of nets; a retired fisherman listening out for the small fleet on an old radio; a curled, mouldering photograph found in a hut by the shore; the shape of the rocks at either side of a cove.

Often, I walk with a camera and photograph the birds – the kestrels and the pair of choughs who made their home in an old mine stack not far from here, fulmars that nest on the cliffside, the seabirds I glimpse far out across the water leading lives of which I can hardly conceive. Watching them, it was easy to see how a tradition like that of the Conway Gulls might come about, the idea that seabirds represent the souls of those who have crossed the bar, flying above the profound sea.

Abby didn't know this when we arranged to meet there, but the place we were standing was, and still is, particularly important to me. Not far from where we had set up the monitoring equipment is the place I come to sit and stare when I need to think. I find the act of thinking easier here, standing on the fringe, where the land drops off, looking out across deep water. It is something to do with the size of the canvas, perhaps. The uninterrupted view and the sea's seeming featurelessness are huge enough to deal with thoughts and emotions that are hard to process logically.

A kestrel hovering above the cliffs.

Inspiration for a story is rarely found in the realm of logic and it is here I find it easiest to play with ideas. It is also the place I come to process happiness and grief, as though looking outwards with no visible boundary before me allows me to investigate more easily what is within. Perhaps it is in part a result of the sea's mutability, some metamorphosing property of its vast depths and breadths that is engrained in our collective psyche – the sea as a metaphor for the unconscious mind – that allows this. Look out from the shore for long enough and you'll see what I mean.

This regular perch on the rocks is the place I brought a very personal grief, a loss with which I struggled for years and one that sometimes still catches me with my defences down, the stillbirth of our first son.

My memories of that time come back in nested freeze frames too. Sitting on a broken chair in a quiet hospital room opposite a window that overlooked a paved courtyard in the centre of which stood a long-dead tree. An endless procession of forms that required signatures. The grey walls around a cemetery, the monotonous regularity of its gravestones. A larger memorial stone that was festooned with toys, cards and flowers, all wrapped in cellophane against the rain. The sensation of being hemmed in. Over the days and weeks that followed, the walls of our small house became constrictive too. The house filled up with flowers sent by friends and family. The planes that flew over every few minutes from Heathrow seemed somehow to press down on the roof. I began to feel the draw of the sea in my bones. It was exactly as Masefield wrote, 'a clear call and a wild call that may not be denied'.

So, in late December 2011 we made our way west to Cornwall for some respite after the events of the previous month. In the carpark at Chapel Porth I stripped down to my shorts and walked across the rocks down towards the shoreline. I had been thinking about doing this for a few weeks, reminded of the ritual I had performed so often as a child when, upon arriving at a beach, I would wade into the surf just to feel the waves break over me. I ran past a few bemused and warmly dressed dog walkers, beyond the shelter of the cliffs, where the wind blew sand horizontally across the beach, and into the white water. There, I stood chest-deep, battered by incoming waves that felt as though they were run through with ice, for as long as I was able. And for a few moments the grief wasn't silenced so much as confronted by a wall of deafening white noise muting its constant scream. The sea's great indifference was a comfort in a way I can't easily explain, and it continues to play its part.

We were still a year or so away from making our decision to move our lives wholesale to Cornwall, though when we returned to our landlocked home, I took back with me the memory of that moment of relief and it was balm. During sleepless nights, I recalled the sensation of the freezing waves as I listened to the litany of the Shipping Forecast both on the radio and in my head.

I had taken to memorizing the forecast areas as an aid to sleep in times when sleep was hard to find. I worked my way clockwise around its areas in the way Catholics might recall the stations of the cross – Southeast Iceland, Faeroes, Fair Isle, Viking, North Utsira, Cromarty, Forties . . . and tried to recall the shapes of each of these areas on the forecast charts. When I mention this to other people it has surprised me how many do something similar, how comforting that listing of location and visibility, wind direction and strength is to those on their sofas or in their beds on land, the strange way in which the forecast 'Lundy, Fastnet, south 7 to severe gale 9', which might sound alarm bells for the sailor heading north from Cornwall, can reassure and calm a restless mind on land.

Standing side by side, looking out to sea, I told Abby the whole story and she told me about the draw she had felt when she was pulled away from the coast by the sudden and serious illness of one of her children. They had been playing on the beach when he became sick and, after taking him to A&E, within an hour, they were helicoptered to the hospital at Bristol where he was diagnosed with a brain tumour.

'We went in a Coastguard helicopter, and it was so loud and I remember thinking, above the noise during that 40-minute trip that he was going to die and I had to accept that.'

He did not die, though his treatment and recovery in the hospital in Bristol took five months, with another eight months of treatment back in Cornwall, during which she stayed with her son. Abby recalled that the sea, and the thought of one beach in particular, stayed in her mind as her son went through his long treatment, through brain surgery and radiotherapy, through the months of chemotherapy and physiotherapy, and during the long rehabilitation in which he had to learn to walk and talk again after the surgery.

'I remember being outside the hospital in the middle of Bristol and thinking I cannot wait to be back here, walking my dogs on the cliffs,' she said above the rising wind. 'This was such a key place for me to come back to.'

The first thing they did as a family, when they finally left the hospital, having gone through all the layers of bureaucracy that surround a child's discharge after so serious an illness, and the surrealness of being told they could leave after more than twenty weeks in hospital, the extended family, gathered at Abby's home, headed down to the beach.

'We had this surreal moment of thanks that we were there,' she said. She talks about the sense of expansion and relief that surrounded that time, the comfort she took from being by the sea again. Her son is now much recovered and the immediacy of the powerful emotions a parent feels when their child is seriously ill are starting to fade, though talking about it brings the memory of those emotions back in waves.

The intensity of my grief and the constancy of it ebbed over time, though when we moved to Cornwall in 2013, I returned to the cliffs above the point where I had swum that December and cast my mind out into the expanse beyond. There I performed one-sided conversations, though others might call them prayers or communion, meditation or a form of therapy. I didn't expect an answer, though what I found was by casting my thoughts out off the edge of the island they often returned to me transformed, having undergone a sea change.

When I turned away from the sea it was almost always with a lighter heart, a sense of perspective. There, I experienced some-thing of what I imagine the cathedral builders sought to achieve when they lifted the clerestories to the sky, creating a huge space to inspire awe and to humble, to lift the heart, a space filled with light and wonder. I imagine they were emulating what can be found here on the cliffs naturally. That is how this place appears to me at least, a place to heal and give thanks. It is, at least in part, how I imagine our ancestors felt when they made their pilgrimages to their holy sites by the sea, the Ness of Brodgar on Orkney, Goat's Hole on the Gower Peninsula, the holy islands of Iona and Lindisfarne.

A few months ago, I was visiting the remains of the Iron Age village at Halangy Down on St Mary's. My family was finishing the picnic in the outline of one of the houses and I had walked up to the top of the site and was standing at the entrance to one of the houses. Another man broke away from his family group and joined me there and we stood together, looking out to sea.

'Do you think they appreciated it like we do? The view? Or do you think their lives were too hard for them to stop and think about it?' He voiced exactly what I had been thinking.

Scilly has one of the highest concentrations of prehistoric carns, entrance graves and villages in the country, and the vast majority, like Billy Idol on St Martin's, face out to sea. And on the tiny island of Nornour, there is a shrine to the Romano-Celtic goddess Sillina, whose name is thought to have inspired that of the Isles of Scilly. The celebrated historian and archaeologist of all things Cornish, Charles Thomas, believed Sillina may have been a particularly important god on the islands. It would make sense if that was the case. The people who lived here were at the mercy of a capricious sea, and of those who travelled across it too, and it is hard to believe they did not also see the sublime and the sacred on its face and in its depths.

'I can't imagine you'd look out from here and not feel that sense of beauty and awe,' the man continued, before returning to his family. 'No matter how long ago.'

Back on the clifftop, the wind was getting up and there were shadows on the sea's surface everywhere I looked, shapes that seemed, for a moment, to be fins or dolphins breaching before resolving themselves time and again into waves. Aside from these sea shadows, we saw no sign of the great beasts that live beneath the waves and Abby said we were unlikely to see anything out there now. Above a certain sea state it is difficult to see anything. Far, far out at sea, there were gannets, bright white against the dark clouds. I saw them in flashes of movement and in the explosions as they entered the water. And closer in, gulls appeared in right front of us, riding the updraught, coming level with us and eyeing us for a moment before veering off with the wind, souls glanced fleetingly. We recorded them on the survey sheet, the gulls and the gannets, before packing up our equipment and turning our backs on the sea again.

13

Songline Shaper

Beach art at Porthcurno

F ROM THIS FAR ABOVE, the figure on the tiny sand
bar below barely seems to be moving. Watch for long
enough though and you see he is walking in broad,
sweeping circles. Behind him, as he passes over the sand,
he leaves thin lines, curves and spirals, ellipses, a parabola,
concentric circles of the sort you see made by rain falling into
a still pool, the line of a wispy cloud on the horizon. Look
through a pair of binoculars and you see he is dragging a
metal rake behind him on the sand. It is hypnotic, meditative,
watching the creation of these patterns. A spiral becomes a
wave that rears, crests and curls in on itself as it approaches
land. Other lines settle themselves into the parallel curves
of an approaching set and yet others seem to stretch out
towards the horizon. His sand island sits in a sheltered bay,
an arm of outstretched rocks curved protectively around it.
The water around it shifts from deepest green to jade as the
tide retreats to its lowest point, as the shallowest water around
the drying sand drops off into a deeper channel. Watch for
long enough and you see the island itself changes shape. It
broadens and swells and takes on an oval shape in the bay,
like a brooch on an elegant coat.

On the falling tide at Pedn Voundr.

Couples and families swim across to the island from the beach or wade across at the shallowest part. When they emerge, some of them walk round the island's far edges, keeping their feet in the small waves that lap at the space that has opened up around the expanding pattern, not willing to step onto the canvas. They circumnavigate and stand at the island's far side, looking out off it towards the horizon. Others walk straight across the drawing, jumping or hopping as their paths intersect with the lines of the pattern. They come and go, come and go.

One woman pauses for a while after she has waded across from the beach and stepped into the drawing. She follows the lines the man has already made, as though she is following a thread he has laid out for her through a labyrinth. She does this for several minutes. Eventually, the man approaches her. You think she is going to leave but after a brief conversation the man hands her a rake that is lying on the sand nearby and she begins to fill in some of the gaps between two lines of a Fibonacci-like spiral.

The woman finishes the colouring in and waits at the edge of the huge spiral. It is unclear what she is waiting for until the man returns from where he has been working on the opposite side of the island and they talk again, though you are far too far away to make out anything they might say to one another. The man draws a connecting line from the shape on which she is standing to the next shape along and again she follows the path made by the rake, unwilling to step off it, and starts on another section of the drawing, filling in some of the smaller circles by raking them over. After 20 minutes or so, she breaks free of the lines that are already there and begins to create her own spiral, right on the edge of the island.

The woman eventually lays down her rake and wades back across to the beach and the artist is alone again. How can he keep the pattern in his head? Surely, he can't see what he has created from down there? He has been working for almost an hour now and the oval sandbank, surrounded by jade water is covered in patterns, as though tattooed. It looks celestial, like a star map or a map of the currents and tides carved onto a piece of bark like the Polynesian navigators would draw, or like a songline, a journey of the mind.

It has just gone midday and the tide is now at its lowest. The man stops, picks up his rakes and wades back across to the mainland. In another hour, the drawing will be gone, lost to the waves as the tide reclaims the tiny island.

I had received the text message out of the blue the night before. It was from the artist, Tony Plant, and read, 'Thinking of Porthcurno, tomorrow, low tide.' When the message came through, I was standing on the roof terrace outside my house, looking up at a blood moon that had risen above the valley, stark in the sky, bright and huge. I had been waiting for this text for months.

When I arrived, Tony was already there, sitting on a rock at the top of the cliff, watching the water below. I joined him and we sat in silence for a while, watching the patterns in the water just off the beach at Pedn Vounder, the last beach in the UK before the first in Bermuda if you were to trace a line directly ahead of us.

'See that patch of turbulence there? That's what we're watching,' he said after a while. I followed the line of his arm and made out an area of disturbed sea just offshore where the waves were more chaotic, butting up against one another. 'All that action there will fade out and hopefully there will be a line around the whole thing. I'm hoping it will make an oval. I've been waiting for this for ages. It will take an hour or two to make, and it will only last an hour or so once it's finished, but it takes years to plan. And even then, things can get in the way – weather, storms, lockdowns. You have to wait until everything lines up.'

He had been waiting for just the right combination of winds, tides and weather, the moon poised in just the right place, to create a sandbank of the shape and size for the artwork he had in mind for six years. And now we were sitting above the last beach in the country on the last of the low, low tides of the season, waiting to see if his prediction would come through. There was something beautifully obsessive, lunatic even, about the whole endeavour.

He asked me if I had seen the crazy moon the night before. 'Do you know why they call it a blood moon? I didn't know this, but according to my daughter's science teacher, the colour of it is the reflection of all the sunsets taking place across the world.'

The colours around the patch of turbulence shifted. The water in one particular area was much lighter now, the sand covered and uncovered as small waves ran across it in all directions. That particular shade of green, the one for which this beach is so photographed comes from the mica that crumbles off the cliffs. The sandbank that would later become Tony's canvas would be framed too by this green with a shadow on the back side of the shape and framed too by the waves bouncing back off the rocks.

Digging in his bag, he pulled out a small, white feather.

'I've been thinking about my dad recently,' he said, holding the feather up so it danced in the breeze. 'He died a couple of years ago. I was kicking around the house yesterday and this thing kept blowing around. We've always equated these loose feathers with people. We always say when we see them that it's my dad, or it's Alice's mum. And it is. It's following me round. I thought I'll take it down here and I'll drop it. It can go now, to where it needs to go. When I'm drawing, I get a lot of time to think about things. All I need to think about really is what's ahead, so I get a lot of time to remember things. Either that or I'm looking for signs. I might decide to stop at the next cracked mussel shell. That might be the signal to stop, change directions.'

As we watched, the waters receded further, revealing the smallest island, with ridged, puckered sand that began to dry almost immediately. That patch of drying sand, the first part of the island to appear, would be the last to go when the tide returned.

Shortly after, a young couple came into view far below us, swimming out from a point we could not see from where we were sitting. The man was out of the water first.

'A tenner says he's going to build a castle,' Tony said. 'Right there. Next to treading paths around the coast, it's the most natural thing in the world.'

I should have taken the bet, as he did not make a castle, though the couple strode around their tiny kingdom proprietorially and looked beautiful standing on the very edge staring out to sea for a while before getting back in and swimming out of view again.

This is what Tony watches – the paths people take to the sea. Several months before we had been walking on a different beach and he had pointed to the different people we came across and talked about the way they moved around the beach. A dog walker will take a totally different path to a metal detectorist, or a surfer or a beachcomber who has come down here to look for driftwood, he told me. Each of them has a different way of getting to the sea. Tony's work traces these desire lines, the hidden paths we take when we are drawn to the sea, though it also echoes the fault lines in the cliffs, the shapes of rock formations formed millennia ago, the patterns of approaching waves and those they make as they bounce back off the cliffs.

There are other lines at Pedn Vounder too – lines that are less visible. Tony pointed some of them out to me in the face of one of the cliffs besides where we sat. I could see nothing to begin with, though as I stared, two parallel lines emerged from the rocks, like shapes hidden within a magic eye puzzle, cables running parallel down the cliffs and into the sea. Once I could see them, I couldn't believe I had overlooked them, these two straight black lines in a landscape in which there were no other straight lines.

The cables we could see were part of the first cable connection from the UK to the rest of the world. Just a little further up the coast, there is a hut with labels of all the places the cables emerge: Gibraltar, India, Malta, the Americas. Although they were the fastest means of communication of their time, revolutionary technology that linked continents that until then had to rely on the packet ships for news, these cables were redundant now, the copper cable having long been superseded by fibre optics. Where we were sitting felt about as remote as it is possible to be in Cornwall, but Porthcurno is the site of what was once the most important telegraph station in the world, and although the cables we could see were now defunct, there was satisfaction to be had in the knowledge that the fibre optic cables that connect Britain to the world still run from Porthcurno, that this tiny corner of Cornwall connects the island to the rest of the world, much as it had when the packet ships sailing out of Falmouth connected England to its colonies from the time of the Stuarts, in the mid seventeenth century, through to the mid-nineteenth century. The first telegraph line was laid not long after the packet ships stopped sailing, in June 1870. This first cable linked England to India, a copper cable that snaked hundreds of miles across ocean and land. It was an epic feat of connection. I tried to get my head round the distances involved but it was dizzying.

Without warning, Tony jumped up, driven by some sign only he could see in the water below. He picked up two metal rakes lying in the grass, slung them across his shoulder and all but sprinted down the path, down the boulders that need to be navigated to reach the beach. A couple of minutes later, I watched as he waded across to the island, which was becoming longer and more oval-shaped by the minute.

Artist Tony Plant makes his first marks on the island beach.

As Tony started to create his huge sand drawing, I recalled something he told me about his work when we first met, clambering across the rocks of my local beach. It was a story about a father with two young daughters who happened to be walking along the cliffs one day as Tony was drawing on the sand below. He noticed that they stopped for a while to watch and later, when Tony had finished and came up onto the cliffs to look at his work from above, they were still there, the two girls wrapped up in their father's coat, leaning into him. The father did not talk about the work so much as the fact that seeing Tony there had slowed him and his daughters down for long enough to observe the tide go out and then come in again. It was something he had never done before, he said; he had never stopped to watch the progress of the tide, his children neither. He wouldn't forget it, he said, though Tony thought the thing he might not forget was that time he had spent with his daughters as much as the artwork itself or the watching of the tide. We all know this happens, this planetary breathing in and breathing out, twice a day, every day, forever – we are taught about it in school – though it is something we rarely stick around long enough to observe, and it would be easy to believe that it didn't happen if we never stopped to watch it happen.

Looking out to the horizon from here it would be easy to believe the sea went on forever, that it would take all we could throw at it and then some. It is the kind of thinking that got us to where we are now, the kind of thinking that runs along the lines that the seas are big enough to restore themselves, that they will continue to provide as they always have done, that the warning signs we are seeing now are blips or passing grumbles.

Many of the conversations I had with the disparate, far-flung tribe of ocean activists – marine biologists, conservationists and people deeply involved in the sea from sailors to swimmers, mermaids to surfers, wreckers to artists – turned inevitably to the climate crisis, to concerns about the health of the seas they love. It is the story of our time and everywhere I travelled it seemed there was a growing awareness that we are all caught in a narrative that will define our lives and those of our children and their children. It is the songline we will leave to them.

When I talked to the marine biologist, Heather Koldewey, sitting on opposite ends of the oversize paddleboard just off St Michael's Mount, I asked her if she still considered herself as incurable an optimist as she had in a talk she gave some ten years' before. She told me that a frustrated optimist would be more accurate now.

'On the plus side the ocean is being talked about more than it ever was,' she said as we peered down into the shallow waters through her bathyscope – a tube with lenses at either end for us to peer beneath the surface – she had strapped to the board.

'It makes the news and people are relating to it whether they're from a coastal place or not. Ten years ago it was difficult to get anyone to even talk about the ocean. The biggest frustration I feel now is the big stuff that feels out of control – it feels really fragile. You hear about so-called ambition around climate change and it's just a lot of talk. You need that big change at the top – action requires a different way of thinking. It requires us to act in a way that we've never done before. And that worries me. There were something like 35,000 papers on climate change in 2020, so it's not like the science isn't there.'

Scientists and campaigning organizations like Surfers Against Sewage are calling this the ocean decade, a chance to act before too many irreversible changes take place. To Heather, the phrase ocean decade is not just semantics, it is not just another piece of ocean branding, but a meaningful, important message.

'That's all we've got,' she said. 'That's it. If we're going to turn things around that's great, as we've defined that period of time. But we don't have the luxury to say we didn't quite meet it or to say let's push it back another ten years. Policymakers have been doing that for years about all the targets they've agreed to. We can't say, "Oh, we only managed to protect one per cent of the oceans instead of ten – let's give ourselves another ten years to get to four per cent."'

We are living in the last few moments at which it is possible to alter the course of our planet, and of the seas over which we have, through our ancestors' and our actions and inaction, inherited stewardship. From high on the rocks above Pedn Vounder, I hope that, like the synchronized swimmers I watched in the lido in Penzance, we are able to change our behaviours, to begin to undo the damage rather than continuing along a course that seems destined to end up in a place that no one wants to imagine.

Jeffrey Levinton, in his afterword to a reissue of Rachel Carson's seminal book, *The Sea Around Us*, wrote that for millennia, seafarers had battled the oceans and that, most of the time, the seas had come out on top. Now, he asserted, we have conquered the seas, though at what price? It would, he wrote, take a new kind of strength to save the seas we have trashed.

We will have to return to the seas and with a zeal to undo the damage we have wrought on it that matches the zeal with which we set out on ships to explore and conquer. He penned this call to action in 1989, over three decades ago, and he was by no means the first. We have some catching up to do.

Another day on the water, this one in early autumn, sitting on my longboard just off the beach with hundreds of other activists – surfers, sailors, kayakers, paddleboarders and swimmers – during a protest paddle out, I felt a glimmer of hope. We shouted and splashed on the water and the noise was tremendous. Similar protests were going on across Cornwall and across the country and in other countries across the world too. Surely, it would be impossible to ignore this kind of noise, to ignore this kind of sea swell?

The paddle out has been a worldwide symbol of the surfing community for decades. Like so much surf culture, we imported the ritual from Hawaii via the United States. In the small villages on the north coast, where I live, it's still a big deal, especially when a well-known surfer dies. Friends will paddle out at their local surf spot, beyond the breaking waves, and form a circle in which they will remember the life and waves of the dead surfer. It's an act of respect and remembrance, but it is also, in its solemnity and ritual, one of defiance, and has been used to protest the destruction of reefs and to demand action on oceanic pollution. No one there wanted to have to do this again to mourn the death of the seas, though it was a subtext of the paddle out and within the shouts there was real frustration, real fear too, a call for real change.

Tony stopped dead on low tide and waded back across. He returned to the sheltered spot on the cliffs and we sat in silence again for a few moments at still water, the earth's momentary breath hold before it exhales again.

I put the thought to him that the whole thing felt like a meditation to me, the grand artwork below a kind of mandala.

Lines taking shape.

'From up here, maybe,' Tony replied, still sweating from the exertion. The island looked perfectly flat from up here, though it was just the distance that had flattened the canvas. What I thought looked effortless was actually a strenuous trudging up and down of sand ridges.

An elderly woman stopped to talk to us. She lived just a few hundred metres away, in Porthcurno, and walked past this beach every day, though, she said, she didn't often stop for that long, and not to look at that sandbank. It had caused her to pause, to look at a familiar place with new eyes.

'When you're drawing in the landscape, the idea isn't to get people to look at the drawing there, it's to move the eye across the surface to somewhere else, to a natural form. It's like skimming stones. The thing I create is pointing towards something, drawing the gaze towards something else. I'm drawing to that,' Tony said and pointed towards the outstretched ridge of rocks. 'I want their eyes to bounce off it to these hard-edged, fractured granite rocks over there. My shapes are soft. They won't look a million miles off the structures and patterns the waves are making, the lines of the tidal flow, the tracks across the land, the cracks in the granite, the meandering paths of the people we see walking around the beach, swimming off shore and the lines the birds are making as they cross the sky above it.'

Another figure approached and Tony waved her over. It was the woman who had taken up the second rake for a while, who I had watched fill in some of the blank spaces. As she approached, Tony told me the reason she stopped and waited for him to come over to her was that she felt she couldn't walk off what she called 'the path'.

'I had to draw her a shape from one place to another. I had to draw her a bridge between shapes, so she could walk it.'

Lisa, it turned out, was only visiting. She lives on the Somerset Levels, where it often floods and she had come down to the far south-west to rest and reset. She talked to us about the healing power of being by the sea, the strength she took away from it, and I took away from the conversation a sense that she was storing up memories for later.

'You wouldn't get a conversation like that in a gallery,' Tony commented as she walked away. And it's true. We are drawn to the sea because we can take so much away from it when we leave and there is a limitless amount it can give, though all the signs we have suggest that the health of these seas we love is conditional on our stewardship, on us giving it a chance to bounce back, to regroup and replenish.

We have cut up the land with roads and paths, we have criss-crossed it with telegraph wires, with motorways, canals and railway lines. The sea does not hold these traces. It asks of us that we make our own way there, and once we are there, that we make our own way across it, within it, above it. No boat covers exactly the same course twice. Even the signs of our approach to it and departure from it will fade. After a few hours the incoming tide will cover our tracks and the next time we go down to the sea, we will have to decide on which path we take afresh. The sea was not subject to enclosure, like the land, parcelled and fenced off. Of course, in some senses it is not quite as open as it might seem. Most of the UK's foreshore – the area between mean low and mean high tide – is technically owned by the Crown Estate or private landlords. However, though there is no general right to roam on beaches, this has rarely been tested and probably for good reason. We go down to the sea for a taste of freedom, a taste of the borderless and expansive. I wouldn't want to be the authority that tried to challenge that.

So, as you go down to the sea you take your own path. If you surf, you have your eyes on the swell, the rip, the points at which the wave breaks, its power and direction. If you are a beachcomber or rock pooler, you linger in the intertidal zone, that space that opens up for just a few hours a day. If you are a coastal walker or runner, you keep the sea to one side, put your head down when squalls blow in from where they have been brewing out at sea and keep going. If you are a fisher, you watch for the roiling mass of herrings from the cliffs or for where the gannets dive, or you trust your intuition as to where and when you should lower a line into the water. If you are a photographer or a painter, you watch the shifting light, and if you are a diver, you breathe deeply, fill your lungs from the belly up through the chest to the throat, and surrender to the water as you dive down into the profound blue.

The sea is your teacher, your mentor. It reminds you, time and again, by its changing moods, its endless mutability, that you are in control of little and that realization, in itself, is a liberation. Whether you lose yourself in the moment of timelessness as you surf the glassy face of a wave – or in the case of those who are able to, drop into the green room of a barrelling one – or mess around in the foam alone or with your children, or walk or sail a section of the coast, or watch the dawn rise as you float offshore or sit on the cliffs, what are you doing once you reach the sea except momentarily renouncing the ticking of the clock? And when you return you are changed by it, refreshed and renewed.

The land, apportioned, allotted and allocated as it has been ever since enclosure, is the realm of the clock, whereas at sea you step outside of your time-bound life and, for a few moments, experience deep time. Instead of grappling with endless deadlines, racing against a clock that will always, in the end, win, you experience respite from time in the rhythm of the waves. And that, perhaps, is what the sea is – respite from time. It is everything the land is not.

The tide is coming in again. You have stopped for long enough to experience the world breathing out and breathing in again, the slow inhalation and exhalation that takes place twice a day and has taken place twice a day ever since the world began. In another hour or so, the artwork below, which causes you to grin to your bones when you look on its exuberant, lunatic, looping lines, will have completely disappeared and when the island emerges again tomorrow, it will have been wiped clean. The only way in which these invisible pathways exist now are in the memory of those who happened to be walking along the cliffs on this particular morning and those who found their way to the sea. And in photographs: by the time that temporarily tattooed island has gone, there's a fair chance someone watching will have pinged a photograph of it to someone else on the far side of the planet.

You find yourself wishing that all your interactions with the sea could be like this, and with the land too, impermanent and fleeting, that you could be caught off your guard by the profound more often. You have longed for a sea change, to be transformed into something rich and strange and whether you realize it or not, that change has occurred, and you carry it with you as you turn your back on the sea again until the next time. You carry with you the sing of the shore, *mordros*, the term the Cornish use for the grinding sound of the sea. Later, you will mistake that *mordros* for that of the traffic passing by outside your window, like the protagonist of Grace Nichols's poem, 'Island Man'. For now though, you leave the water's edge with the feeling that the trace we leave on the coast and on the sea should be no more than a line carved into the face of a wave or a wake trailing behind a rudder, and you resolve to do everything in your power to protect it, this sacred space.

The completed canvas, Pedn Vounder.

A GLOSSARY OF SEA WORDS

Bathophobia The fear of depths and in particular the fear of deep water.

Bathyscope Sometimes called an aquascope or a marine telescope, a bathyscope is a simple device used to see underwater and observe marine wildlife without getting wet. Formed of a tube or cone with a glass or plastic lens at each end, one end is lowered into the water, often from the side of a boat, and the viewer peers into the underwater world through the upper lens.

Beamer A beamer or beam trawler is a type of outrigger trawler. It uses a tower with a strong outrigger boom on each side, each towing a beam trawl.

Birch bark Rolls of bark from birch trees are often found washed up on the tideline, having been carried on the tides across the Atlantic from the forests of the northern United States and Canada. In Shetland, these rolls of bark are sometimes known as Loki's candles, an allusion to Shetland's Viking history, and they were once known for their fire-lighting properties.

Bow thrusters Small propellers fitted to the bow and/or stern of a ship in order to manoeuvre the ship in the close quarters of a dock or harbour. In particular, bow thrusters are useful for docking.

*Bremming** The old Cornish term for the glow caused by a school of mackerel as it disturbs phosphorescent blooms.

By-the-wind-sailor The common name for *Vellella velella*, an oval-shaped bluey-purple colonial hydroid. By-the-wind-sailors have a small sail which catches the wind and propels them across the ocean. They are truly strange animals, or rather, collections of animals. Like the Portuguese man o' war, they are made up of a colony of much smaller animals. Also like the Portuguese man o' war, they are often mistaken for jellyfish, as they have tentacles that hang beneath them, which they use to catch prey. They are found in their hundreds, washed up on the shore after storms, often accompanied by violet sea snails, which get their distinctive shell colouring through eating the by-the-wind-sailors. Little is known about their lives on the open ocean.

Cetaphobia   The intense and irrational fear of whales.

Charybdis and Scylla   Mentioned in Homer's *Odyssey* and Ovid's *Metamorphoses*, Charybdis and Scylla were monsters from Greek mythology who guarded the narrow passage of water at Messina, between mainland Italy and the island of Sicily. Charybdis, the daughter of Pontus and Gaia (the first gods of the sea and earth) is thought to be the personification of a whirlpool, and Scylla, a sea monster with 12 legs and six heads on long necks is thought to have derived from a dangerous underwater ledge or reef that might tear open a ship's hull. To be 'between Charybdis and Scylla' is to be caught between a rock and a hard place.

Cowsherny*   An old Cornish term for a sea the colour of cow dung.

Cthulhu   The most famous fictional monster created by the writer of weird fiction H. P. Lovecraft, Cthulhu was introduced in the short story 'The Call of Cthulhu', in which the monster was described as being 'of vaguely anthropoid outline, but with an octopus-like head whose face was a mass of feelers, a scaly, rubbery-looking body, prodigious claws on hind and fore feet, and long, narrow wings behind'. A kind of agglomeration of sea-based anxieties, in the story the deeply troubling (and purposefully difficult to pronounce) Cthulhu is hibernating in an underwater city in the South Pacific.

Cymophobia   The intense and abnormal fear of waves and sea swells, and a phobia closely related to aquaphobia, the broader fear of water.

Dive reflex   All mammals, including humans, are born with the diving response, or mammalian dive reflex, which allows us to dive underwater for extended periods. It describes a series of reactions that occur when the face is submerged in cold water. First described in the late 1930s, the dive reflex consists of apnea (the cessation of breathing), bradycardia (slowing of the heart rate), and peripheral vasoconstriction (the narrowing of blood vessels in the peripheries which allows oxygen-rich blood to be redirected towards the body's core). It is strongest in sea mammals, such as Weddell seals, which can dive for up to 80 minutes on a single breath, to depths of 2,300 feet, and in humans it is strongest in babies. While the reflex weakens as we age, it can be strengthened with practise. In those who freedive, there are two other markers of the dive reflex: blood shift, in which blood is shunted from the extremities to the vital organs and chest cavity, occupying the space created by the compression of the lungs as the diver reaches depths at which the pressure is much increased; and at depth, splenic contraction takes place, in which the spleen kicks out additional oxygen rich blood into circulation.

Dredger   A boat towing a dredge, a heavy steel frame that forms a scoop and which is dragged along the floor of the sea, collecting bottom dwelling fish and crustacea. Some dredges have teeth called tynes along the bottom side which rake through the mud or sand on the sea floor before being hauled back to the surface with the catch. They are often used to catch scallops, mussels, oysters, clams and crabs, and are profoundly damaging to the marine environment. In some areas, there are specific rules around dredging, for example in the Fal Estuary in Cornwall, where oysters can only be dredged by sail or oar, the last fishery in the world where this is practised.

Drethan*   Old Cornish for a sandy patch at the bottom of the sea.

Dumha thuama**   The sound the sea makes against the sand dunes (The Mullet Peninsula, County Mayo).

Finfolk   In the folklore of Orkney, finfolk are shapeshifters who live half their lives underwater and half on land. They wreck boats and abduct fishermen and women, taking them down to the deeps or to their hidden island as unwilling husbands and wives. Resembling humans, they can be distinguished up close by the presence of their fins. Unlike the selkies of Celtic mythology, sorcerous and cunning finfolk are vengeful, malevolent and best avoided.

Fisherman's kisses   Net mending offshore tends to result in many tiny offcuts which are jettisoned or wash overboard and which wash up on beaches. Often taking the form of an X, with a knot in the middle, they are one of the most recognizable and common forms of marine litter around the South West coast. In 2020 and 2021, members of the conservation group, Rame Peninsula Beach Care, collected over 10,000 fisherman's kisses in just a few visits to beaches in the area.

Foxy*   A deceptive lull between storms (Old Cornish).

Glan*   A synonym of bremming (Old Cornish).

Gleo**   The sound of a loud sea, similar to that of a loud machine and which often precedes bad weather (The Mullet Peninsula, County Mayo).

Guskins*   Parts of the sea that are in the lee of the land and therefore sheltered (Old Cornish).

Hurricanes and storms (naming)   Weather scientists around the world meet regularly to decide on the names large storms, such as hurricanes, cyclones and typhoons, will be given, making them easier to discuss in news and weather bulletins. In most parts of the world storms are given people's names, though in the western North Pacific and North Indian Oceans, the names of flowers, animals, birds and trees are used. Only large storms, expected to cause damage, are named. Each year, the naming of storms is reset, starting at A and proceeding in alphabetic order (though Q, U, X, Y and Z are not included), alternating between boys' names and girls' names. When the 21 letters are exhausted, as occurred in 2021, a supplementary list of names is used.

Jörmungandr   The world serpent of Norse mythology, Jörmungandr was thrown into the ocean as a baby and grew so large that it circled the world, gripping its own tail in its mouth. In the myth, when Jörmungandr lets go of its tail, Ragnarök, the end of the world, will arrive.

Left   A surfing term for a wave that, from the surfer's perspective, breaks to the left. Looking at it from the beach, the wave will appear to be breaking to the right.

Lung squeeze   Lung squeeze (alternatively lung barotrauma or thoracic squeeze) is an injury sustained by some freedivers, and is caused by the rapid changes in lung pressure that take place at depth. At 30 metres below the surface, the lungs shrink to about a quarter of their size at the surface. During the dive, the increase in pressure causes air spaces in the body to compress and in cases of lung squeeze the lungs may collapse or tear.

Marine megafauna   The catchall term for the giant animals of the sea, from the blue whale which can reach lengths of over 100 feet, to oarfish, Southern elephant seals, giant clams, Caribbean giant barrel sponges, giant ocean manta rays with wingspans of up to 23 feet, giant squid, the giant Pacific octopus, and Japanese spider crabs.

Monofin   A single broad fin used for freediving, which attaches to the diver's feet. The diver uses a technique called the dolphin kick, which uses the whole body to propel them through the water. Used as an alternative to stereo or bi-fins.

Mordros   Cornish is one of the few languages to have a word specifically for the sound of the sea or, in some translations, the sound of the surf. Other languages that have a specific word for this sound include Polynesian and Greek.

Narcosis   While nitrogen narcosis, the symptoms of which mimic alcoholic intoxication is more often associated with traditional diving, the same principle applies in freediving. Occurring when nitrogen builds up in the brain, divers can experience failures in logical thinking, drunkenness, tunnel vision, euphoria or fear, and eventually a gradual loss of consciousness.

No-Limits   No-Limits freediving is a discipline in which the diver descends using whatever method they like, often a weighted sled, and can ascend using inflated vests or balloons. Using this method, it is possible for divers to achieve great depth, though as this discipline has resulted in several deaths, it is banned in most competitions.

The world record-holding no-limits freediver, Herbert Nitsch, when attempting to beat his own record, achieved a depth of over 253 metres, though suffered severe injuries and retired from competition afterwards.

Nurdle   Lentil-sized plastic pellets, billions of which are used each year to make almost all of our plastic products, and many of which wash up onto beaches across the world. They are among the most common beach contaminants and have been found in the digestive systems of fish, seabirds and crustaceans and have shown to cause ulceration in animal's stomachs, as well as preventing them from eating other foods, leading to starvation and death.

Pilly*   A sea floor that is, in part, rocky with seaweed and in part sandy (Old Cornish).

Pitted   Surfing slang for the experience of riding the hollow centre of a barrelling wave. Getting pitted is considered a peak surfing experience.

Prinkle*   The sparkle of phosphorescence (Old Cornish).

Right   A surfing term for a wave that, from the surfer's perspective, breaks to the right. Looking at it from the beach, the wave will appear to be breaking to the left.

Ro-Ro   A truncated name for roll-on, roll-off ferries, which have in-built ramps for the loading and unloading of cars and trucks. Ro-Ros are often used on short crossings, such as the English Channel between England and France.

Sea beans   Also known as drift seeds, sea beans are seeds that wash up on beaches, having travelled hundreds or thousands of miles from where they originated and often years or decades later. Many wash up on the coasts of Cornwall and Devon from as far afield as Brazil, the Caribbean and Central America. For some beachcombers, the smooth, tactile seeds are considered talismanic and in the past they have been associated with witchcraft and used as amulets for childbirth. In her memoir, *Held by the Sea*, Jane Darke describes growing a vine from a nickarnut she and her husband Nick found on the beach, which reached 6 feet in six months.

Scranner   The term used in Orkney for a wrecker or beachcomber.

Seech*   An Old Cornish term for the foaming edge of a wave as it makes land, or that of the edge of the sea as it inundates the land at high tide.

Spindrift   Spray blown from the crest of a wave.

Stranach**   The murmuring made by the moving of the sea into and out of a cove (Achill Island, County Mayo).

Superior mirage   A superior mirage, or *Fata Morgana* (named after the sorceress from Arthurian legend) is an illusion of the sea in which an object on the horizon, often a ship, appears to float above the horizon line. One explanation for sightings of the folkloric *Flying Dutchman* is that it is a superior mirage sighting.

Tuaimneacha**   The noise of powerful, ceaseless waves against the rocks (Magheroarty, County Donegal).

Uaigneas an chladaigh**   The sense of loneliness felt on the shore, or the sensation of the presence of people long dead (The Mullet Peninsula, County Mayo).

Umibōzu   A humanoid sea spirit in Japanese mythology and one of the yōkai or folkloric spirits. Umibōzu, which translates as Sea Monk, appears to sailors in calm seas, heralding a storm in the form of a beautiful woman, a hairy whale or a giant black head rising from beneath the sea.

Violet sea snails   Also known as the bubble raft snail, these sea snails spend their lives at sea, feeding on Portuguese man o' war and by-the-wind-sailors. They are entirely blind and float, ingeniously, by means of a raft of bubble-filled mucus which they use to create a kind of raft.

Wrecker   The Cornish term for a beachcomber or for someone who collects from the beach items washed up from wrecked ships. In popular legend, encouraged by a few writers in the eighteenth and nineteenth centuries, wreckers lured ships onto the coast, employing false lights on the cliffs to trick sailors into running their ships aground, and though there are a few unsubstantiated accounts of wrecking in this way and a law passed in 1735 that made it illegal to make false lights, there is no evidence that this actually ever happened and no one was ever prosecuted for the crime.

---

* These words were collected by R. Morton Nance and are described in more depth in his 1963 *A Glossary of Cornish Sea-Words*.

** Originally described in Manchán Magan's 2020 project *Sea Tamagotchi*.

NOTES

EPIGRAPH

p. 9. The epigraph is a quotation from the documentary, *The Wrecking Season* by Jane Darke, a film that follows her husband, the playwright Nick over the course of a stormy winter as he scours the beaches of Cornwall's north coast and records his finds. These words represent Nick's final lines of the documentary, which was made shortly before he died, and the extract is used with Jane's kind permission.

STRANDLINE GLEANER

p. 15. *Just a day before, the M6 buoy...* The Marine Institute M6 buoy, situated about 200 nautical miles west of Ireland recorded the 30-metre wave, the highest wave ever recorded in Irish waters, at 0300 on 30 October 2020. vis.marine.ie/dashboards/#/dashboards/weather?buoy=M6&measurement=Hmax

p. 16. *...the storm namers had already turned to the Greek alphabet...* The standard naming of storms large enough to warrant a name in the Atlantic begins each year with the letter A and follows through to W, often using people's names. In 2020 there were so many storms of this calibre, one of the many worrying results of climate change, that meteorologists turned to Greek letters. The practice of naming storms is designed to make communications about them easier, though in March 2021, meteorologists ended the practice of using Greek letters, stating that storms named Zeta, Eta and Theta sounded so similar that it got in the way of effective communication. From 2021, a new supplemental list of names has been used, and a similar new back-up list for the Eastern Pacific has been developed too. Source: Associated Press, 'Bye Alpha, Eta: Greek alphabet ditched for hurricane names' Seth Borenstein, 17 March 2021.

p. 19. *Moments after, recalling the lecture I'd been given...* As part of the Svalbard Environmental Protection Act, all traces of human activity dating from before 1946 are automatically legally protected, including the skeletal remains at whale and walrus slaughter sites and artefacts associated with spring guns for polar bears, and must not be removed from where they currently sit. www.regjeringen.no/en/dokumenter/svalbard-environmental-protection-act/id173945/

p. 22.   *Cornwall has the longest shoreline…* It is technically impossible to measure the length of any coastline – the coastline paradox, defined by Lewis Fry Richardson and Benoit Mandelbrot, which results from the fractal properties of coastlines, means it is not possible to define a length, as the measurement would continue to increase the more accurate the measurement device used was. However, a rough measure of the length of coastline by walking has Cornwall at 1086 kilometres, with the county of Essex coming in second at 905 kilometres.

p. 22.   *… 'so besieged … with the ocean that it forms a demi-island in an island'…* R. Carew, *Survey of Cornwall,* 1603.

p. 23.   *…while the term wreckers brings to mind false lights…* Bella Bathurst, in her book *The Wreckers*, discusses the difficulty of substantiating claims of false lights or 'active wrecking' and, like many commentators and historians, she casts doubts on claims of ships wrecked by false lights, though she suggests that the temptation to actively wreck in times of hardship may have been strong. Bella Bathurst, *The Wreckers: A story of killing seas, false lights and plundered ships*, Harper Perennial, 2005, pp. 19-26.

p. 23.   *The first recorded beachcombers…* Herman Melville, in his possibly autobiographical – book, *Omoo* (1847), refers to beachcombers on South Pacific islands, though the first explanation of the term appears in Chamber's *Journal of Popular Literature, Science, and Arts*, in the 5 February 1881 edition, claiming it as a word of American origin and applying to those whose occupation is to pick up whatever the long waves rolling in from the ocean wash up. Early depictions of beachcombers are almost always of male Europeans, often castaways or deserters, who found they needed, or in some cases chose, to find their food and living along the shoreline.

p. 24.   *When Hawker arrived there…* Much of Hawker's work in his parish at Morwenstow was based around the proper burial of those who died at sea on this dangerous stretch of coast. Hawker describes wreckers and the practise of wrecking in his book, *Footprints of Former Men in Far Cornwall* (1870), in which he writes 'My people were a mixed multitude of smugglers, wreckers, and dissenters of various hue.' Hawker alleges the use of false or 'treacherous' lights in this book, though he gives no specific account of the practice. However, some have suggested that Hawker was not always a reliable witness, and that his use of hearsay clouds things. C.E. Byles, in the introduction to the 1903 edition, wrote, '[Hawker] never lets facts, or the absence of them, stand in the way of his imagination.'

p. 24.   *Though, technically, everything that washes up on the shores…* In answer to a question raised in the House of Commons in 2009 about who owns the foreshore (Hansard, 10 February 2009, column 1847W), the government replied, 'The Dutchy of Cornwall owns all the Isles of Scilly foreshore and the majority of the foreshore in Cornwall,' with Dutchy ownership extending to the Mean High Water mark.

p. 29.   *...the eighteenth-century treasure hunter Chunosuke Matsuyama...* The story of Chunosuke Matsuyama is widely told, including in the news article for National Geographic: 'Oldest Message in Bottle: Behind History's Famous Floating Notes', Jeremy Berlin, 20 September 2012. www.nationalgeographic.com/science/article/120918-oldest-message-in-a-bottle-science-history-messages

p. 30.   In his 1972 Shell Book of Beachcombing... Tony Soper, *The Shell Book of Beachcombing* (David and Charles, 1972). I originally came across this quote in the essay, 'Gleaning and Dreaming on Car Park Beach', Humanities, 2 April, 2018.

p. 34.   *...I had flicked to the news pages...* According to the International Organisation for Migration in Switzerland, between 2018 and 2021 at least 52 migrants drowned in the English Channel while attempting to reach the UK.

p. 34.   *Two of Rasul Iran Nezhad and Shiva Mohammad Panahi's children...* Source: 'Four Iranians who died crossing Channel were part of same family', Michael Safi, Akhtar Mohammad Makoii and Jamie Grierson, the *Guardian*, 28 October 2020.

p. 34.   *Eleven containers lost overboard in the Bristol Channel...* The incident, reported on 20 October 2020, involved 11 containers lost overboard from an unidentified containership close to Land's End, causing a hazard to ships in the Bristol Channel. One of the containers washed up at Bucks Mill in North Devon and a second near Breaksea Point. Source: 'British Authorities Search for Containers Overboard in Bristol Channel', The Maritime Executive, 27 October 2020. www.maritime-executive.com/article/british-authorities-search-for-container-overboard-in-bristol-channel

p. 34.   *...the plastic that washes in is not the biggest problem...* According to Surfers Against Sewage, our seas currently contain approximately 51 trillion microscopic pieces of plastic, amounting to 269,000 tons. SAS reports that one in three fish caught now contains plastic. Source: www.sas.org.uk/our-work/plastic-pollution/plastic-pollution-facts-figures/

ISLAND FISHER

p. 39.   *The idol has watched over the boats...* Historians and archaeologists, Ashbee and Thomas originally believed the stone to be Romano-British, about 2,000 years old, though they later revised their estimate later to 4,000–5,000 years old, believing it more likely that it is a Neolithic or Bronze Age statue. Source: 'Scilly's statue-menhir rediscovered' by Paul Ashbee and Charles Thomas in *Antiquity*, vol. 64, 1990, pp. 571-75.

p. 39.   *It has watched over the incursion of the seas that transformed...* At the lowest tides, it is possible to walk between some of the islands of Scilly and the circuitous routes taken by the shallow draft tripper boats between the islands speaks to the shallowness of the seas. The Romans referred to the area as *Scillonia Insula*, indicating, possibly, a single island. Though rising sea levels around AD 400–500 are thought to have caused Ennor's split into an archipelago, as recently as the time of Henry I, most of the islands are thought to have been joined. Source: Robert Duck, *This Shrinking Land: Climate Change and Britain's Coasts*, Edinburgh University Press, 2019, pp. 14-15.

p. 41.   *On the Isles of Scilly tourism accounts for 85 per cent of the local economy...* Source: duchyofcornwall.org/newton-park-estate.html

p. 45.   *He was, it turned out, the Canadian friend Keith had mentioned...* According to the Marine Life Information Network, conger eels can grow up to 2.75-metres long, making Keith and his friend's claims possible if not probable.

p. 47.   *In 1860, Sir Walter Besant wrote...* 'There is a shipwreck story belonging to every rock of Scilly, and to many there are several shipwrecks.' Walter Besant, *Armorel of Lyonesse*, 1890.

p. 48.   *...the Western Rocks were inaccurately located on charts written before 1750...* Bella Bathurst notes in *The Wreckers* that the whole of the Scillonian archipelago was often depicted as being 10 to 15 miles further north of its actual position in charts made before this date. Bella Bathurst, *The Wreckers*, 2005, *op. cit.* pp. 122-23.

p. 48.   *crisscrossed like Jenga blocks off Thicasus Ledge...* Thickasus Ledge, or Lethergus Ledge is another example of a site named differently by different families on Scilly.

p. 48.   *...Jof's great-grandfather, Steven Lewis Hicks...* In a confusing quirk of island life, there are several families with the name Hicks on St Agnes. The majority of eleven Hicks men who were on the Agnes lifeboat that went out to the Lawson were of a different branch of the family to Jof's.

p. 48.   *The* Lawson, *the largest schooner ever built...* There are several slightly conflicting accounts of the events that followed the wreck of the Lawson. For this retelling, I consulted a variety of sources including John Hicks's *An Absolute Wreck: The Loss of the Thomas W. Lawson*, Scotforth Books, 2015, and Thomas Hall's *The T. W. Lawson: The Fate of the World's Only Seven-Masted Schooner*, The History Press, 2006. It is worth noting, especially in light of the later discussion of the wreck of the *Torrey Canyon*, that the wreck of the *Lawson* represents what is almost certainly the first example of an oil tanker wreck.

p. 48.   *...the six-oared* Slippen... *Slippen* is still in service, though of a different kind. She is now raced by gig crews on St Mary's.

p. 49.   *Although the last recorded gig rescue was...* The last recorded rescue by a gig boat gook place in 1955 when the *Sussex* gig from Bryher, Scilly, helped to rescue the crew of the Panamanian steamship *Mando*, which had gone aground in fog. Source: John Clandillion-Baker, 'The Pilot Gigs of Cornwall and The Scilly Isles', *The Pilot*, Autumn 2007, No. 291.

p. 49. *Jof was born on St Agnes, though...* Most of the inhabited islands have a small primary school and St Mary's, the largest, has a secondary school, though all tertiary education involves moving to the mainland.

p. 51. *...'to send a wreck before morning'...* Robert Heath, in his 1750 book, *A Natural and Historical Account of the Isles of Scilly*, mentions the well as a source of ritual activities and alludes to the practice of appealing to the saint to draw wrecks towards the shores of St Agnes.

p. 55. *As the American marine biologist, Sylvia Earle put it...* Earle has reiterated this quote and quotes like it several different times in several ways, though I first came across it through a tweet she put out on 1 August 2019.

p. 56. *act as a kind of smokescreen for the bigger problem...* The nets to which I refer here are those of the biggest trawlers, those that are more than 80 metres long, with nets the size of a sports stadium, and which catch indiscriminately. In contrast to the small fishing boats many of us imagine when we think about the fishing fleets, these boats can catch and process 250 tons of fish each day.

ROCK POOL PILGRIM

p. 61. *...no one really understands what causes the moon illusion...* The moon illusion is the name given to the trick our brain plays on us that makes the moon appear to be larger when it is rising or setting. There is still no convincing scientific explanation for why this is the case. Source: solarsystem.nasa.gov/news/1191/the-moon-illusion-why-does-the-moon-look-so-big-sometimes/

p. 61. *...or the fact that your bike stays upright when you are in motion...* It sounds improbable, but physicists do not yet have a full answer to the question of why some nuts rise to the top of a bag of mixed nuts, and why a bicycle is stable when in motion. www.newscientist.com/article/mg22730370-400-how-does-a-bicycle-stay-upright/

p. 62. *Richard Carew in his 1602 survey claimed the bizarre catches...* R. Carew of Antonie, *The Survey of Cornwall*, 1602.

p. 62. *I like the description that surrealist painter Ithell Colquhoun gave...* Ithell Colquhoun, *The Living Stones*, Peter Owen Publishers, 2016, p. 145.

p. 67. *He was on honeymoon on St Martin's in March 1967...* The descriptions of the *Torrey Canyon* disaster are taken from a range of contemporaneous and after the fact news articles, including: Adam Vaughn's article, 'Torrey Canyon disaster – the UK's worst ever oil spill 50 years on', the *Guardian*, 18 March 2017, and Bethan Bell and Mario Cacciottolo's article, 'Torrey Canyon oil spill: The day the sea turned black', BBC News, 17 March 2017. Among the most damning indictments of the fallout from the *Torrey Canyon* oil spill were the findings of a 1968 report on the disaster by the Marine Biological Society, which concluded, 'We are progressively making a slum of nature.'

p. 69. *In the documentary,* The Wrecking Season... *The Wrecking Season*, director Jane Darke, Boatshed Films, 2004.

p. 69. *These creatures, like the St Piran's hermit crab...* The St Piran's crab
        (*Clibanarius erythropus*) almost entirely disappeared from UK shorelines
        after the *Torrey Canyon* oil spill. The hermit crab with its equally sized
        claws, in contrast to other hermit crabs, and its distinctive black and
        white eyes, was given its common name in 2016 after a public vote on
        BBC Springwatch, shortly after it was rediscovered. In the legend, St
        Piran, Cornwall's patron saint, was tied to a millstone by the Irish and
        thrown into stormy seas, though as he entered the waters, they becalmed
        and he floated across the Irish Sea to Perranzabuloe beach in Cornwall,
        where he became a hermit.

DEPTH PLUMBER

p. 80. *Incidentally, among Lovecraft's many fears...* H.P. Lovecraft, *H.P.
        Lovecraft: The Complete Fiction*, Barnes & Noble, 2011. A long list of
        H.P. Lovecraft's fears appeared in an article by Lucy Sante, published
        in the *New York Review* in October 2006, titled 'The Heroic Nerd'. The
        extensive list of the author's terrors includes invertebrates, temperatures
        below freezing, caves, old age, dreams, gases, whistling and brittle
        textures, as well as Lovecraft's well-documented xenophobia and racism.
        Sante concludes that a list of things Lovecraft was not frightened of
        would probably be shorter.

p. 81. *The watery areas on the edge of charts in the Middle Ages...* Charts such
        as Ortelius's 1570 *Theatrum Orbis Terrarum* depicted imagined sea
        monsters sinking ships and mermaids. Contrary to popular belief, the
        phrase 'Here be dragons' was rarely used on charts, appearing only on
        the 1504 Hunt-Lenox Globe (and here it appears as the Latin phrase,
        'HC SVNT DRACONES') and its prototype, the Ostrich Egg Globe.
        The Fra Mauro Map of 1450 shows an island of dragons, an imaginary
        island in the Atlantic, and an animal resembling a dragon appears on
        Oluas Magnus's 1539 *Carta Marina*, a map of Scandinavia. A whole
        other area of interest for which there was no space in this book is the
        practice of drawing mythical or phantom islands onto charts, which
        often speaks of a spiritual aspect to our relationships with the sea
        and which is explored in depth in Malachy Tallack's *The Undiscovered
        Islands*, Polygon, 2016; Edward Brooke-Hitching's *The Phantom Atlas:
        The Greatest Myths, Lies and Blunders on Maps*, Simon & Schuster, 2016;
        and Alastair Bonnett's *Off the Map: Lost Spaces, Invisible Cities, Forgotten
        Islands, Feral Places and What They Tell Us About The World*, Aurum, 2015.

p. 81. *Official observers on commercial fishing boats...* An investigation for
        the *Guardian* by Karen McVeigh found evidence of harassment and
        sexual assault against observers on commercial fishing boats, and the
        death of between one and two observers while on duty each year since
        2015. 'Disappearances, danger and death: what is happening to fishery
        observers?' the *Guardian*, 22 May 2020, p. 23.

p. 81. *And fishing itself continues to be one of the most hazardous professions...*
        While the sea is a distinctly dangerous place to be (according to the

Maritime and Coastguard Agency (MCA) Annual Reports and Accounts 2020–21, on average 400 people drown in the UK each year and a further 200 commit suicide in waters around the UK). According to the MCA's fatality figures for 2017–18, the industry suffered a fatality rate of 62 per 100,000 workers, making it the 'most fatal' profession in the UK. Source: B. Hendry, 'New figures show fishermen six times more likely to die at work', *The Press and Journal Evening Express*, 14 July 2018.

p. 82.   *George is a six times UK national record holder...* 'Georgina Miller – The Life of a Professional Freediver', PADI blogpost by Danielle Schofield. blog.padi.com/georgina-miller-life-professional-freediver/

p. 83.   *In one, a world record attempt, the Slovenian freediver, Alenka Artnik...* Artnik's record-breaking dive took place on day four of the Vertical Blue 2021 competition in the constant weight (CWT) discipline. www.youtube.com/watch?v=DQRPaLZ0Q2M

p. 83.   *The current world record for depth...* www.cmas.org/news/new-world-records-were-set-in-the-vertical-blue-freediving-world-series

p. 84.   *The absolute record for depth...* Nitsch, one of the pioneers of the sport who is taking it to its far limits, achieved this in 2007 in the No-Limits discipline of freediving, in which divers use a weighted sled to descend and a balloon to come back up. This discipline has been excluded from competition due to the dangers involved. In attempting to break his own record in 2012, in which he used a torpedo-design sled for extremely fast descent, Nitsch reached over 253 metres deep, Nitsch injured himself seriously and subsequently suffered severe decompression sickness and several strokes.

p. 87.   *In 1860, Charles Darwin wrote to his friend Charles Lyell...* This line appears as a postscript to a letter of 10 January 1860 from Darwin to the geologist, Charles Lyell, shortly after the publication of *On the Origin of Species*, in response to criticism of his ideas.

p. 87.   *A similar idea resurfaced a century later, in 1960...* 'Was man more aquatic in the past?', Alister Hardy, *New Scientist*, 17 March 1960, p. 642. Hardy's theory was that a branch of apes had fed on the seashores, forced by competition for food in the trees by other apes, and took refuge in the sea, in time beginning to dive for food at great depths. His theory was based on observations of human's diving skills, our furlessness, subcutaneous fat deposits and streamlined shape, which stands in contrast to that of other apes.

p. 87.   *...we retain the ability to dive to great depths...* Some freedivers posit that we may have forgotten our true potential to dive, and that we actually have much greater potential to dive and breath-hold than is currently thought, citing stories from antiquity of divers able to hold their breaths for up to 15 minutes.

p. 88.   *...freedivers' hearts have been known to slow to...* Source: www.livescience.com/divers-brain-oxygen-level-lower-seals.html

p. 89.   *...until the diver reaches a plate set at a specific depth...* The main disciplines of depth diving are: CWT, constant weight, in which the freediver uses fins or a monofin to dive to depth; CWF, constant weight without fins, which is thought by many in the freediving community to be the purest of the diving forms as the diver relies on nothing more than their own body to propel them down; and FIM, or free immersion in which divers pulls themselves down a rope.

p. 91. *I tell Daan I have been watching some of the films…* Daan's films are available at www.youtube.com/channel/UCU4OkffdV-G9PyRkmYcNiDA

p. 94. *A lobster fisherman, Michael Packard, was swallowed whole…* Cape Cod lobster fisherman, Packard was swallowed by a humpback whale while diving for lobsters in 2021. He estimated he was inside the whale for about 40 seconds before it spat him out with only a few superficial injuries. He was not the first Cape Cod fisherman to be swallowed by a whale. 150 years earlier, Captain Peleg Nye was swallowed whole by a sperm whale while hunting it. As with Packard, he escaped unharmed. Source: Doug Fraser, '"I was completely inside": Lobster diver swallowed by humpback whale off Provincetown', *Cape Cod Times*, 11 June 2021.

p. 100. *The Japanese have a word for sunlight filtered through trees…* While there is no direct translation for the Japanese term, *komorebi*, which is a popular word choice in haiku, a rough translation might be, 'sunlight leaking through the trees'. A related Japanese word, though less well-known beyond Japan, and less popular in haiku, *hamorebi* describes sunlight peeking through the leaves.

p. 100. *Poet Gerard Manley Hopkins coined something similar…* The term 'shivelight' appears in Hopkins's poem, 'That Nature is a Heraclitean Fire and of the Comfort of the Resurrection', written in 1888, shortly before the poet's death.

p. 101. *Later, I look up a TED talk by the French freediver, Guillaume Néry…* Guillaume Néry, 'The Exhilarating Peace of Freediving', 2016. Used with kind permission. To watch the full talk visit TED.com.

CAUL CHILD

p. 105. *The superstition that it is lucky to be born with…* A caul birth is also known as a 'mermaid birth' or 'veiled birth' or being 'born in a mermaid's purse'. Source: Ed. Lauren Dundes, *The Manner Born: Birth Rites in Cross-Cultural Perspective*, Altimera, 2003, pp. 120-26. Fletcher Bassett cites the 1658 will of Sir John Offley, who left a caul as part of his legacy, as well as an advertisement in *The London Times* on 21 February 1813, reading, 'To persons going to sea, a child's caul, in a perfect state, to be sold cheap' as evidence for the ongoing superstition of the power of a caul. Source: Fletcher Bassett, *Legends and Superstitions of the Sea and of Sailors: In all Lands and at all Times*, Belford, Clarke & Co., 1885, pp. 459-61.

p. 105. *Occurring in about one in every 80,000 births…* This is an often repeated statistic, though it is difficult to verify and may be treated with some suspicion. Source: 'The Veiled Child', blogpost on the website of

Surgeon's Hall Museums, 10 January 2019. surgeonshallmuseums.wordpress.com/2019/01/10/the-veiled-child/

p. 105. *A sea captain bought the caul with which Lord Byron was born...* Royal Naval Captain James Hanson bought Byron's caul from his mother's midwife. Source: *The Works of Lord Byron* – Part II, Vol. 1., John Murray, 1902, p. 9.

p. 105. *Although it did not protect the captain from drowning...* Source: Fiona McCarthy, *Byron: Life and Legend*, Faber & Faber, 2003.

p. 106. *The caul-protected Lord Byron, inspired by his support...* The line 'to woo,— and Lord knows what beside' forms part of the satirical poem, 'Written after swimming from Sestos to Abydos' that served as Byron's report of his swim, an experience he claimed to prize above all his poetic achievements. Incidentally, I suspect that Byron, more than anyone, perhaps, could imagine the possibilities that lay within the phrase 'what beside'.

p. 106. *...to prove it could be done...* Byron was a keen swimmer throughout his life, and as well as his poetry and promiscuity, many consider him to be the father of modern open water swimming.

p. 106. *The caul superstition is just one of hundreds of sea-related shibboleths...* Sources include Fletcher Bassett, *Legends and Superstitions of the Sea and of Sailors: In all Lands and at all Times*, Belford, Clarke & Co., 1885, and R. Nance Morton, *Glossary of Cornish Sea Words*, Federation of Old Cornwall Societies, 1963.

p. 107. *As the story goes, Tom sailed out in a great storm...* Mike O'Connor, *Cornish Folk Tales*, The History Press, 2010, p. 57.

p. 107. *Methods of surfboard production have barely changed...* Roger Mansfield, *The Surfing Tribe: A History of Surfing in Britain*, Orca Publications, 2011, pp. 220-21. Jock Serong, 'Are we trashing the places we love? The toxic truths at the heart of surfing', *the Guardian*, 16 March 2017. Todd Plummer, 'Think plastics are bad for the environment? Take a look at what surfboards are doing', *Los Angeles Times*, 1 June 2019.

p. 108. *...increasingly working with less toxic materials...* Just a mile or so up the coast, the St Agnes-based clothing company Finisterre is in the process of perfecting the recyclable wetsuit and many local surfers use their natural Yulex rubber suits, which are less environmentally damaging than the traditional neoprene suit.

WIND WORKER

p. 116. *I must go down to the seas again...* The quotes from John Masefield's 'Sea Fever' are used with kind permission of The Society of Authors, as the literary representatives of the Estate of John Masefield.

p. 116. *Masefield had trained on the Conway too...* Source: Alfred Windsor, *HMS Conway: 1859–1974*, Witherby Seamanship International Ltd, 2008, p. 52.

p. 117. *A three-masted, wooden, 92-gun battleship... Ibid.* A Windsor.

p. 118. *If I was not aware before that I am engaged…* Francis Spufford, *I May Be Some Time*, Faber & Faber, 2018.

p. 121. *The hollow earth story enjoys brief spells of popularity…* Source: David Standish, *The Long and Curious History of Imagining Strange Lands, Fantastical Creatures, Advanced Civilisations, and Marvellous Machines Below the Earth's Surface*, Da Capo, 2007.

p. 126. *It is a painfully beautiful sight…* Seamus Heaney, 'Postscript', from *The Spirit Level*, Farrar, Straus and Giroux, 1996.

p. 129. *…after losing his previous job…* While anyone can travel to Svalbard without a visa, there are strict rules on those who can stay there. Without a job, you must ship back to mainland Europe fairly quickly.

p. 133. *As we approach the Russian mining town of Barentsburg…* With almost 450 inhabitants, Barentsburg is the second largest settlement on the Spitsberg archipelago. While it is technically under Norwegian jurisdiction, like the rest of Svalbard, the settlement is predominantly Russian and Ukrainian. Having a Russian consulate, the town is the most northerly diplomatic mission in the world.

p. 134. *The archipelago of Svalbard is one of the fastest warming places on earth…* Source: Laura Paddison, 'Deep in the Arctic, a town fights for zero emissions', *Wired*, October 2021.

p. 136. *In my last few moments on board…* Gerard Manley Hopkins, 'Inversnaid' (1881).

MEMORY KEEPER

p. 143. *In some parts of the world, shell collecting is…* the major sources for this section was Bin Yang's *Cowrie Shells and Cowrie Money: A Global History*, Routledge, 2019.

p. 146. *…40 knots as it passed the Bishop Rock…* The 32-metre long *Maxi Edmond de Rothschild* is a foiling catamaran, though it arguably flies rather than sails, and is capable of mind-blowing speeds of 55 knots. When it is on its foils, hardly any of the boat is in the water at all.

p. 146. *In the third book in the Earthsea cycle…* Ursula Le Guin, *The Farthest Shore*, Gallery Books, 1972, p. 44.

p. 149. *By the time the* Tokio Express *cargo ship…* Andrew Male, 'Monopoly houses, toy soldiers and Lego: the museum of plastic lost at sea', the *Guardian*, 4 April 2020, and Mario Cacciottolo, 'The Cornish beaches where Lego keeps washing up', *BBC News Magazine*, 21 July 2014.

p. 150. *People seek Tracey out with their finds now…* There are still bits of rare LEGO seaweed Tracey said she would like to find. She found one of the rare octopuses in 1997 when they first started to come ashore, in a sea cave and it was another 18 years before she found another. She refers to the one that got away as the 'elusive green dragon' and, even decades later, her neighbour, who found one, signs her Christmas cards, 'Mary, keeper of the green dragon.'

p. 150. *In February 2021, some Yemeni fishermen found 127 kilograms...* Adam Forrest, 'Yemeni fishermen find £1.1m of "vomit gold" in sperm whale carcass', the *Independent*, 1 June 2021.

WAVE RIDER

Note: Elements of this essay first appeared, though in a different form, in the Spring 2020 edition of *The Marine Quarterly* under the title, 'In The Balance'.

p. 163. *In his surf memoir, Barbarian Days...* William Finnegan, *Barbarian Days: A Surfing Life*, Corsair, 2016.

p. 166. *Soooo Pitted!...* (image) In a show of socially responsible graffiti that seems to me very much indicative of this stretch of coast, much of the rest of the wall art at the site at which I took this photograph takes the form of eco-conscious slogans along the lines of 'Stop single use plastic' and 'Down with palm oil'.

p. 166. *The way St Agnes surfer, Minnow Green, tells it...* Audio extract from The First Wave archive. thefirstwave.co.uk/surfers/minnow-green/

p. 167. *Da Hui were also known as Black Shorts...* Isaiah Helekunihi Walker, *Waves of Resistance: Surfing and History in Twentieth-Century Hawai'I*, University of Hawai'i Press, 2011.

p. 169. *...informal code of conduct...* The basic rules of surfing are, roughly:

1. The surfer closest to the peak (the highest point of the wave) has right of way.

2. Don't drop in – in other words, don't take off on the same wave in front of someone who is already surfing it. In short, one rider per wave.

3. Observe the line-up – the surfer who snakes around others who are already waiting for the wave is an unpopular surfer. It's the equivalent of cutting into the queue.

4. In general, the surfer who is furthest out from the shore has priority on the wave. This rule gets a little grey in some areas when it comes to long boarders and paddleboarders, who are able to catch waves further out than short boarders, so discretion is key (it is the reason for some of the animosity between shortboarders and other wave riders).

5. Communicate your intentions – indicate whether you intend to go left or right on a wave, or that you are paddling for it. The same goes for listening – listen for other surfers who have shouted their intention on the wave.

6. Don't ditch your board – keep control of it.

7. Give respect – to the order of the line-up, to local surfers, to the skill and experience of the other surfers in the water.

8. Know your limits – as the often-quoted phrase goes, 'if in doubt, don't paddle out'.

p. 170. *Only a few days before, I had been in the water at dawn...* On that morning, as we paddled out, James had shouted over to me, cheerily, 'Don't eat too much shit out there.' To 'eat shit' in surfing slang also means wiping out on a wave or. To wipe out is also known, less prosaically, as 'going over the falls'.

p. 171. *And further out we can see the large white dome of Nancekuke…* Nancekuke itself might be a strong contender for the reason this area is named Badlands. Nancekuke was formerly an outstation of the chemical defence research centre at Porton Down where the nerve agents VX and sarin were produced, over 20 tons of the latter. The base was closed in 1978, but in the early 2000s the *Independent* newspaper claimed that waste from the chemical weapons testing site had been dumped down mine shafts when the site was abandoned, leading to chemicals leeching into the groundwater and the sea and the production and handling of chemical agents at the site were implicated in the deaths of at least 41 employees and former employees. The Ministry of Defence denied the allegations, though instigated a huge clean-up operation. We don't have the best record when it comes to getting rid of our inconvenient waste; in the mid 1990s, the MoD admitted it had lost the records for more than a million tonnes of munitions and the details of 24 chemical weapon ships dumped in the sea around the British Isles between 1945 and 1963. Among the chemicals jettisoned were 14,500 tonnes of rockets filled with the chemical weapon, phosgene, which were dropped into the Irish Sea at the end of the Second World War. The site where these chemicals were 'loose dumped', Beaufort's Dyke, a trench that sits between Northern Ireland and Scotland, was the military's main dumping site during the mid-twentieth century, a convenient place to get rid of inconvenient chemicals and weapons. However, there are few details as to the conditions in which these chemicals were dumped, nor much information on what chemicals are still contained within the rusting containers, though the ordinance dumped there, including anti-tank grenades, occasionally washes up on beaches in Northern Ireland and on the Isle of Man, offering chilling clues.

OCEAN WANDERER

p. 178. *Even the huge Egyptian vulture that appeared…* The vulture, spotted in a tree on Tresco in June 2021, is believed to be the first seen there in over 150 years. Source: 'Leonie Chao-Fong, Egyptian vulture seen in UK for first time in 153 years', the *Independent*, 17 June 2021. Of the two other known sightings, the vulture spotted at Bridgewater Bay, Somerset in 1825, and the other at Peldon, Essex in 1868, were both shot. Source: 'Egyptian Vulture arrives on Scilly' *Birdguides*, 14 June 2021. www.birdguides.com/news/egyptian-vulture-arrives-on-scilly/

p. 180. *In 2011, a polar bear was recorded having swum…* Source: Anne Casselman, 'Longest Polar Bear Swim Recorded – 426 Miles Straight', *National Geographic News*, 22 July 2011.

p. 180. *We have history with the walrus…* Anne Birgitte Gotfredsen, et al., 'Walrus history around the North Water: Human-animal relations in a long-term perspective.' *Ambio*, vol. 47, Suppl 2, 2018: 193-212. doi:10.1007/s13280-018-1027-x

p. 183. *She hopes he will find it, use it and stop...* 'Walrus in the Isles of Scilly', *Isles of Scilly Wildlife Trust* news, 3 August 2021. www.ios-wildlifetrust. org.uk/walrus-in-the-isles-of-scilly

p. 185. *In his book, Blue Mind...* Wallace J. Nichols, *Blue Mind: How Water Makes You Happier, More Connected and Better at What You Do*, Abacus, 2018.

p. 185. *Marine disturbance, the problem Lizzi is concerned with...* 'Marine disturbance in Cornwall triples in six years', *Cornwall Wildlife Trust* news, 18 August 2021. www.cornwallwildlifetrust.org.uk/news/marine-disturbance-cornwall-triples-six-years

p. 186. *In 2020, a new aggressive behaviour was noted in orcas...* Victoria Gill, 'Have rogue orcas really been attacking boats in the Atlantic?' *BBC News*, November 2020. www.bbc.co.uk/news/extra/buqvasp1rr/orcas-spain-portugal. And Helen Fretter, 'Orca attacks: Rudder losses and damage as incidents escalate', *Yachts and Yachting News*, 2 September 2021. www.yachtingworld.com/cruising/orca-attacks-rudder-losses-and-damage-as-incidents-escalate-133968

p. 187. *Earlier in the year, when the Colombian singer Shakira...* Jessica Glenza, 'Shakira says two wild boars attacked her in Barcelona park', the *Guardian*, 30 September 2021.

p. 187. *We are, the boars and orcas seem to be saying...* Herman Melville, *Moby Dick: or The White Whale*, The St Botolph Society, 1922, p. 528.

p. 189. *The walrus is a keystone species...* The walrus is widely considered a keystone species, an animal that helps to define an entire ecosystem. It is also listed on the IUCN Red List. Kovacs, K.M. 2016. *Odobenus rosmarus ssp. rosmarus*. The IUCN Red List of Threatened Species 2016: e.T15108A66992323. https://dx.doi.org/10.2305/IUCN.UK.2016-1. RLTS.T15108A66992323.en

p. 189. *Decade on decade, the Arctic is experiencing a 13 per cent loss...* Data from NASA's Global Climate Change website pages on the extent of Arctic Sea Ice. climate.nasa.gov/vital-signs/arctic-sea-ice/

p. 190. *The International Panel on Climate Change report...* Data from IPCC special report on the ocean and cryosphere in a changing climate. www. ipcc.ch/srocc/chapter/chapter-4-sea-level-rise-and-implications-for-low-lying-islands-coasts-and-communities/

p. 190. *According to the US Geological Survey...* Data from the US Geological Survey professional paper, Storlazzi et al., 'The Impact of Sea-Level Rise and Climate Change on Department of Defense Installations on Atolls in the Pacific Ocean (RC-2334)'.

p. 191. *...this story has a happy enough ending...* The story of the bottlenose dolphin ends less happily. In mid-September, his carcass washed ashore in Cork Harbour in Ireland. He had been killed by a propeller strike.

DAWN PATROLLER

p. 195. *Similarly, when I saw St Ives photographer…* For a short film about the Dawn Days project and example photographs, visit www.nickpumphrey.com/Portfolio/DawnDays/

p. 201. *About the same time, branded 'wild swimming'…* Rory Carroll, 'Shivering Dublin Bay swimmers slighted for their "fancy fleeces"', the *Guardian*, 25 November 2020.

p. 201. *One of the biggest of these revivals occurred in the early eighteenth century…* Various sources including Susie Parr, *The Story of Swimming*, Dewi Lewis Media, 2011.

p. 201. *On Cornwall's north coast at Portreath, there are no fewer…* My father-in-law, Jonathan Griffin has provided an overview of the Basset baths on his *A Cornish Journey* blog at acornishjourney.wordpress.com/2020/09/08/the-basset-baths-at-portreath/ and there is a broad overview of rock-cut baths in Cornwall in the article 'Rock-cut Baths in Cornwall' by Michael Tangye, in the journal *Cornish Archaeology*, no. 36, 1997, pp. 186-200.

p. 203. *In Cornish dialect, there are words for things for which…* R. Morton Nance, *A Glossary of Cornish Sea Words*, The Federation of Cornish of Old Cornwall Societies, 1963.

p. 203. *Dig deep into many languages and there are…* The Irish words quoted are taken from Manchán Mangan's Sea Tamagochi archive at https://www.manchan.com/sea-tamagotchi

p. 204. *Looking through Nick's photographs, though, reminds me…* Extracts from Gary Coyle's performance, 'At Sea', are available at garycoyle.ie/performances/at-sea-stage-performance/

p. 204. *The Forty Foot is an iconic piece of Irish…* James Joyce, *Ulysses*, Dover Thrift Editions, 2018, p. 3.

p. 207. *I experienced it more recently too, over summer…* Even the strongest swimmers will lose against a rip and the advice given by the RNLI, should you get caught in one, is to swim perpendicular to the direction of the rip (often this means swimming parallel with the beach) until you are out of the rip, at which point you can swim back to shore.

p. 210. *"Oh, how beautiful!" For the great plateful…* Virginia Woolf, *To the Lighthouse*, David Bradshaw, 2008, p. 14.

p. 210. *As it grows lighter still, the mist…* Roger Deakin recounts this experience in *Waterlog*, Vintage, 2000, pp. 136-40.

p. 213. *Then there are the well-documented benefits…* M. Gibas-Dorna, Z. Checinska, E. Korek, J. Kupsz, A. Sowinska and H. Krauss, 'Cold Water Swimming Beneficially Modulates Insulin Sensitivity in Middle-Aged Individuals'. *Journal of Aging and Physical Activity*, 2016; 24:547–554. P. Huttunen, L. Kokko and V. Ylijukuri, 'Winter swimming improves general well-being'. *International Journal of Circumpolar Health*, 2004; 63:140–144. C. van Tulleken, M. Tipton, H. Massey and C.M. Harper, 'Open Water Swimming as a Treatment for Major Depressive Disorder', *BMJ Case Reports*, 2018. L. Buzzell and C. Chalquist (eds), *Ecotherapy*,

2010. Sara S. Patterson et al., 'A Color Vision Circuit for Non-Image-Forming Vision in the Primate Retina', *Current Biology*, 2020.

p. 215. *Many artists have suggested that there is something special...* M. Bird, *A Quality of Light: A Collaborative Visual Arts Event, May – July 1997*, St Ives International, Penzance, 1997. M. Bird, *The St Ives Artists – A Biography of Place and Time*, Lund Humphreys, 2008. B. Tufnell, *On The Very Edge of the Ocean – The Porthmeor Studios and Painting in St Ives*, Tate St Ives, 2006. T. Cross, *The Shining Sands – Artists in Newlyn and St Ives 1880–1930*, Halsgrove, 2008.

p. 215. *In an article in* The Studio, *Norman Garstin...*The Studio Vol. VI, No. 33, Dec 1985.

p. 215. *I see what D.H. Lawrence meant...* In his letter of 1916 to Katherine Mansfield and John Murry, Lawrence was discussing the view of the sea from Zennor. James Boulton (ed.), *The Selected Letters of D.H. Lawrence*, Cambridge University Press, 1997, p. 123.

p. 215. *...and what Mel Gooding described as...* From the essay, 'A Marine Light' by Mel Gooding, in *A Quality of Light: A Collaborative Visual Arts Event, May – July 1997*, St Ives International, 1997.

p. 216. *Byron was once quoted as having said, 'I delight in the sea...'* Ernest J. Lovell Jr, *Medwin's Conversations of Lord Byron*, Princeton University Press, 1966. The less-referenced ending to this quote is, 'If I believed in the transmigration of your Hindoos, I should think I had been a *Merman* in some former state of existence or was going to be turned into one in the next.' (p. 118)

OAR RAISER

p. 222. *There are other fixed seat boats...* British Rowing article, 'Fixed Seat Rowing'. www.britishrowing.org/go-rowing/types-of-rowing/fixed-seat-rowing/

p. 222. *Modern pilot gigs are all built to the same design...* K. Harris, *Azook! The Story and History of the Pilot Gigs of Cornwall and the Isles of Scilly 1666–1993*, Dylannsow Truran, 1994.

p. 224. *They were swift and low in the water, with a shallow draught...* Cornish gigs and pilot cutters were used, often interchangeably, for lifesaving, salvage, trade, pilotage and smuggling. In *Pilot Cutters Under Sail* (Seaforth, 2013) p. 22, Tom Cunliffe discusses the case of pilot, James Nance, who was also a successful smuggler, having rowed back and forth between Britain and France no fewer than 25 times.

p. 224. *The six swimmers are at the beginning...* Richard Cockram et al., *The Newlyn Tidal Observatory*, Newlyn Archive, 2018.

HORIZON SCANNER

Note: Sections of this essay first appeared in Edition 1 of *Elementum Journal*, a journal of nature and story, ed. Jay Armstrong, and subsequently on the website for Writers' Rebel, the writing arm of Extinction Rebellion.

p. 240. *It was exactly as Masefield wrote…* The quote from John Masefield's 'Sea Fever' is used with kind permission of The Society of Authors as the literary representatives of the Estate of John Masefield.

p. 243. *Scilly has one of the highest concentrations of prehistoric carns…* Source: Charles Thomas, *Explorations of a Drowned Landscape*, Batsford, 1985.

SONGLINE SHAPER

p. 250. *The cables we could see were part of the first cable connection…* Source: 'Our History: Codename PK' pkporthcurno.com/discover-pk/our-story/

p. 253. *Jeffrey Levinton, in his afterword to…* Rachel Carson, *The Sea Around Us*, Oxford University Press, 1991, p. 243.

SELECTED BIBLIOGRAPHY

Baring-Gould, S., *The Cornish Wreckers*, Cambridge University Press, Cambridge, 1910.

Bassett, F., *Legends and Superstitions of the Sea and of Sailors: In all Lands and at all Times*, Belford, James Clarke & Co., Cambridge 1885.

Bathurst, B., *The Wreckers: A story of killing seas, false lights and plundered ships*, Harper Perennial, New York, 2005.

Bird, M., *A Quality of Light: A Collaborative Visual Arts Event, May – July 1997*, St Ives International, Penzance, 1997.

Bird, M., *The St Ives Artists – A Biography of Place and Time*, Lund Humphreys, London, 2008.

Boulton, J., (ed.), *The Selected Letters of D.H. Lawrence*, Cambridge University Press, Cambridge, 1997.

Bowley, R., *The Fortunate Islands: The Story of the Isles of Scilly*, W.P. Kennedy, Edinburgh, 1945.

Bradshaw, E., et al., *A Century of Sea Level Measurements at Newlyn*, Southwest England, Marine Geodesy, 39:2, 115-140, DOI: 10.1080/01490419.2015.1121175 (2016).

Buttivant, H., *Rock Pool: Extraordinary Encounters Between the Tides*, September Publishing, Tewkesbury, 2020.

Byron, G.G., *The Works of Lord Byron* – Part II, Vol. 1, John Murray, London, 1902.

Carson, R., *The Sea Around Us*, Oxford University Press, Oxford, 1991.

Cockram, R., et al., *The Newlyn Tidal Observatory*, Newlyn Archive, Newlyn, 2018.

Colquhoun, I., *The Living Stones*, Peter Owen Publishers, London, 2016.

Cross, T., *The Shining Sands – Artists in Newlyn and St Ives 1880–1930*, Halsgrove Publishing Group, Wellington, 2008.

Cunliffe, T., *Pilot Cutters Under Sail*, Seaforth, Barnsley, 2013.

Darke, J., *Held by The Sea*, Souvenir Press, London, 2011.

Darke, J., *The Wrecking Season*, Boatshed Films, Padstow, 2005.

Deakin, R., *Waterlog*, Vintage, London, 2000.

Duck, R., *This Shrinking Land: Climate Change and Britain's Coasts*, Edinburgh University Press, Edinburgh, 2019.

du Maurier, D., *Vanishing Cornwall*, Virago Press, London, 1967.

Finnegan, W., *Barbarian Days: A Surfing Life*, Corsair, 2016.

Fowles, J. and F. Godwin, *Islands*, Jonathan Cape, London, 1978.

Gibson, F., *Gig Racing in the Isles of Scilly*, privately published, 1986.

Gill, C., *The Isles of Scilly*, David & Charles, Newton Abbot, 1975.

Girling, R., *Sea Change*, Transworld, London, 2007.

Halliday, F.E. (ed.), *R. Carew of Antony, The Survey of Cornwall*, Adams and Dart, 1969.

Hamilton Jenkin, A.K., *Cornish Seafarers – The Smuggling, Wrecking and Fishing Life of Cornwall*, J.M. Dent, London, 1932.

Harris, K., *Azook! The Story and History of the Pilot Gigs of Cornwall and the Isles of Scilly 1666–1993*, Truran, Saint Agnes, 1994.

Hawker, R.S., *Footprints of Former Men in Far Cornwall*, J. Lane, 1870.

Heaney, S., *The Spirit Level*, Farrar, Straus and Giroux, New York, 1996.

Heath, R., *A Natural and Historical Account of the Isles of Scilly*, 1750.

Holmes, R. and D. Wilson, *You Should Have Been Here Yesterday: The Roots of British Surfing*, SeasEdge Publications, 1995.

Hunt, J., *Islands Apart*, Wruff Publications, 1989.

Jenkin, M. (dir.), *Bait*, Early Day Films, 2019.

Keats, J., *Complete Poems*, Book of the Month Club, 1993.

Le Guin, U., *The Farthest Shore*, Gallery Books, New York, 1972.

Lopez, B., *Arctic Dreams: Imagination and Desire in Northern Landscape*, Vintage Classics, London, 2014.

Lovecraft, H.P., *H.P. Lovecraft: The Complete Fiction*, Barnes & Noble, New York, 2011.

Lovell Jr, E., *Medwin's Conversations of Lord Byron*, Princeton University Press, Princeton, 1966.

Manetta, J., *Looking for Something to Find*, Toad Hall Press, Cornwall, 2015.

Mansfield, R., *The Surfing Tribe: A History of Surfing in Britain*, Orca Publications, Newquay, 2011.

McCarthy, F., *Byron: Life and Legend*, Faber & Faber, London, 2003.

Menmuir, W., *The Many*, Salt Publishing, Cromer, 2016.

Mothersole, J., *The Isles of Scilly: Their Story, Their Folk & Their Flowers*, The Religious Tract Society, London, 1914.

Mumford, C., *Portrait of The Isles of Scilly*, Robert Hale, London, 1970.

Nance, R., *A Glossary of Cornish Sea Words*, The Federation of Old Cornwall Societies, 1963.

Néry, G., 'The Exhilarating Peace of Freediving', TED, 2015.

Nestor, J., *Deep: Freediving, Renegade Science and What the Ocean Tells Us About Ourselves*, Profile Books, London, 2015.

Nichols, W.J., *Blue Mind: How Water Makes You Happier, More Connected and Better at What You Do*, Abacus, London, 2018.

Otter, J., *Do Make: The Power of Your Own Two Hands*, The Do Book Co., London, 2020.

Parr, S., *The Story of Swimming*, Dewi Lewis Media Ltd., Stockport, 2011.

Payton, P., *Cornwall*, Fowey Rare Books, Fowey, 1996.

Pearce, C.J., *Cornish Wrecking, 1700—1860: Reality and Popular Myth*, Boydell Press, Woodbridge, 2010.

Sprackland, J., *Strands: A Year of Discoveries on the Beach*, Vintage, London, 2013.

Spufford, F., *I May Be Some Time*, Faber & Faber, London, 2018.

Tallack, M., *The Undiscovered Islands: An Archipelago of Myths and Mysteries, Phantoms and Fakes*, Polygon, Edinburgh, 2016.

Thomas, C., *Explorations of a Drowned Landscape*, Batsford, London, 1985.

Trubridge, W., *Oxygen*, Harper Collins, London, 2017.

Tufnell, B., *At the Very Edge of the Ocean – The Porthmeor Studios and Painting in St Ives*, Tate St Ives, 2006.

Turk, S.M., *Seashore Life in Cornwall and the Isles of Scilly*, D. Bradford Barton, Plymouth, 1971.

Walker, I.H., *Waves of Resistance: Surfing and History in Twentieth-Century Hawai'i*, University of Hawai'i Press, Hawai'i, 2011.

Wigglesworth, A., *People of Scilly*, Sutton Publishing, Stroud,1994.

Windsor, A., *HMS Conway: 1859–1974*, Witherby Seamanship International Ltd, Livingston, 2008.

Winton, T., *Breath*, Pan Macmillan, London, 2009.

Woollett, L., *Sea Journal*, Zart Books, Redruth, 2016.

Yang, B., *Cowrie Shells and Cowrie Money: A Global History*, Routledge, London, 2019.

ACKNOWLEDGEMENTS

My thanks to everyone who showed me the beaches, shorelines, tidal zones, waves and waters of Cornwall, Scilly and Svalbard through their eyes and to those who sailed, surfed, dived, swam, paddled and wandered with me while I researched and wrote. While the interests and backgrounds of the people featured in this book vary wildly, they are all connected by their passion both for the seas and for its preservation. It has been a privilege to share time on, in and by the water with you and I am proud to consider you my friends.

To the crew who helped to bring the book into being: my agent, Peter Straus, whose knowledge of the waters of publishing is second to none; my editor, Katie Bond, for her vision, drive and masterful navigation of the ship; Aruna Vasudevan, Phoebe Bath, Viviane Basset and the Aurum team, who have championed this book from the moment we laid the keel; Colin Midson for PR par excellence; Holly Ovenden for gorgeous cover design; and Oli Udy for superb author photos.

So much of any success this book experiences will float on the expertise of the sea-going communities around Cornwall and Scilly and beyond and, predictably, I owe many thanks.

For Strandline Gleaner, to Jane Darke, Lisa Woollett, Claire Wallerstein and the volunteers at the Cornwall Wildlife Trust's Strandings Hotline. As I mention in the opening chapter, I never got the chance to know Nick Darke, though I would have loved to have been able to thank him for his influence on this book and on the way I have come to see the sea.

For Island Fisher, to Jof Hicks. To the late and much-missed Keith Low – when he said to me it was important to pass these stories on because otherwise they would be lost when he died, I didn't expect it would happen so soon after the telling. Rest well, Keith. To the staff and volunteers at the Isles of Scilly Museum, in particular Kate Hale, and to Jeremy Brown, Tammy Bedford, Piers and Rachel Lewin, Maddie Hicks and Marthe Broadhurst and the staff and students of Five Islands School. To Callum Roberts and Julie Hawkins for sharing expertise and knowledge just moments after you arrived in Cornwall, and to Heather Koldewey, not least for the best of all interview spots on a SUP board off St Michael's Mount.

For Rock Pool Pilgrim, to Heather Buttivant and family, and to Richard Pearce. To Helen Scales for introductions, suggestions and pointers.

For Depth Plumber, to freedivers and instructors extraordinaire, George Miller, Daan Verhoeven, Alex Atkins and Luca Anselmi, and to mermaids extraordinaire Emma Harper and Tracey Frowde. And to the Kernow Freedive Tribe, who are supportive and kind-hearted in the extreme – thank you for sharing the depths with me.

For Caul Child, huge appreciation to James Otter and to Buddy, Ali and Chris at Otter Surfboards. And in particular to Fiona Francis for sharing the story of her recovery and return to the sea.

For Wind Worker, firstly, to my grandfather, Patrick Menmuir, for stories of smuggling and for planting the idea of the sea in my head from an early age, and to my dad, Richard Menmuir for helping me to appreciate the sound of the water on the hull and the wind in the sails. Tusind tak to Rasmus Jacobsen for allowing me to join the crew of his ship, and the team at Venture Sail in Truro, who organised for me to join S/V *Linden*. My particular thanks to Captain Nikolai Anderson, Thomas Andreasen, Emil Fagerli, Sixten Hüllert, Laura Lerche, Tomas Salem and Linn

Langeng for sublime sailing, ice-cold swims, late-night saunas, excellent meals, tempestuous card games and friendship.

For Memory Keeper, to Sue Hill and to the memory of the much-missed Bill Mitchell, whose legacy continues to be felt across Cornwall, and to Tracey Williams.

For Wave Rider, to Chris Hines. To Johnny Manetta, Drustan Ward and Sam Bleakley. And to Ryan Manetta for reminding me that the purpose of surfing is to smile.

For Ocean Wanderer, first and foremost to blue mind guru Lizzi Larbalestier. To Charlie Elder for allowing me to use his photographs of the walrus in Scilly. And to the communities of the Isles of Scilly, who have made me welcome since I first landed on the islands as a travel writer for the *Guardian* back in the dim mists of time. Scilly and its shallow and treacherous seas will always have a special place in my heart.

For Dawn Patroller, to Nick Pumphrey and James Warbey. To Jonathan Griffin for many hours under sail, for expertise in anything involving boats and ships and for indulging me in my obscure and sometimes ridiculous questions.

For Oar Raiser, the incomparable Anna Murphy, and the crews of Pendeen Gig Club, in particular the Ladies' B crew – you are all superstars. To the members of Penzance's Out of Sink synchronised swimming group.

For Horizon Scanner, to Abby Crosby.

And for Songline Shaper, to the talented and visionary Tony Plant.

To Hugo Tagholm, Amy Slack, Pete Lewis and the team at Surfers Against Sewage. Having been embedded with you during COP26, I got to see first-hand the tirelessness with which you approach campaigning for cleaner waterways, your dedication and energy. And similarly, to Ruth Williams, Matt Slater and the teams at Cornwall Wildlife Trust and Isles of Scilly Wildlife Trust, as well at British Divers Marine Life Rescue. We all need to do more to protect our seas and if you are looking for ways of helping, wherever you are, please consider supporting these organisations and the many others that campaign, educate, champion and protect the oceans, their creatures, habitats and plant life.

To Arts Council England and Falmouth University for funding my research trip to Svalbard and for my sabbatical in which to write and research without interruption.

To the Society of Authors for awarding me the Roger Deakin Award, which allowed me to dedicate much-needed time to a book the scope of which expanded rapidly. To the Q-Fund for supporting my research trip to the Isles of Scilly. To the staff of Kresen Kernow, Redruth and the archives team at the library at Falmouth University. And to the photography and underwater photography stores at Falmouth University for the loan of cameras and advice on how to use them.

To Cathy Rentzenbrink for good advice and sea swims, and Liz Jensen for unswerving belief. To my colleagues at Falmouth University's School of Communication, and to Amanda Harris, Helen Reynolds and Polly Roberts at the Writers' Block for support and encouragement.

In 2016, Jay Armstrong asked me to write what was to become the first article for her new journal, *Elementum*. I titled it 'The Draw of The Sea' and it was that article that started me off on the journey that led to this book. Elements of that essay appear in this book, and I thank Jay for commissioning that first article for her stunning journal of story and nature and for including it in her beautiful publication.

Above all, my love and thanks to Emma, Lana and Tom, with whom I continue to explore the waves and the waters.

INDEX

Page numbers in *italics* refer to illustrations